THE TOWN
THAT FOUGHT
TO SAVE ITSELF

THE TOWN THAT FOUGHT TO SAVE ITSELF

By **ORVILLE SCHELL**

WITH PHOTOGRAPHS BY **ILKA HARTMANN**

PANTHEON BOOKS

A DIVISION OF RANDOM HOUSE, NEW YORK

Library of Congress Cataloging in Publication Data

Schell, Orville.
The Town That Fought To Save Itself.

1. Cities and towns—Planning—United States—Case studies.
2. Municipal government—United States—Case studies.
3. Environmental policy—United States—Case studies. I. Title.
HT167.S26   309.2′62′0973   75-39122
ISBN 0-394-48498-3   ISBN 0-394-73169-7 pbk.

Manufactured in the United States of America

Design by Kenneth Miyamoto

FIRST EDITION

ACKNOWLEDGMENTS

Grateful acknowledgment is made to the following for permission to reprint previously published material:

The Associated Press: "Town Opts Out Via Chain Saw," from the *Oakland Tribune*, May 3, 1972, and article by Lewis Mumford from the *San Francisco Examiner*, 1973. Copyright © 1972, © 1973 by The Associated Press. Reprinted by permission of The Associated Press Newsfeatures.

Newsweek: "Return to the Guild" from *Newsweek*, August 20, 1973. Copyright © 1973 by Newsweek, Inc. All rights reserved. Reprinted by permission.

Fred Rose Music, Inc.: Four lines of lyrics from "I'm So Lonesome I Could Cry" by Hank Williams. Copyright 1949, renewed 1976 by Fred Rose Music, Inc., Nashville, Tennessee. All rights reserved. Used by permission.

San Francisco Chronicle: "Skinny Dipper Victory" from the *San Francisco Chronicle*, December 15, 1973. Copyright © 1975 Chronicle Publishing Co.

TO JONATHAN—

a wonderful brother

O.S.

Für meine Mutter

I.H.

POEM

Words themselves are medicine.
By telling the events of our time,
we give meaning to them.
Words themselves are medicine.

It was considered a sacred place.
The mountain is considered a sacred mountain.

It is said that they lived here peacefully,
naked, that they hunted quail, rabbit, deer.
By the bay, in the village that is now
Briones, the people lived. They are
all dead now, sang songs no one remembers
nor can tell the things they danced to,
when time was called moon of the black cherries,
moon when the ponies shed their hair,
moon when the deer shed their horns.
Olema they named, for the coyote.
Petaluma they named, that means
flat hill. Whales, then many whales
swam past the coast in the time
of water, in the time of darkening
light, swam south to mate.

The Miwok tribe lived here.
Before the Gold Rush, before the
lumbering started, when the land
was still peopled with giant redwoods
when trees still spoke, were revered,
before spanish, portuguese, irish, or
italians, before chinese or japanese
came here, the Miwoks lived here,
or near here. Some say this place
was such a sacred place that no one
was bold enough to live here, but
came here only to get strong, be healed.

                                        BLACKBIRD

PROLOGUE

A TOWN which is a community is a delicate organism. As yet, it has virtually no legal means at its disposal by which to protect itself from those who choose to search it out. Unlike an individual, it cannot sue for invasion of privacy. It cannot effectively determine how many people can live in it. It cannot even decide for itself the number of visitors with which it feels comfortable. The roads are there; anyone may travel on them. A commercial establishment is free to advertise the town's name and its desirable attributes in the hopes of attracting people to it in order to make money. If the people who call that town home find the influx of people, cars, and money unsettling, they have little recourse.

A town is public property not only for its residents, but for the world. In many ways, it is at the mercy of forces existing outside its boundaries, and of people whose names it does not know and whose faces its inhabitants will never see.

Thus, it is with some trepidation that we have recorded the events of our town for people who do not make it their home and naturally may not be as concerned over its welfare as are those of us who live here. The reader will discern as the narrative proceeds that many people in our town are uncertain and apprehensive over the consequences of increasing notoriety. Notoriety seems to inevitably attract people and money. People and money in themselves are not necessarily bad. But there is an inclination in this town to view them with utmost caution and scrutiny, lest they end up destroying the very qualities which originally attracted the people.

Our town does not crave publicity and does not want to become a subject of glancing fascination for the media. We cannot think of anyone who lives here who would be desirous of boosting our town into celebrity status. And yet, many of us who have lived here for some time and participated in recent events have long felt that certain aspects of our experience may suggest new pathways—and perhaps give some new hope—to people elsewhere who find themselves confronting similar situations. It is the process rather than the town which is offered, and it is offered to anyone who finds it instructive, encouraging, or enjoyable.

In a more immediate sense, however, this narrative is offered to the town itself, and to the people about whom it is written. The story belongs to the town. Were it never read by anyone outside the town, it would have been justification enough for setting it down. And, while it is a highly personal rendition of events (into which we intrude with complete abandon), it is our hope that in some small way it will serve to bind the town together by recalling for all the process by which we arrived at the present.

Having talked to a great number of people in the town, we have decided to change the name of the town and the names of several people who do not live there. One hesitates to be secretive or to play games by trying to hide a name. No doubt, those who are interested will easily learn the actual names. This is as it should be. To others it will be irrelevant. For there is nothing extraordinary to come to see in this place. There are roads, houses, trees, fields, ocean. What is extraordinary is what has happened, and the ways in which people in this town have enjoyed living with one another.

This book is the product of all the people who participated

in the events which it records, who wrote things which are included, took the photographs, and helped edit the manuscript. They all appear throughout the narrative. And we thank them for the help and good times.

To Tom Engelhardt, our outside connection, we can only say, "Thank you for reading the early manuscript more carefully than we did ourselves . . . and for not letting us get off easily with an unfinished job."

To Carol Lazare and Jim Peck, our editors, we can only say thanks. Your editing was superb.

ORVILLE SCHELL
ILKA HARTMANN

1975

THE TOWN THAT FOUGHT TO SAVE ITSELF

Mine is a proud village, such as it is.
We are at our best when dancing.

MAKAH INDIAN POEM

OIL-SOAKED GREBE

INTRODUCTION

THE OIL SPILL was a beginning, or perhaps it would be better to say another beginning. For the town has doubtless witnessed many past milestone events since the Spaniard Don Gregorio Briones first brought his family over the mountains on horseback in the 1830s. But, the thick black "bunker C" oil, which covered the coastal waters and littered the beaches with carcasses of tar-soaked birds, seals, and sea lions, affected the town profoundly. Day and night, people waded out into the oily surf to save dying seabirds. Crews of local people worked nonstop for days to rig booms and keep the oil out of the Lagoon, a wildlife sanctuary. And then, for weeks, the cleanup dirge on the beaches surrounding the town on three sides went on. The town was transformed into a strange kind of combat outpost. The main street and the beaches were covered with piles of heavy equipment, timber, bales of hay, emergency supplies, generators, piles of tools, wireless radios, and men in hard hats from Standard Oil. The restaurants, churches, and community buildings became barracks and dining halls for all the volunteers.

The oil spill was indeed a disaster, especially for the animals who made the ocean their home. But it brought people together. Until the oil hit the beaches, many people in town looked on themselves as escape artists. They were people who had moved to Briones from the city in search of peace and solitude.

I think many of us were surprised to encounter so many other congenial people on the beach during those days. New friendships were made. And, I think, many of us began to sense the vulnerability of our escapes as we wrestled those two-hundred-pound blobs of oil and seaweed up onto dump trucks. But the town seemed to congeal. When it was all over, people began to look back on those exhausting weeks with warm feelings. The oil spill began to be remembered as the town's 1776.

The town's chemistry began to change. A group of oil spill veterans rented a room downtown across from the Bar, and called it the Briones Future Studies Office. By this time the cause was not oil, but a sewer. The local community Public Utilities District (PUD) had hatched up an $8.1 million sewage treatment plant and collection system which would have hooked us up with the neighboring town like a Siamese twin. It was obviously too expensive, too big, and would have opened the whole peninsula to possibilities of runaway development. I think it was the development threat which really got people upset.

The sewer came to be known as the "Kennedy Plan," after the engineering firm in the city that had designed it and become its main champion.

At first, most of the town seemed resigned to the sewer. They didn't like the high cost, and dreaded the day when construction would begin, digging up the town from one end to the other. But people seemed gripped by a profound fatalism. I remember one lady standing at the meat counter at the Store, and saying to a friend, "Sure, it's the end. But you can't stop something like this." Other people talked about waiting until the bulldozers came, and then moving away.

It was then that Greg, Russ, and Peter began to get the Future Studies Office fired up. They got out a letterhead, put in a phone, began raising money, and started collecting information on sewers, our PUD, and all the other governmental agencies somehow involved in the project. Gradually a larger group gathered around them. We fanned out into the town, banged on doors, passed out leaflets (and even some comics), started having town meetings. The farther we got into the Kennedy Plan, the clearer it became that the whole project was a dinosaur which almost no one would support once it was understood. Among other things, it promised to run a force main full of sewage right across the San Andreas Fault. It called for a million-dollar outfall pipe which would have fed partially treated chlorinated sewage out onto one of the state's most renowned tidal pool marine habitats. It proposed to hook up almost every house in the area (even those on septic tanks) to solve the problem of 187 houses which allowed sewage to flow into the Lagoon through an ancient collection system. Hookup was to be at the owner's expense.

It would not be an overstatement to say that the town soon became electrified over the subject of sewage.

We ended up petitioning for a recall election of two of the PUD board members. We had sewer salesmen and engineers visiting town every other day explaining their ideas and their company's products. We asked busy officials from the county and state (most of whom were only dimly aware of what was happening) to come out and take a walk by our old outfall pipe, where we would sit and talk about sewage and what the town wanted as we watched clouds of dishwater, shreds of toilet paper, and shit float up into the channel. The wall above the outfall pipe became something of a shrine.

We all agreed that something should be done about it. The question was, "What?" Matters got so sewer-conscious that Halloween that year saw Ilka and me at the Halloween Ball dressed as two outfall pipes (hers and his). By the time we all got done, I doubt if there were more than ten people in town who didn't know about the Kennedy Plan.

We had a really good time defeating that sewer. There were parties, benefit dances, potluck dinners, bull sessions. One of the things we learned was that not too many villains were really involved. Very few people truly wanted the sewer. It had just happened. It was a dumb, expensive, professional solution to a relatively small problem. There were some dark moments of doubt, mostly, I think, because none of us had ever stopped a multimillion-dollar project before.

By the time the state finally decertified the project and killed the plan, the Future Studies Office and a large part of the town were well into an election campaign to win control of the Utilities District Board, composed of five locally elected members. The board is the only locally effective governing body in town. The issues had broadened from sewage to include land use, water, agriculture, development, local control, and self-sufficiency.

We took a look at the California Public Utilities District Act to see what kind of powers our seemingly insignificant PUD might have:

> A district may acquire, construct, own, operate, control or use for supplying its inhabitants with light, power, water, heat, transportation, telephone service or other means of communication, or means of disposal of garbage, sewage or refuse matter. . . .
> A district may acquire, construct, own, complete, use, and operate a fire department, street lighting system, public parks, playgrounds, recreation buildings, buildings to be used for public purposes; work to provide for drainage of roads, streets and public places including but not limited to curbs, gutters, sidewalks and pavement of streets.
>
> CALIFORNIA PUBLIC UTILITIES
> DISTRICT ACT
> SECTION 16461 & 3

I remember Greg's remark after reading the Act. "Pretty wide," he said with a grin.

That November we won the two recall seats, plus the two others up for election. I was one of the newly elected directors, and we would soon find ourselves inaugurated and part of the incumbent status quo of American officialdom.

This was another beginning. And it is from here that the narrative about our town begins.

THE CREATURE FROM THE BRIONES LAGOON

A LONG TIME AGO, THERE WAS A SLEEPY LITTLE TOWN CALLED BRIONES, 30 MILES NORTH OF SAN FRANCISCO...

SOME PEOPLE CALLED IT A "PSYCHEDELIC PEYTON PLACE", BUT TO MOST FOLKS IT WAS JUST DOWN-HOME AMERICA.

A POCKET OF BEAUTIFUL BEACHES AND RURAL CHARM WITHIN EASY REACH OF THE CITY.

ONLY TROUBLE WAS, 187 DOWNTOWN TOILETS FLUSHED DIRECTLY INTO THE BEAUTIFUL LAGOON... 20-45,000 GALLONS OF RAW SEWAGE EVERY DAY! THE SWIMMIN' WAS PRETTY SHITTY AT THE "WRONG END" OF THE BEACH, AND, NEEDLESS TO SAY...

THE POLLUTION ATTRACTED SOME UNUSUAL WILDLIFE TO THE AREA...

SAN ANDREAS CRACK

MMM... SNORF! SNORF!

BUT, LIFE MOVED ON FROM SEASON TO SEASON, AND THE CALIFORNIA LIVIN' WAS MIGHTY EASY... SO NOBODY DID ANYTHING...

BLURP!

UNTIL:

WARNING BEACH QUARANTINE
NO

I TELL YA, M'BOY, THERE'S GOLD IN THAT LITTLE SEWER SITUATION IN BRIONES — WE'RE GONNA BUILD A SYSTEM THAT'LL HANDLE 75,000 PEOPLE!

HEH! HEH!

THE BIG PLAN

THE DUMB CITIZENS WILL FOOT THE BILL, AND WE'LL MAKE A KILLING 'CAUSE THE WHOLE AREA WILL BE OPENED TO DEVELOPMENT! BEAUTIFUL TRACT HOUSES EVERYWHERE!

I'LL BE ABLE TO RETIRE TO A NICE QUIET VILLAGE UP THE COAST!

NOBODY THOUGHT IT WAS IMPORTANT TO ASK THE RESIDENTS OF BRIONES AND NEIGHBORING PROCTOR BEACH IF THEY WANTED A GIANT SEWER SYSTEM... IT WASN'T EXACTLY A DEMOCRATIC SITUATION... BRIONES AND STINSON WERE UNINCORPORATED, SO THE BIGGEST LANDOWNERS AND THE COUNTY OFFICIALS CONTROLLED THE FATE OF THE TOWNS...

FOR TWO YEARS THE PEOPLE LISTENED TO THE MUSIC OF JACKHAMMERS AND BULLDOZERS, AS EVERY STREET WAS TORN UP TO LAY PIPE TO EVERY HOUSE... FINALLY, THE GREAT DAY CAME...

HERE

NOW INSTEAD OF 187 TOILETS DUMPING A LITTLE SHIT INTO THE LAGOON, 1500 TOILETS DUMPED TONS OF CHLORINATED SHIT 3000 FT OFF THE COAST (AND ON TO DUXBURY REEF).

MEANWHILE, THE FAUNA IN THE LAGOON WAS DISTRESSED BY THE NEW ECOLOGICAL IMBALANCE.

WHERE FOOD?

BUT FORTUNATELY THE NEW OUTFALL PIPE...

WAS WITHIN EASY PADDLING DISTANCE!

SNF SNIF

YEARS PASSED... THOSE TRACT HOMES WENT LIKE HOTCAKES.

SAFEWAY
NOW LEASING
Marina Vista
LUXURY HOMES
BY THE SEA

INCREASED POPULATION MEANT MORE SUNDAY VISITORS!

THE DEMAND FOR A NEW HIGHWAY TO OPEN UP THE RECREATIONAL POSSIBILITIES OF THE AREA COULD NOT BE IGNORED!

AS THE YEARS WENT BY, WHAT HAD STARTED AS THE SIMPLE NEED TO STOP THE POLLUTION OF THE BRIONES LAGOON NOW BECAME A CRAVING NECESSITY TO HOUSE AMERICA'S SWELLING POPULATION...

MORE YEARS. THE LAGOON? OH, THAT WAS FILLED WHEN THEY BUILT THE INDUSTRIAL PLAZA AND THE RACETRACK!

CONTINUED NEXT ISSUE

MEANWHILE, ON THE BOTTOM...

MMM... DAT CHLORINATED SHIT TASTES ALMOST AS GOOD AS BUNKER OIL!

TIME PASSES SLOWLY...

WHEN YOU'RE LOST IN A DREAM...

EVERY CITY HAS A MILLION STORIES... THIS IS ONE OF THEM...

IN AN EXPENSIVE APARTMENT ON THE MESA, "FAST EDDIE" PEREZ COUNTS HIS PROFITS.

OPEN UP IN THERE!!

CHRIST! THE PIGS!

BLAM BLAM

1,000 HITS OF "PINK LIGHTNING" LSD

MOMENTS LATER:

OM!

KAFWOOM

GLOM

WITHIN MOMENTS AMERICA'S EVER DILIGENT ECOLOGY PATROL STRIKES OUT RUTHLESSLY AGAINST THE DISGUSTING MANIFESTATION FROM THE LAGOON!

ATTENTION ALL ECO-UNITS!! ALIEN LIFE FORM INTERFERING WITH INDIGENOUS FAUNA OFF DUXBURY REEF!

 BROLEENUS?

 BROLOGNAS?

 BROLONGUS?

BLUB... FUCK IT!

IT'S BEEN A LONG TIME SINCE HE LEFT HOME, BUT OUR CREATURE'S INSTINCTS DIRECT HIM UNFAILINGLY BACK TO HIS MOTHER—

KRRR...

UNFORTUNATELY HE'S GROWN A BIT SINCE THOSE HALCYON DAYS WHEN HE SWAM WITH HIS FRIENDS IN THE DEEP CAVERNS OF THE SAN ANDREAS FAULT!

SCHWEEZE

MOM, IT'S ME, LITTLE BIMBY!

KRUMBLE KRUMBLE KRRRUMBL!

THE EARTH'S 7-YEAR WOBBLE... THE SIDEWAYS PRESSURE BUILDING SINCE 1906!... THE COMPLEX ARRANGEMENT OF MOON, SUN, AND STARS — ALL THIS, AND ONE MUTATED TUNAFISH GOING HOME—

KKKRRRAAASSSSHH!

ONCE A MAN WALKED THE PEACEFUL COAST WITH HIS WIFE, WROTE POEMS AND RAISED A FEW KIDS... THEN CAME THE SEWER... NOW, LIKE ATLANTIS OF OLD, HIS LIFE HAS SUNK BENEATH THE SEA, BANISHED BY FATE FROM THE ROUGH SOIL, THE SMOOTH STONE, THE SOFT GRASS. MAYBE NEXT TIME HE'LL LOOK BEFORE HE FLUSHES.

Irons/Veitch · 71

TOWN FACT SHEET

Total land area: 3,600 acres

Estimated population: 2,000

Registered voters (June 1974):   1,000

Existing dwellings: 650

Assessed valuation (1974–75): $6,600,000

Utilities District Budget (1974–75): $174,000

School District Budget from local property taxes (1974–75):
     $338,000

Fire District Budget (1974–75): $24,000

Median income: $7,000–$9,000

Example of Homeowner's Tax Obligation (1974–75)
Assume a $30,000 appraised value. Minus homeowner's exemption, the assessed valuation (which is one-quarter of appraised valuation) would be $5,750. The following breakdown occurs:

	Rate*	Amount
County Government Services	$2.38	$137.14
Special District rates (Fire, PUD)	$2.59	$148.98
Schools	$6.05	$348.28
		$634.40 yearly taxes

* The rate is computed on so many dollars per $100 assessed valuation.

FALL

You won't have any trouble in your country as long as you have few people and much land. But when you have many people and little land, your trials will begin.

THOMAS CARLYLE, SCOTTISH ESSAYIST,
WARNING NINETEENTH-CENTURY
AMERICA OF 25 MILLION PEOPLE

THE OFFICE of the Community Public Utilities District is located in the biggest building in town, a huge rambling wood-frame structure built in the 1920s. The PUD office is an anonymous institutional room which expresses no one's taste, good or bad. Plywood veneer has been put up as part of a recent remodeling to hide the old yellowing particle board walls. Fluorescent tubes cast a cold, white-green light from the ceiling onto two tables below, which are covered with plastic woodgrain finish.

A time clock on the wall is surrounded by maps of proposed pipeline projects and sewer plants. There is an aerial photo of the town over the electric coffeepot, which stands amidst an almost bizarre assemblage of old non-matching coffee cups. The tables are piled with blueprints, engineering reports, and copies of *Public Works* magazine, with cover pictures of smiling municipal officials posed proudly in front of huge water treatment plants or garbage incinerators.

On the wall over the duplicating machine is a calendar. For each month a platinum blonde in a bikini embraces a large Rigid brand pipe wrench and wears an expression of feigned satisfaction. Old Glory and the California bear flag hang limply on either side of the far wall. The California flag is emblazoned with the word, "Eureka" ("I have found it!"), which Archimedes is reputed to have said (yelled?) upon discovering the principle of specific gravity, and which Californians cried after they discovered gold.

The district clerk sits in a small alcove near the safe and the Xerox machine and runs the office. To his back is a door leading into a large meeting room, the PUD Grand Ballroom, which is built around a massive brick fireplace.

Today is the day that the "new" PUD board will take office. Two seats have been won in the recall by Bill, a schoolteacher and future pig farmer, and Greg, a town organizer listed on the ballot as "volunteer worker." Two other seats have been won to fill expired terms by me and Mimi, a woman in her forties who is a reading specialist at the School.

The four of us sit on folding chairs with fifteen or twenty other people in the audience, as the "old" board convenes the meeting for the last time. The atmosphere is somewhat muted. Members of the audience talk in low voices as they wait.

Joe the fire chief, the retiring president, picks up his small wooden gavel from the table top, gives a few cautious raps, and calls the meeting to order. Minutes of the last meeting are read and approved. With no further words or to-do, we are asked to come forward to the seats at the front.

As the four older men leave, they do not seem overjoyed. The election and our clear victory have been unsettling experiences. But they are gracious.

We take our seats in the wooden chairs with arms which traditionally have been reserved for directors. We look out at the audience in which we have been accustomed to sit ourselves. There is an awkwardness about this moment. Attempts to relieve it are made by smiling and making a few amateurishly humorous remarks.

Our first order of business is the election of a chairman. We unanimously elect Mimi, who better than any of us has succeeded in bridging whatever gaps exist between different groups in the community. She immediately distinguishes herself by placing on the table a small pink plastic bell which she rings when discussions get too heated or out of hand.

The most important item on our agenda is the proposed moratorium or new water hookups. There is an acute summertime water shortage within the district. In order to make do, the district has been forced to pump water out of Pine Gulch Creek at a temporary site in back of the School.

For most of us on the board, a water moratorium, which

THE PUD BOARD: ROB, MARK, MIMI, ORVILLE, BILL, AND GREG (FROM LEFT TO RIGHT)

would stop further building, was one of the main reasons for seeking office. Not only was water short, but the town had been growing at an unsettling rate over the last few years. We needed to find a way to stop, reevaluate, and plan. A water hookup moratorium presented us with the only legal means available to stop runaway growth.

More than an hour of discussion ensues. The issue is extremely sensitive, although most people in the room support the motion. The consequences are clear: hundreds of people will be left holding land on which they cannot build, and which they cannot easily or profitably sell.

The motion, which Mimi has written, comes to a vote. It passes four to one. The only opposing vote is cast by the member remaining from the old board. The resolution reads:

> *Whereas*, The land areas encompassed by the BCPUD contain canyons, ridgetops, mesas, a lagoon, and ocean beach frontage, which in total comprise a unique and irreplaceable combination of natural features providing a habitat for a variety of life forms, including quail, for which part of the above described land serves as a Refuge; and
> *Whereas*, The existing water supply is inadequate to meet the health and safety standards, and creates in the summer months a serious fire hazard that is dangerous and constitutes a threat to human life and property; and
> *Whereas*, The water delivery system is in need of repair in order to meet the minimal needs of the District's inhabitants, and that any further extension of its water delivery service would tax the resources of the District *beyond* the *reasonable limits* of its *facilities*; and . . .
> *Whereas*, Further extension of the *dedication* of the District would seriously impair the ability of the District to provide water to its users;
> *Therefore, be it resolved*, That the BCPUD hereby limits dedication to the territory and the water consumers that the District now supplies with water, and do hereby declare that its policy is to establish, as of this date, a moratorium on providing its service of water to new construction requiring same, until such time as a thorough and comprehensive evaluation of the entire area is made; to which this Board is committed in its capacity as a Public Utilities District.

It is 1971. We become the first town in America that we know of to have a zero-growth control limitation.

OUR town is a dead end. The road comes out onto this small peninsula of land and ends. We are not even geologically part of the continental land mass. We lie on the western side of the San Andreas Fault. Our town sits on one of the few outcroppings of the Pacific Plate which protrude above water.

As it is now, one must leave by the same road on which one arrives. From the white Methodist Church, one passes the empty lot where the bus stops; goes over Finney Hill past Ben Meyer's horse barn, trailer, and pasture; then down to Gospel Flat, where the road straightens out by the Christian Science Church and the School. Here, people are tempted to speed. It is not uncommon to hear someone scream, *"Slow down!"* as a car whizzes past one of the many children riding horses or walking into town.

The road turns at the Catholic Church just after it crosses Pine Gulch Creek, favorite spawning ground of salmon and steelhead. The nursery is on the right. Although the town has no official boundaries, since it is unincorporated, to most people it seems to end here where the road widens and runs along the Lagoon to the highway and what is known as "over-the-hill," or the rest of the world.

Downtown Briones consists of two streets which bisect at the old Methodist Church. One hosts the post office, liquor store, laundromat, hardware store, and a real estate office. The other is lined with the garage, Community Center and library, bookstore, Tarantino's Seafood Grotto, the Store, Snarley's delicatessen, Scowley's eating establishment and hangout, a curio shop, and a secondhand clothes store in the old livery barn. On the other side are Smiley's Bar, a motel, an art gallery, and another real estate office.

Both streets dead-end at the beach.

Today is a weekday. It is late in the afternoon. There is almost no traffic on the street. The usual array of pickup trucks and "sensible" foreign compact cars is parked in front of the Store. Kids speed by on their bicycles doing wheelies in the street. The horses are tied up to the picket fence in front of the Bar. Most of the pickets have long since been pulled

GOSPEL FLAT

DOWNTOWN

loose by earlier horses and ponies left tied by their owners.

Several people sit under the umbrella in front of the delicatessen drinking wine and eating salami. It is five o'clock, and several of the many carpenters in town pull in with their pickups to have a beer, shoot a game of pool at the Bar, or buy some food for dinner at the Store.

Three women with children stand by the bulletin board on the Store wall and talk. An uncountable number of dogs wash back and forth across the street sniffing garbage cans, growling, or running after their masters. As a temporarily friendly pack, they are interested in some fish which has just arrived from the dock up in front of Scowley's. Josh, a young man in baggy coveralls, bare feet, and bushy blond hair is cleaning a salmon on the hood of an old De Soto and slicing it into steaks.

DOWNTOWN

Don't be too hasty
to trace
all evil to
the marketplace.
TOM CLARK

THE Grand Ballroom of the PUD building is filled to capacity. A folding table has been set up in the front of the room next to a large stand-up blackboard. Collapsible chairs are lined up in obedient, neat rows facing the table. There are many unfamiliar faces among the people who are seated and waiting.

A large group stands in the rear of the room. Some sit up under the eaves of the loft to get a better view. A progression from age to youth is discernible as one moves farther and farther to the back.

"It's almost like a ghetto back here," someone whispers. "All the straights are up front, and the freaks are in the back."

The first meeting of the nascent Briones Property Owners Association is about to be called to order. Some have attended

THE STORE

as supporters. Others have come out of curiosity to see what motives they can divine for the new group. Membership costs five dollars a year.

A small number of people from town are in the seated section. They are mostly the older and more conservative group who supported the old board and the defeated Kennedy sewer. But the majority of new adherents are absentee landowners. They have come from a great variety of distant places. Most of them evidence concern over the new water moratorium and the future of their property. Some own only one or two lots (twenty by one hundred feet). Others have considerable holdings. Some talk of retirement on their land. Others speak more guardedly of profits and sale.

An uncustomary tenseness is in the room. There are rumors of pending lawsuits against the district.

"Well, we could all just join, and then take over the organization," says Bill with a sly smile.

"Aw, come on!" says Greg. "We *need* this opposition to keep our trip together."

Peter E. is the association's apparent organizer. He is a

PETER E. AND REX

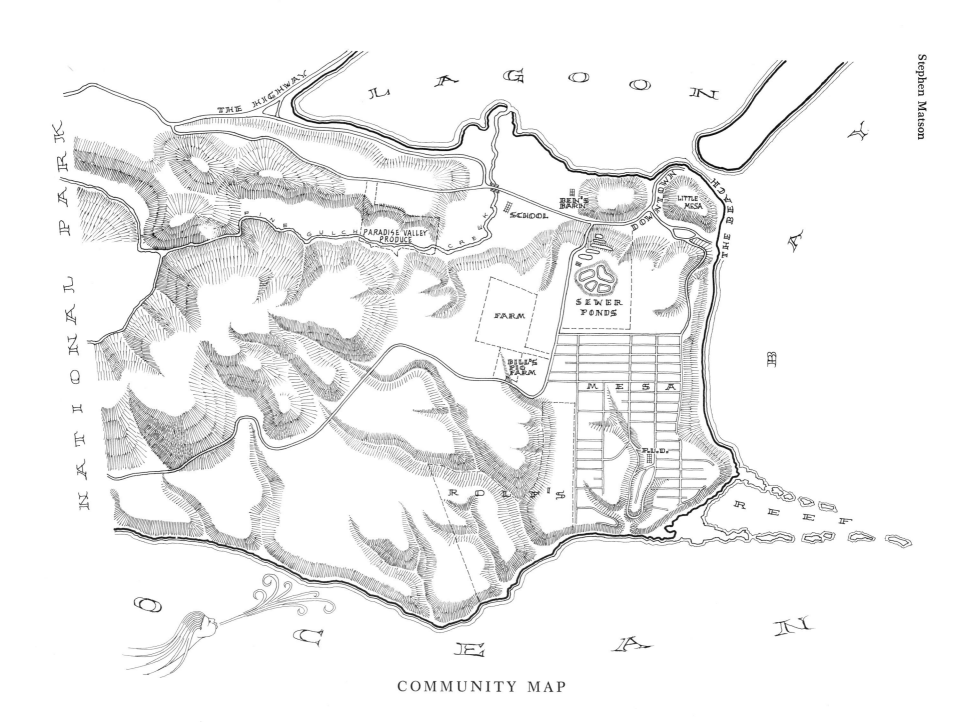

Stephen Matson

COMMUNITY MAP

slight, tense, pipe-smoking man whose family has lived in Briones for many years. He works in the city as a librarian for a state historical society. He and his brother, an engineer, were two of the most ardent and active supporters of the old sewer.

He half stands, half leans on the front table with his forearms extended in a straight-arm position. He calls the meeting to order somewhat nervously. He explains that the organizing committee has decided that all residents may attend the meetings, whether or not they own property. Non-property owners may not, however, join or vote. There is murmuring from the back of the room.

An election of directors ensues. A list of names "recommended" by the nominating committee is written on the blackboard. One nomination is made from the floor.

The voting proceeds without a hitch. As though the script had already been written, the "recommended" slate wins overwhelmingly. Since most of the absentee landowners know neither each other nor the nominees, they are left with little room for judgment. It is clear that they are voting against the moratorium. And, it is equally clear, although never stated outright, that the new directors are like-minded.

"What I can't understand," says Nancy, "is why Peter is interested in organizing a group like this for people who don't even live here."

The newly elected directors take up their positions behind the table. Peter is quickly elected chairman. The remaining official business takes only a short time to transact. Then, almost before people have settled down inside, the meeting is over. The room empties back out into the PUD parking lot.

It is cool and pleasant under the tall cypress trees that arch over the old Catholic Church. The tombstones stand in the hot sun behind the church marking graves of forgotten townsmen. Someone has mowed the cemetery. But already the blackberry vines and thistles are moving back in around the headstones.

Some of the dead are covered with a blank concrete slab; a Catholic habit in these parts. Others lie strangely alone out in the grass with nothing more than a leaning headstone covered with lichen to mark their final resting place.

Gophers have irreverently dug their burrows in and around the graves.

Well-wishers have put coffee cans and jelly jars of flowers and lilies on many of the graves. Most have been tipped over by the wind and lie on their sides in the weeds with the dried stems of flowers still protruding. On other graves, plastic flowers have been stuck incongruously in among the dried grass and weeds; lusterless blossoms which ignore the seasons.

It is strange to be walking among the faceless dead out of the past of this town, people from distant places who once called this peninsula home.

In Sacred Memory of
JANE
Beloved wife of John McCoy
August 27, 1883
Aged 46 years, 3 months, 7 days
Native of Ireland

JOSEPH LANINI
Born at Frasco,
Canton Ticino, Switzerland
Died August 7, 1894
Age 34
R I P

In memory of
REV. BLASIUS MOORS
Born 1874
Ordained 1903
Died January 17, 1920
Native of Belgium

What brought these people to this town from the other side of the world? Did they work in the booming lumbercamps sawing down virgin redwood on the ridge to build San Francisco? Did they work the dock loading timber, tallow, dairy produce for gold-crazed California? Or did they keep one of the many saloons or hotels in town which clustered first in Dog Town and later around Wharf Road? Or maybe they ranched or drove the stage over-the-hill.

In any case, they are all now erased, and the land has been passed on to another generation, most of whom have not the faintest sense of those who went before. Their passing might just as well have been a thousand years ago. Only the tombstones remind us that we have a history.

In one corner, buried under a tall, white marble turret overlooking the Lagoon and the mountains, is Pablo Briones. He came by horse with his father, Don Gregorio Briones, in 1837 from the Spanish settlement of Yerba Buena, now San Francisco. They built an adobe structure on Pine Gulch Creek just across from the old Catholic Church, from whence they ranched the surrounding land. The Spanish government in Mexico gave them a land grant to the whole peninsula.

They were the first white men to live in this town. They rode over this same land and spoke Castilian Spanish.

TODAY, Greg, publicly elected Director of the Utilities District, goes to jail.

Twenty days in the "Big Pink" (the county Civic Center) slammer and on the Sonoma County Farm: payment for his gross indiscretion wherein he (A) got drunk on assorted beers, wines, and liquors; (B) busted all the windows out of a real estate office with a mop handle, while yelling, "I've had enough of this shit!"; (C) slashed all the tires on the shiny new black Lincoln Continental owned by an active spokesman for the newly formed Property Owners Association; (D) charged a parked truck and broke his collarbone, which ultimately led him to the hospital at 3:30 in the morning.

[18]

GREG

People of all political persuasions could not fail to recognize various repressed political motivations in these acts. For some, they were the well-plotted acts of the Antichrist in an assault on private property and law and order. For others, the incident represented fulfillment of unspoken yearnings.

The affair put the whole town in the hot seat. It was the kind of evening that one thinks at the time is unsurvivable. It opened the schism between the two contending forces in town which had heretofore sniffed around each other like two dogs with their backs up, deeply suspicious, growling a lot, but with no outright fighting.

The broken windows and slashed tires confirmed the deepest fears of many people who had previously looked upon the political takeover by the younger group with distaste. Greg's rampage gave them palpable cause for fear and animosity. The young people themselves were upset, lest the incident cast a shadow over all that they were trying to do. But then, many of them knew Greg personally and respected him, which gave them a certain reassurance.

Dick and Nancy expressed the thoughts of many in the *Paper*, a sometime town publication.

The New Society is not here yet. . . .

Briones is a mellow town, but only if one is speaking from a comparative point of view. We do not know how to reach each other. We are only beginning to sense that we must learn how.

At present we are still in a phase wherein, laid low by our own fear and mistrust, we seek release in an impersonal lawsuit on our neighbor, or by smashing his impersonal windows.

We have disparate visions of an ideal society. Does it have to be a choice between ours and theirs? Or will we learn to live and let live? Until the Golden Age, it seems necessary to learn to tolerate one another—bare feet, Continentals, tents and vans, real estate offices, rock music, and all. Perhaps someday we will be able to communicate with a clear heart and mind.

Judith writes a song which she is frequently requested to play on her guitar at jam sessions and social events:

BALLAD OF A REBEL

Sit down friends and strangers
And listen to my song,
I'll sing about an outlaw, and I know it won't take long.
Way out in California, in the County of Marin,
They said he done a bad thing, but I know it was nothing.

Oh, the times we are livin' in seem very strange to
    me,
Why prosecute a good man for goin' on a spree?
Why don't we jail our leaders, who vote for guns
    and bombs,
And spare the poor young people, whose crime
    never hurt no one?

This rebel was a drinker
And at gamblin' he did shine.
And my best friend once told me, that at lovin' he was fine.
But his drinkin' got the best of him, and to prison he did go
For slashing someone's tires, and breaking some windows.

Well, you can take a small-town hero
And lock him up in jails.
But when you let him free again, you'll see how our system
    fails.
For his friends will gather round him more loving than before
And swear to change the system, or vow to break the law.
                                        JUDITH WESTON

WORD reaches town that the California Department of Highways wants to widen and straighten the coastal highway past the turnoff to town.

It will reportedly cost them (us) over $6 million if they follow through on all three projected phases. They have the whole job divided up like salami into slices. And since each slice is relatively thin, they have filed a negative declaration of environmental impact on the first phase. This means they will not have to do an environmental impact statement. But if you add up all the small project slices, you get a huge undertaking.

Even the State Department of Highways people are unable to pinpoint the genesis of the project, or who supports it.

[19]

Vague talk of "safety" and "easier maintenance" is offered by a ranking bureaucrat over the phone.

Who decided to do it?

"It's just been in the works for several years," reports the voice on the phone.

The project has a momentum of its own.

We ask the department to send some representatives to a town meeting to discuss the matter. They consent.

A date is picked. Word is spread.

SINCE the recall election, nothing has visibly changed in the PUD office. No pictures of Che or posters of Chairman Mao have materialized on the walls. The flags still hang at attention, and the time clock still ticks away on the wall. But the atmosphere has been transformed. More people are there, now—working, reading, having a cup of coffee, using the phone, talking sewers, hanging out, waiting for rides downtown.

The PUD office has become a social hub, a place to which people drift with great purpose, and with no purpose at all.

IT is 7:30 and already dark.

Slowly, people start arriving at the PUD Grand Ballroom for the town meeting on widening and straightening the highway. There is a reassuring mixture of people. They sit together in apparent obliviousness of their wildly diverging habits of dress. A young woman in long flowing granny dress and home-embroidered jacket is next to a gray-haired older woman in a pants suit, carrying a cardigan sweater and holding a flashlight. The men are mostly in work clothes embellished in various ways with colorful patches and embroidery.

The men from the State Department of Highways arrive bearing briefcases and tubes containing maps and charts. They sit down in the front row looking somewhat out of place and uneasy.

Finally, their PR man gets up and gives a short description of the project and the various stages in which it will be undertaken. One can feel the tension. People are leaning forward in their chairs just waiting for a pause in which to get out a question. The PR man is bucking a strong tide. He keeps telling the assembled people *how* they are going to do the project, when we want to know *why* they are going to do it.

People start interrupting. The three silently seated engineers turn nervously around to see who is butting in with the hostile questions.

"Who wants this project, anyway?" asks a young man in overalls, boots, and long hair in a ponytail.

The PR man tries to hedge around the *who* part of the question. He mentions safety. He is becoming apologetic. He is a mild, intelligent person who does not appear to be convinced of the project's wisdom himself.

"I'll blow up your lousy trucks if you fool with that road," says Rex in an uncharacteristically angry outburst. He is tall, gray hair and beard, red bandana around his neck, blue jeans. He is a retooled industrial chemical salesman who is now the operator of a ranch and an independent building contractor.

The PR man turns to the engineers who sit mutely with their drawings of cut-and-fill sections. They have no answer for Rex.

"This is my home!" yells Don, a local architect. "And I don't want your goddamn road so people can go faster!"

"Hey, why don't you do your road somewhere else?" asks a woman from the back.

People are angry. The meeting is out of control. Then people begin to talk to one another softly as the PR man and the three engineers discuss what to do next. I see a few smiles around the room on the faces of some of the bolder residents. There is a feeling among most of the seventy-five people in the room that the highway project will never happen. The feeling is strong and obvious.

"Well, if we can't stop it before it's begun," says one seated young man, "we'll stop it when they get their equipment here."

"I haven't had a chance to lay down in front of a bulldozer since we stopped them logging Briones Ridge over three years ago!" exclaims Jack.

All the veterans of the Kennedy Sewer Plan fight still have stratagems filed away in their heads: pipes disappearing at night, trenches mysteriously backfilled, survey stakes in the wrong places, vehicles that won't start.

"If you guys are gonna build that highway, you better hire us all as night watchmen!" yells Patrick.

Someone calls for a straw vote. The hands shoot up. Only one person wants the new highway.

Everyone starts clamoring at once, demanding to know whom they should write in protest. Whom should they see? Whom should they lobby? The PR man finally gives his boss's name and address. Everyone writes it down.

The meeting trails off into groups talking together and with the highway engineers. It doesn't end. It disintegrates. It is clear that most people do not need to hear any more to know where they stand.

For the past week, the Department of Highways maintenance crews have been cutting back a cliff around a sharp corner where the highway borders the Lagoon.

It is not related to the larger project under contention. But some town alarmists see it as a symbol of what is to come.

Today the crews removed a large yellow bulldozer from the cut-and-fill site on a lowboy heavy equipment trailer.

"What happened?" responds the flagman on the job. "Well, what happened is that some guy ripped out all the wires on that cat. And they must have put something in the diesel tank. It's all plugged up! Won't budge by itself!"

Some people think prayers may help.

PRAYER FOR AMERICA'S ROAD BUILDERS

Oh almighty God, who has given us this earth and has appointed men to have domination over it; who has commanded us to make straight the highways, to lift up the valleys, and to make the mountains low, we ask thy blessing upon these men who do just that. Fill them with a sense of accomplishment, not just for the roads built, but for the ways opened for the lengthening of visions, the broader hopes, and the greater joys which make these highways a possibility for mankind. Bless these, our nation's road builders, and their friends. For the benefits we reap from their labors, we praise thee; may thy glory be revealed in us. Amen. THE OFFICIAL PRAYER OF THE AMERICAN ROAD BUILDERS ASSOCIATION

The theater-like seats with ashtrays on the back are filled with well-barbered realtors, developers, lawyers, and us. The room is a study in sartorial contrast: suits, ties, well-shined shoes vs. army jackets and sweaters, blue jeans, boots and sneakers.

We are all attending the supervisors' meeting at Big Pink, our pink cement Civic Center done in a Tibetan–Howard Johnson's mode by its architect, Frank Lloyd Wright. The pink cement is topped off by a tinny-looking brass molding and a bizarre turquoise roof.

The county supervisors, the legislative body of the unincorporated areas of this county, are in session. They are discussing which parcels of land will be taken out of Agricultural Preserve* and "made available for development," as one realtor describes it.

---

* The state of California has made provisions under the Williamson Act to reimburse counties for land which receives a substantial tax reduction by the owner's promising to remain in agriculture for an extended period of time. Large ranches (usually two hundred acres or more) are able to sign "contracts" which bind the owner to using the land for agricultural purposes for a given number of years. The rancher then pays approximately a quarter of what would be his standard tax load.

The Williamson Act has been a boon for real farmers who are in the Agricultural Preserve zone, and who do not want to be driven off by high taxes caused by rapidly rising speculative land prices based on development-potential valuations.

On the other hand, the Williamson Act has also benefited large banks and corporations who want to buy land for relatively long-range speculation. Their land appreciates rapidly in value while they pay fractional amounts of standard taxes because they have signed "agricultural contracts." When these expire, they do not renew, and thus have a nice little piece of real estate ready for development with an inflated price on it. Their goal is not the preservation of agriculture, but low-cost investment.

"Agriculture is dead in this county," says one rancher who looks too prosperous to be convincing. "And by keeping this land tied up in this here preserve . . . it's like condemnation without payment."

Taxes are high. Cattle feed prices are rising. But so is the price the land can command for development. If agriculture is dying, most ranchers and realtors are not complaining.

The supervisors listen. No one expresses joy in owning land, land of incomparable beauty. Get an overwhelming sense from these people of the burdens of land ownership. All hardship and trouble. Everyone trooping over to the Civic Center to make sure they can convert their land into as much money as possible.

The poor land. It's not at the supervisors' meeting. Nor are the hawks, the deer, the insects, the trees.

The land is chased by taxes into a spiral of profit-taking.

"The best and highest use."

The best for whom?

The land is a commodity. Like a transistor radio or a hair dryer. It is bought and sold.

The supes are playing a shy game with no rules. They are not so much trying to protect the land as to keep a respectable middle ground between the developers, the conservationists, and their own better judgment.

Five men sit behind plastic name plaques and make decisions which will endure for centuries about land on which most of them will never have a chance to walk.

They are overburdened with work. They get as close as they can by staring at maps and reading assessment figures, and are sometimes treated to slides by a really aggressive or big-time developer.

People's backyards disappear in the process.

They don't own that thousand acres which they have looked at for fifty years. Or perhaps they have looked on it only for a month.

"Improvements." The backward, black-is-white language of a world gone crazy on change.

A developer stands up. Walks to the speaker's mike.

He wants one hundred units. The supervisors throw around some environmental lingo, tell him to plant more trees, and give him eighty units.

Private property.

BRIONES. Subdivided in 1927 by Arthur Smadback into several thousand twenty-by-one-hundred-foot lots. He took the old Vierregio Tract and sliced it into squares like a tray of fudge.

He built a "clubhouse" (the present PUD Building) and whooped it up about Briones Beach (no mention of the summer fog).

Sales sagged.

A San Francisco newspaper decided the answer to its declining readership was to throw in a Briones lot with each six-month subscription. They ran a full-page ad:

$69.50 PAYABLE! $9.50 DOWN! $3.00 A MONTH!
SUBSCRIBE FOR ONLY SIX MONTHS TO THE
SAN FRANCISCO BULLETIN!!!

The ad shows a picture of women on a beach in one-piece bathing suits with frilly leggings. The women wear strange hats that look as if they were covered with fruit.

The ad promises "a big real estate boom in the county."

Our town: postage-stamp-sized lots, carved out to sell a newspaper. And now the San Francisco *Bulletin* is dead. Only our subdivided mesa remains. Smadback moved on to become a big-time operator and investor in the New York Coliseum.

When I was a kid, into dry-cereal culture, there was a brand of shredded wheat which gave away "one square inch of Alaska" with each box. You got a keen little deed, the whole shebang. It excited me to think that as a nine-year-old I could become a landowner just by eating the right kind of cereal.

Training for the future.

Our town is just a microcosm. This strange peninsula, covered with a man-made patchwork of lots and roads.

THE TOWN

Was it someone's vision of the future?
Was it yours, Arthur Smadback?

WHILE driving downtown, I see the bent-over figure of old George standing on the roadside. He wears his plastic fedora, suspenders, and green trousers. He is waiting for a ride to the post office, his daily pilgrimage to the outside world.

I stop and pick him up.

"I was born in 1891," he says, after slowly and meticulously working his stiff body and feet into the cab of the truck. "So, you figure it out. I won the Golden Gate Lottery back in thirty-six for five hundred dollars. So I went in on a new Ford sedan with a friend.

"Well, we landed down at the beach in that old car one day, and then finally came up here to Briones."

He makes a gesture of finality with his arm.

DOWNTOWN AT THE TURN OF THE CENTURY

"Hell," he says. "You know, in them times a fella could get lots for ten dollars up here. No one wanted them. There wasn't nothing up here."

SUNDAY. It is a clear and beautiful fall day. A strong wind blows down across Double Point from the headlands.

There is an almost continual line of cars on the road coming into town past the School. It is not the normal flow of pickup trucks, vans, VW's, and compact cars. Most cars are new, shiny, and filled with couples and families. Lots of sports cars with barely muffled engines which snarl up Finney's Hill as their drivers downshift for the stop sign.

A beer can sails out of the window of a red Porsche and lands in the blackberry bushes by Ben's pasture.

Almost all the parking spaces are filled downtown. People cruise Brighton Avenue for spots near the beach. There is a miniature traffic jam out in front of the Store as people pause, looking for a place to park. Six people in unmistakably well-cleaned and pressed clothes stand in front of the Bulletin Board, reading and smiling.

"Hey, get this, Bob," says one man in a windbreaker and a golf hat as he points out to his friend some ad or message.

Six or seven motorcycles roar down the street driven by a group of acid barbarians. They park in front of the Bar, then disappear inside.

A brown Buick with a leatherette roof, towing a massive Aristocrat Trailer like a barge, comes hesitatingly down the street. The driver, like some animal digging too far down a narrow hole, senses danger in the way the street becomes so meager and indistinguishable from the sidewalk.

Gandoff, Scowley's watchdog, walks out and starts barking. The Buick with appended trailer has become the center of attention. People stop and stare, waiting to see what will happen.

The driver is flustered. The car behind honks. The trailer lurches forward again. The driver seems to be animated by

THE HIGHWAY AT THE TURN OF THE CENTURY

embarrassment and self-consciousness rather than by any clear conviction to press on. Cars are piling up behind him. No place to maneuver. Behind the rolled-up windows, his wife cranes around looking backward for some solution.

There is none. They drive forward several hundred yards to where the road hits the seawall and beach. They unhitch the trailer and spend forty-five minutes turning themselves around with the help of some surfers. Then they drive out of town back to the state highway.

THE supervisors' meeting on the County Master Plan finally ends about 10:30. Everybody's wiped out.

Lydia offers to give me a ride back to town from over-the-hill.

Out on the dark road, she smiles and says nothing when I ask how old she is. She is a retired teacher. A short woman with graying hair. She takes the Senior Citizens' Bus over-the-hill each week. She has lived in the area for many years. And although her husband was one of the people recalled from the old PUD board, she still attends every meeting faithfully. She brings a pad and pencil, and takes notes.

"It's a habit I learned taking all those courses when I was a schoolteacher," she says.

She believes that it is not right to keep people out of town who want to move or build here. At the same time, she views the growth of Briones over the years with some sorrow.

"Well, I don't know," she says. "It just isn't the same."

Years ago, she used to teach out at a one-room schoolhouse way out on the end of the Point near the McClure's Ranch.

"Of course, all the roads were dirt then," she recalls as we speed home on an asphalt highway. "There were some fisher-men down at the Gallagher Ranch on the Bay. And they would take me across the Bay in a boat to a small depot called Hamlet. Then I'd catch the train. We'd pick up my sister, and then ride all the way into Sausalito where we would catch the ferry for Oakland. And that was our weekend."

You can still see the old roadbed alongside the Bay going up the coast to Sonoma where they loaded lumber. All that remains now is rotting timber and a few shaky bridges.

"Well, it was just crazy," says Lydia. "Now, why did they have to go and take those trains out? It was such a beautiful ride down the coast of the Bay. We used to bring something to eat and crossword puzzles, and this man, Donahue, who later became assessor over at the County, would help us."

The children at the ranches on the coast used to take the train up to the high school in the next town in the morning, and then take it back again in the afternoon. They had two trains on the weekdays. On the way back they used to load fish and oysters at Hamlet and Millerton for the city. Then on the weekends they'd run three or four trains with what they called "picnic coaches." They went all the way up to the resorts on the Russian River.

At first, the train was fueled with wood. There were huge piles of cordwood stacked where the drugstore now stands. All of it was cut by hand on the Shafter Ranch by two men on bucksaws. It was hauled by horse and wagon to the depot.

Then the train switched to oil. Hauled mostly hay and other freight for the ranches along the coast and in the valleys. The ranchers had to drive their wagons into the depot, buck the 350-pound bales onto wagons, and drive them home.

Then the trucks came. The road was paved. Two years later the train was dead.

On July 31, 1933, the last train headed up the coast.

"Well, I guess when the trucks came in, they could take the goods right to the ranchers' doors. That was it for the train right there," says Lydia.

She stops talking for a while. We both stare out the window of her car as the headlights illuminate endless fenceposts. Then we slip into a redwood grove. The car winds around the large shaggy trunks.

"Oh well, yes," she says. "In those days everyone knew every-one else. We used to have the grandest old time. Weenie roasts on the beach. In those days, you know, we could still have fires on the beach."

She speaks of the old unwritten understandings in town.

"And then a whole lot of people began to come," she says without hostility. "Why is it," she asks, "that for so long we just stood still? And then all of a sudden people started flooding in?"

What is it like to live in Briones now after all those years?

"Well, that's a hard one to answer." She smiles. Maybe she senses a loaded question. I feel the rootlessness of our town, our state, our society. So little local history. No oral or written tradition from the past. Everyone moving around too fast to pick up the antecedents. Each generation acting as though there were nothing to learn from the past, and no future beyond our immediate lives.

. . . As though the world would end with us.

FRANK is sixty years old. He has been a carpenter all his life. An old leftist from the days of the Wobblies and the Spanish Civil War.

He has been around town for some time. A gentle, kind man.

FRANK

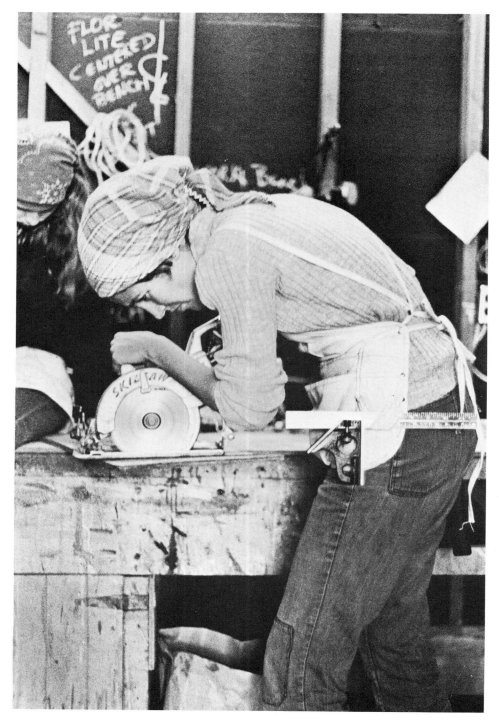

He is partially deaf, but never quite gets it together to trade in his old hearing aid for a new one which works. Sometimes at meetings he turns the volume up so high you can actually hear static crackling and snapping from twenty-five feet away.

Frank has been living in Bob's barn and Lucy's garage. He seems eternally burdened with the tornado of a relationship which howls through his life with someone whom he refers to as "my lady friend."

His garage and barn are cold. He cooks on a Coleman stove.

He has rounded up all his old power tools and moved them into Lucy's garage. He and a group of women have organized a women's carpentry class with a nine-hundred-dollar grant from the County Community Action program and a lot of work. They meet each week.

"Carpentry is like sewing," says Linda. "But sewing is too domestic for me. I *know* I can sew. I don't waste time on things I know I can do."

As a present, the women buy Frank an electric blanket.

It's a slow night at the Bar. It's not as smoky as usual. Very quiet. Several people are shooting pool. Several of the regulars sit at the bar staring into their drinks with a stash of money on the counter in front of them in anticipation of more rounds to come. The jukebox is silent. Three dogs wait patiently outside on the sidewalk for their masters to finish their business inside.

Drinking. Thinking.

We are like termites trying to eat out the bottom in this small insignificant town in a day and age when everyone seems to want to settle his problems at the top, at the power centers rather than at the bottom where all the constituents are.

Write a senator!

Telegraph the President!

Try to get in touch with someone who knows a famous movie star or politician!

We are numbed by the habit of thinking that things always

LYNN

THE BAR

happen over-the-hill, in the Civic Center, in Sacramento, in Washington, Moscow, and Peking.

How about right here? Maybe on Elm Road?

A revolution could start right here on Elm Road and Walter Cronkite might never even notice it.

STEAMY, warm, showery. Days of rain trying to end. Thunderheads over the mountain across the Bay make it look like someone has dropped an atomic test bomb. (The Russians? Chinese? French?)

Evening settles. I head downtown, buy a quart of ale, and go up to the Future Studies Office where Russ is practicing his fencing.

The Future Studies Office is the best place on Wharf Road from which to watch "television."

The windows of Future Studies look out to the main street in front of Scowley's restaurant to the Bar on the far side, action central after dark. Watching TV consists of turning off the lights, opening the window, smoking a joint, sitting just inside the window so that your face is not visible from the street, and watching. It is considered bad TV-watching form to speak from behind the screen to any of the actors on the street or in the Bar, since it makes them all self-conscious and ruins the show.

To the untutored eye, the show appears monotonous and repetitious, e.g., dogs lying on the sidewalk, people coming and going to the Bar, the click of pool balls, the sound of the juke-box, an occasional car, and a rare fight or someone getting eighty-sixed from the bar for rowdiness. But to the knowing eye, the show invariably has drama. Single members of couples who are having trouble arrive looking for some relief and possibly diversion. There are the usual drunks endlessly acting out their saddening and depressing alcoholic reveries. There are the unusual drunks, and groups of people drinking together, getting carried away, dancing, singing. People arrive and leave in unexpected combinations. If nothing else, there are

always the dogs: sniffing, growling, wagging, fighting, sleeping.

Roy comes busting out of the bar onto the "screen." Short, swarthy, longish hair, glasses. He is a sculptor and director of the town theater group. He gives Francine a big hug.

The bartender yells from inside, "You all come back again real soon now, Roy!"

"Any goddamn day of the week," Roy hollers back as he wades through the dogs to the curb.

He pauses. Looks up. Sees our silent grinning faces in the window, watching him.

"Hey, General!" he yells. "When are we getting that Briones Army together?"

THE last three years before the moratorium on new water hookups was declared saw an alarming yearly increase in the number of houses built. The first year there were 14. The second year it rose to 26. The third year the figure increased to 64. Altogether, there are about 650 houses in the town.

Many people became alarmed for the same reason that they fought the old Kennedy sewer. Not only was the town physically beautiful, but there was some almost indescribable quality to it which had to do with smallness of scale, familiarity among people, slowness of pace, absence of crowding. These qualities seemed to hang in the balance. No one was quite certain how one went about insuring that these qualities of a small community could endure. But the victory over the sewer suggested that the town possessed immeasurable strength, provided we could again learn how to mobilize and use it.

The County Planning Department had been at work for some time on a new county-wide master plan which the California legislature had legally required all counties to implement. It was to describe what kinds of development and land uses would be permitted throughout the county's unincorporated areas. But naturally, since the county is so large, the planning staff was able to deal with each area in only a general way. They hoped that more detailed area plans could be done at a later date, and in special cases by the communities themselves.

Our town would not be an easy one for which to plan. Beyond the obvious need to preserve the land around us, there was also the subtler need to arrive at ways by which the people who lived here could sustain themselves without commuting or resorting to connections to the big money pot over-the-hill.

Ironically enough, the largest single employed body of people in town were in the building trades. Almost all the work was small-scale building: A carpenter-contractor would hire a few men to build someone a house. Or a plumber, electrician, or carpenter would help someone build his own house. As Peter, down at the real estate office, described it, "There is a good organic relationship between builders and people in this town. It would be a pity to destroy it." Jobs have traditionally been contracted out by word of mouth. There is no unionization and often no withholding or reporting of income.

"It's cool," says Bill. "You make a little less. But what the hell? Good people and no hassles." Somehow planning and efforts toward slow growth would have to deal with this dilemma.

The only other steady jobs were provided by the School, the BCPUD, the Bird Observatory, the restaurants, the Bar, the post office, and the hardware store. Most of these paid very low (around $2.50 an hour), but people were willing to take them because they were congenial and because they did not require an almost impossible commute.

A great variety of other people made varying amounts of supplemental income farming, fishing, baking, baby-sitting, house painting, cutting firewood, hauling junk, gardening.

Then, there were a rather surprising number of writers, poets, artists, sculptors, weavers, architects, photographers, film makers, cabinetmakers, and musicians who managed to make some part of their incomes by working at home, or elsewhere, whenever opportunity knocked.

A sizable group of retired people had found the town to be a good place to plant a garden, raise a few animals (like chickens, goats, rabbits, ducks, geese), and take it easy. There were also a number of retired younger people who lived on family money, and even a few relatively wealthy young people, most of whom lived quite simple and unflamboyant lives of nonconspicuous consumption.

Last, but not least, was the welfare–food-stamp–medi-Cal contingent, an ever-changing collection of people who at one time or another (or more or less permanently) received checks from the county. Some were utterly indolent and undeserving, others undisputedly deserving, and still others saw this paltry means of support as a way to accomplish a variety of other activities which proved to be important to themselves and the community.

For at least two-thirds of the town, making a living was an irregular and uncertain undertaking centering around part-time and sometime jobs. But these people enjoyed the freedom from a full-time, well-paying job (which most could get if they chose to live in the city), and were willing to put up with a high level of anxiety over where each month's rent or mortgage payment was coming from.

But there were limits. People still needed some sort of work, just as desperately as the land and community needed respite from further inundation. The planning process, as always, was on the horns of a dilemma.

Nonetheless, our town jumped at the possibility of deciding on such questions as zoning, road patterns (even closing off some roads), commercially developable land, land to be put in Agricultural Preserve. Although we knew there were no cure-alls for solutions, or even any legally workable way to effect a growth limitation through the planning process, many people in town knew we had to at least wrestle with it as a community. Otherwise we were doomed to death by "growth."

We formed a group. Got Steve, who is a planner and an architect who lives in town, to help and counsel. A large number of people became interested.

After the usual months of meetings, we decided to have a

Land Fair for one whole weekend in the PUD Grand Ballroom. We also decided to distribute a survey around town to ascertain just how people felt about their town, and what hopes they had for it and themselves in the future.

The Land Fair was a marvel. For two days the room was packed from morning until night. The last night there was a large potluck dinner followed by a talent show consisting of the gymnastic group from the elementary school, a four-year-old girl singing a song about Briones, some jazz, poetry, and a slide show on the town.

The fair itself was a series of informational booths all run by different groups of people (plus a bake sale to make money). One booth was on the town's history, with photographs and old documents. Steve drew up ten large-scale maps in colored Magic Markers which showed our town and surrounding area in terms of elevation, house placement, property boundaries, drainage patterns, roads, zoning, land ownership, wildlife. There were photos by local photographers (one mind-blower in which some condominiums were double-exposed by Betty on top of a well-known cow pasture). There were booths showing labeled samples of local fauna, and a display on wildlife in the Lagoon. The PUD had an exhibit on water and the town water system (which is very leaky). There were videotapes of local people (experts?) talking about water and sewage and of some of the older people talking about the town.

The Land Fair generated a lot of excitement, and got people thinking about the town. It got us all together for a good time and helped us begin to ask for what seemed to be the impossible.

BRIONES PLANNING GROUP

Dear Briones Resident:

This letter accompanies a survey put together by the Briones Planning Group. The purpose of the survey is to supply general demographic information about the town and the people who live in it. There is also an opinion section intended to uncover attitudes of Briones residents towards the community and its development. The survey is absolutely *anonymous*. When you (and everyone in your household over the age of 18) have completed all the questions you wish to answer, please put the questionnaires in the envelope provided and seal. (The envelopes will not be opened until all the questionnaires are in.) The person who delivered them will be back to pick up the envelopes with the questionnaires enclosed.

The survey will be delivered to every house in Briones. We are such a varied community that a partial sampling would leave out important information; we are hoping for a near-100% response rate. By the same token, we hope you will answer every question in the survey; however, if any question seems inappropriate, by all means leave it blank.

You, as a resident of Briones, are a member of the Briones Planning Group. There is a Board of Commissioners which presides at the meetings held on the second and fourth Monday evening of each month at the BCPUD building. These commissioners represent the various community organizations as well as the five geographical sections of town. Everyone is welcome to come and speak out at the open meetings.

With the distribution of this survey comes the first concrete step toward the Planning Group's goal: a locally drawn plan for Briones that will be incorporated into the county's county-wide Master Plan. We hope that the whole community's thinking will be represented in our plan by its response to this questionnaire, and by participation in the meetings, either in person or through its various representatives.

Sincerely yours,

Survey Committee
Briones Planning Group

REVOLUTIONARY DOCUMENT
Judith Weston

The results of the Briones Planning Group survey have been compiled and it is a fascinating document: a blueprint which gives clear guidelines for planning mandated by the residents themselves. Surely it's no secret that in the last year Briones has led the county in seeking revolutionary ways to solve community problems.

The recent election returns for Briones showed the sewer bonds passing 5 to 1, open space bonds 5 to 2, the death penalty losing 5 to 1, Prop. 20 (to establish a Coastal Conservation Commission) winning

5 to 1 and, naturally, the Marijuana initiative winning 5 to 1. These returns were reassuring, proving, in fact that sanity is alive and well in Briones.

EQUAL RESPONSE

Half of the households in Briones were represented in the survey—over 500 people questioned. An equal number of men and women responded. The ages represented show 262 between 18 and 36 and 217 over 35.

Further, respondents who have lived here longer than 11 years outnumbered new-comers (one year or less) by 123 to 108. The bulk of the people have lived here from one to five years, the period which has seen Briones' greatest growth spurt.

Of those people questioned, 237 support the work of the Planning Group, 135 held no opinion and only 15 did not support the group's efforts at local planning. No doubt some who do not support the group chose to not respond to the questionnaire at all. The survey continues with questions relating to income, employment and educational achievement. A well educated community, 238 answered that they are college graduates or hold advanced degrees.

INTERESTING OPINIONS

The last part of the questionnaire dealt with the opinions of the people answering and therefore was by far the most interesting section.

Broken down into percentile figures, these numbers do not represent people, remember, but percentages: Ninety-three percent are glad to be living in Briones; over 72 percent feel a sense of involvement in the community; 76 percent felt Briones should remain about the size it is now; only 6 percent felt that Briones could double in size and still be a desirable place to live.

Sixty-two percent feel there should be a maximum population set for Briones. It isn't surprising then, that 89 percent feel commercial subdivisions are inappropriate for Briones, while only 6 percent felt a Sea Ranch type development would be acceptable here.

An astounding 82 percent feel speculation and profit taking on Briones land should be discouraged; 77 percent felt the number of new homes built in Briones each year should be regulated by the community.

SEWAGE

Directors of the BCPUD might have known that their Bond issue would pass since 78 percent of those surveyed said they would support a bond issue for sewage treatment downtown while 96 percent felt it was important that something be done about the discharge of raw sewage into the Lagoon. Eighty-seven percent felt that decisions affecting the future of Briones should be made within the community, and 63 percent felt Briones should have its own local government.

In questions dealing with open space and preservation, 96 percent felt that preservation of the Lagoon and the Reef were very important, 90 percent felt setting aside land as open space is crucial for any master plan, and 77 percent said they would support a bond issue to preserve open space in the community.

KEEP OUT

Watch out, tourists! Only 8 percent of the people feel that Briones should expand its tourist facilities and only 12 percent favored any straightening and widening of the existing roads from over-the-hill. Almost 40 percent of the residents would like non-resident automobiles restricted from entering Briones.

And perhaps the most revolutionary proposal of all: 77 percent feel that tighter controls on dogs running free should be imposed. Far Out!

What all these numbers and percentages indicate is pretty clear. They say that no matter what our age, our income, our educational background, and the length of time we have lived here, an overwhelming proportion of people living in Briones now love living here and want to preserve our small town way of life. The ways to do that: buying up open space through local bond issues, keeping tourism to a minimum, limits to population growth and to the type of development allowed, and no road improvement received very strong backing.

It is also clear, that Brionesites want a far greater degree of decision making process to be carried out here within our community, by ourselves. The Planning Group, therefore, is now starting to study the question of incorporation.

DIFFERENCES

Interesting, there were some dichotomies which the community will need to understand. Only 22 percent felt that Briones should develop a low-cost housing program, while 49 percent felt that there should be strict enforcement of laws against people living in trucks and temporary dwellings.

But 186 people responding to the questionnaire reported yearly incomes of $7,000 or less. Without resorting to low-cost dwellings, a ceiling on rents or on profit making, how will people with little money be able to afford to live here?

The new-style planners in the West County will be working towards solutions which had not been thought of before, although the idea of population growth limits was actually thought up by the old guard who've lived here the longest (as in: "Why don't you all go back to where you come from?"). It certainly was an idea whose time had come.

NIGHTTIME. Downtown.

Walking down Wharf Road to the beach dreaming about the days when the old schooner *Owl* used to ply the Lagoon Channel from the city, carrying mail, passengers, and supplies which were unloaded on the Briones docks.

But the lumbermen took the trees off the hills to build San Francisco. Virgin Douglas fir and redwoods standing hundreds of feet high were fed into the mills. The creeks flowed with eroding silt, and slowly the Lagoon Channel filled in. The *Owl* stopped coming, replaced by the automobile. Everyone wanted one.

There are only a few small fishing boats around the docks tonight. Just the barest intimation that we live on the edge of an ocean.

The town is quiet.

The light is still on in the laundromat. The liquor store is closed. An occasional car passes. A dyspeptic dog streaks out to challenge an old Nash filled with Don's beautiful daughters.

The town feels right tonight. Not too big, but offering good company. Self-contained without being cut off. A whole worth struggling for.

ROLF is a real estate man. He is in his middle thirties. He drives an Audi. He belongs to the Sierra Club. Has a family. Talks about his organic tomatoes with gladness and satisfaction. He wears well-tailored suits which give him an eastern aristocratic look. He is a reasonable and very likable man, and he owns 210 acres of land in Briones upon which he plans to construct a lodge, condominiums, tennis courts, an amphitheater, and a restaurant.

Today he comes out to talk to various people on the Planning Group about his plans, which have generated almost complete and uncompromising opposition in town.

We walk out across the mesa to where his land lies on the coast. We finally stop and sit down on the cliff top where the sod is sloughing off and slowly raining pieces of earth down on the beach below. We watch the gulls catch the updrafts over the cliff, and glide along its rim. Except for the wind, the surf, and our voices, there is no sound.

We talk. Rolf says he has investigated possible agricultural uses such as artichokes and Christmas trees. They are not commercially feasible, he says. We talk about the possibility of trying a new kind of commercial development, of subdividing into 50-acre family or multifamily farms for people who did not have to depend on all their income coming from the land, a new kind of subdivision with barns, fences, agricultural water supply, windmills, houses.

Rolf is intrigued. But he speaks of the need for a fair profit for himself and his partners.

Profit vs. use. The old problem. When it comes to land, money cancels invention.

WALK up to the PUD office to check with EPA (Environmental Protection Agency) about our sewer grants.

American sewage treatment orthodoxy is just coming out of the Middle Ages. The technology is moving faster than people's ability to absorb and feel comfortable with new ways of treating human waste. Millions are spent for disposal, pennies for reuse.

A sign hangs in the PUD window, showing an ugly little guy with his face all screwed up looking at a turd in his hand. "Tired of the same old shit?" reads the caption. "Vote YES on the Briones sewer bond."

Our sewer is going to be a shrine. It will be small.

People know. Large sewers lead to accelerated development. Can't develop unless you can figure out where to put the puckey. It's nature's protection against man's violence on himself.

Finally the land can't soak up any more water and shit through septic tanks and individual waste treatment facilities. They put in sewers.

The land becomes irrelevant. Its natural carrying capacity is circumvented. Pipes, pumps, force mains, comminutors, trickle filters, activated sludge, blinking lights, chlorine take over. The land loses its ability to slow us down.

We ignore its signs. We substitute technology. We go right on expanding, growing, carving up the land.

When any public works project is built, the most crucial decision of all is, "How big is it going to be?" The size of the pipes determines the size of human settlement. How do public officials usually decide? They plot a growth curve. They look at how fast the town or area has grown in the last few years, add a little, and project it into the future. They think they are simply "accommodating" a natural, unavoidable phenomenon. But, in truth, they are creating it. They are creating growth without ever asking (1) What are it's implications? (2) Is it desirable from a human standpoint? (3) Do people want it?

Will people actually vote to pay more money for water and sewage systems which will crowd their schools, surround them with development, create traffic, require increased commercial services, and pollute their environment?

Explain it to them, and ask them at the ballot box.

Our sewer will be built so it will serve only existing houses and provide for a small amount of infilling. No new areas will be developed because of our sewer.

It is too *small*.

Our shortages are our blessing. Scarcity is our comfort.

In a perverse way, the gods have blessed us with an inadequate water and sewage system.

Our leaks protect us.

I grew up in the City. Watched them wreck neighborhoods for "redevelopment." They tore down the "slums," the candy stores, bars, delicatessens, ice cream shops, magazine shops, and restaurants where people used to hang out and get together. We became strangers in the same building, sharing walls with people whose names and faces were mysteries, cherishing our privacy as a luxury, and wondering at our isolation if Saturday night rolled around and we had not got anything together ahead of time. We were afraid of even walking on the streets. Our locks were our sole comfort.

In this town, people seem to get together with greater ease. Numerous meetings take place in the street, at the post office, in the laundromat, the Store, the Bar, Scowley's, Tarantino's restaurant, on the beach. There are a great number of town events and festivals at which everyone is welcome, such as poetry readings, concerts, film showings, exhibits, potluck dinners, dances, and happenings. One goes if one wants, or stays home if one wants. Such public gatherings create little sense of anyone's being "in" or "out." They engender little social competition. There is no jockeying for invitations to the houses of the select. It is perfectly acceptable for a woman or a man to be alone. The fear of being left out or lonely is diminished. There is a certain democracy of social life, and although I cannot prove it, I know it continues to flourish because we have not allowed ourselves to grow too large.

A guy who manufactures dental plates picks me up and drops me one cloverleaf before I want to get off the freeway.

There is about one-half a mile of freeway between me and the building supply store where I want to buy some plastic pipe fittings. The freeway has been gouged and blasted through a large hill topped like a nut sundae by a housing development.

It is clear that unless I take the freeway I cannot get to Goodman's Building Supply Depot without taking a two-hour walk around the hill.

I head off down the feeder ramp feeling very minuscule.

Smog.

Cars whiz past.

Drivers crane their necks, look behind to see if they are going to be obliterated by a semi as they knife off the feeder ramp into the swift main current of cars.

I walk with my eyes on the roadside searching for nuts, bolts, washers, and other spare pieces of hardware which have spun off the leviathans hurtling past me. A precious and inexhaustible inventory lies amidst the other freeway effluvia.

Freeway shoulders are linear garbage dumps. Transcontinental junk piles of metal, chrome, rubber, plastic, wood, glass, and paper. Each foot of a freeway is unowned, uncared for. Miles and miles of land which is always someone else's responsibility. A means of moving, and a place to throw stuff away. Right, Colonel Sanders?

I continue my journey toward the next turnoff, and am just about to lean over and pop a four-inch carriage bolt into my pocket, when I hear the tires of a car crunching to a stop on the gravel behind me.

"Well, hello, officer."

"What do you think you're doing?"

"Actually, officer, I was hitching because my truck's in the shop, and this guy left me off an exit too soon. Want to get some fittings at Goodman's, and there's no way to get there without taking the freeway. The hill's in the way."

"Well, ya know . . . ."

"Nothing like a pair of feet to save energy, officer."

"Yeah. Well, OK. But ya know it's against the law to walk on a freeway, doncha?"

"Oh yeah? Well, I can see why. I won't let it happen again."

IF you leave the road out of town at the School, and walk up Pine Gulch Creek under the alders for about a half a mile, you arrive in Paradise Valley. It was one of the favorite campgrounds of the Miwok Indians before the white man arrived. There remain several Indian shell mounds near the creek, which still provides clear fresh water throughout even the dry season.

When white settlers arrived, they, too, found the valley an ideal place to live, grow their crops, and raise cattle. The ground was fertile, and it was protected from winter storms by hills surrounding it on all sides. The coastal fog seemed generous, so often hovering just at the ridge top and advancing no farther. Even today, when the town is buried deep in fog, the valley is sunny and warm.

There are still apple orchards in the valley, planted by our unknown and forgotten precursors. The split-picket redwood fences still stand some hundred years later. They follow the grassy ridge on one side, and cross the creek into bay and alder trees where they run up the canyons of the steep wooded western hills. They mark an almost perfectly proportioned and secluded land form, a small universe of its own.

Slowly word filters around town that the lower part of Paradise Valley has been bought. People are curious. Some are apprehensive. Rumors abound. Questions are unanswered. Who bought it? What will happen? Will it be developed? Is a hippie commune moving in? Drugs, transients, VD, noise, garbage?

The land, about forty-eight acres, has been bought by a group in town called the New Land Fund. It is a nonprofit organization committed to trying to work out new relations between people and the land. The land will be leased at very low rent to families who hope to plant orchards, plow the earth for gardens, and build their own houses, barns, and sewage treatment system. The land will be held in trust, removed from speculation, and put back into agriculture. The cost is $187,000, a gift by two wealthy people who see the issue of land as central to the future, and now live and farm in the town.

Ilka and I are one of the eight families, who among them have seventeen children.

The vision is to start a multifamily farm. Each person with his own house. Sharing barns, gardens, trucks, animals, and know-how.

But we are sawing across the grain. We refuse to subdivide into parcels. Don't want electricity or flush toilets as required by the Uniform Building Code. Want to build well but inexpensively, out of used building materials. Try windmills, waterwheels, methane generators, composting toilets, solar heaters, organic agriculture. Pry our way in and around all the codes, laws, permits, red tape, and struggle for money, and position ourselves somewhat closer to the earth, the trees, the sky, the water, our food, our houses, manual labor, each other.

Members of Paradise Valley Produce, as we call ourselves, vary in age from twenty-four years to sixty. We consist of two carpenters, two Public Utilities District directors, a writer, a woodcutter, a school shop teacher, a kindergarten teacher, a weaver, an architect-planner, an illustrator, a photographer, and a gardener-landscaper.

PARADISE VALLEY

Somehow we all got together. It took almost two years, from the time Nancy, Susan, and Renée, three single mothers, first started investigating the possibility of buying a piece of land or a house together. The cost was prohibitive. This was just about the same time that several other people like Greg, Russ, Steve, and Dennis began to get inklings that perhaps Briones was not going to be just another two-year stop on the drifters' circuit. The Kennedy sewer had been stopped, we had won high political office, and were now daily dealing in millions of dollars, but had no homes.

The scenario varied for everyone. But everyone was looking for roots.

"If there isn't a place for people like us to live here," I remember Greg asking, "then what are we fighting for?" Greg was sleeping in his sleeping bag under an old abandoned barn at the time.

Twenty-five different families must have been members of the group at one time or another. People dropped out. Some got disenchanted with the long and sometimes crazy meetings. Others found mates and retreated into single-family lives. New people became enthusiastic and joined. The pot kept boiling, as it still does. Finally, we boiled ourselves down to eight families. We all shared some hard-to-articulate connection with Briones. Many of us had been through numerous political town battles together and all of us had an urge to homestead. None of us had the money. And while I am not sure exactly why, that fact never seemed to bother any of us.

I remember the first time I walked up the creek to Paradise Valley. It was fall. The alders were turning. The creek was low, the fields orange. I sat on the creek bank in absolute silence, and looked across at the place where Dennis would build his house out of telephone poles and fine old wood from a wrecked warehouse. I did not even know who owned the land then. It did not occur to me at the time to wonder. But I recall thinking this was one of the loveliest valleys I had ever seen. But it was not mine. And that day, I walked quietly

through it under the trees wondering if anyone would come and kick me off.

WARREN and Marion contributed the money to buy Paradise Valley and set up the New Land Fund, an incorporated entity with a board of directors consisting of the donors and two members from Paradise Valley Produce.

The fact that $187,000 is a lot of money has not escaped our attention. There is a strange irony in the fact that our efforts to change and reform our relationships to land must first be threaded through a generous gift, a gift of money from a system which we hold accountable for many of our ills.

In most poor countries which have undergone deep changes, the land has been taken, expropriated. In our own country, the rebels must buy their land in order to carry out their rebellion.

Nonetheless . . .

We all hope that Paradise Valley will be the first of several land experiments in town undertaken by the New Land Fund. As Paradise Valley repays it, money will be available for other ventures—more land, or perhaps a feedstore or community freezer.

Warren writes a description of how he sees the Land Fund:

A COUNTERPLOT LAND FUND

A nonprofit revolving fund, the New Land Fund has been created to aid much needed land reform in this country. Twenty-two hundred eighty farmers per week for the last twenty years have been relinquishing their farms. Agribusiness oligarchies increasingly control the land, production, and marketing of the US's food supply. The soil is depleted by chemicals and monoculture. Pesticides are threatening numerous species of wildlife. Mining and clear-cutting are raping the land of natural contours and erosion protection. Leapfrog development blights our open spaces. The story goes on without a sufficient counterplot. The New Land Fund is an attempt to change the story by:

1. Challenging the notion that land itself (apart from

improvements made on it) ought to be owned and speculated on.

2. Aiding people in finding ways to live on and farm the land organically, ecologically, responsibly, and joyfully.

The New Land Fund proposes to achieve these two objectives by establishing a revolving fund which would purchase selected parcels of land for individual farmers or communities wanting to move onto it and work it. Upon purchase, the NLF will lease land to individuals until the land is paid off. Once it is paid off, the individuals on the land will be able to lease it back from the NLF in perpetuity for a token rent. Alternatively, those living on the land could establish their own nonprofit corporation similar to the NLF and receive title to the land.

The NLF sees its function as driving a small wedge into the present structure of land ownership, speculation, and misuse. It seeks to find people who not only want to stay on the land or go back to it, but who also identify strongly with the need to organize locally at a political level to effectively challenge outmoded building codes, subdivision requirements, patterns of speculation, and traditional patterns of energy consumption. The NLF seeks to create a heightened awareness of the potential relations between land and human community.

JOHN

JOHN is a carpenter, one of the best in town. He builds houses, does cabinet work, carves doors, makes furniture. He now lives in Paradise Valley in a half-finished house which he designed and built himself. He shares it with his three children, whom he has raised himself since he and his wife had a parting of the ways years ago. He earns a living, cooks, does the laundry, takes the kids to the doctor.

He has lived in town for over twelve years. He was one of the first of the new wave of immigrants who transformed the town in a matter of years from a predominantly summer and weekend vacation town into a year-round community.

"It sure is easier with a woman around," he says with a sardonic smile.

John grew up in Kentucky and Texas, the son of a pacifist who lost his job teaching during the Second World War.

"Worked oil rigs in west Texas for a while," he says. "Odessa, Texas. Lived in a hotel room, and had to drive a hundred and twenty miles out to where we were drilling. We worked in four-man teams. Spent about every fourth night in town. You know, three guys would sleep, and the fourth would just floorboard out to the job. Driver was half asleep, too. Those guys worked seven days a week. Had those drills going three hundred sixty-five days a year. They had the caps up on two big diesels twenty-four hours a day. Four hours down, four hours up on those big diamond drills. I was a 'weevil,' the lowest guy on the totem pole. I used to grease the crowns on the rigs. It was cold up there in those Texas winters. Just a thin

[39]

dusting of snow. And you could see the mountaintops four hundred miles away across the flat.

"I don't know how those guys did it. Made good money. They worked seven days a week. Two days a week at time-and-a-half. They all bought new cars every year and had a house trailer. But they never had any money. Spent it all! Mostly gambling. Big cardshark would come into town and take it all away. And some whoring, too! I remember one really incredible guy. He says to me, 'Hey, weevil! Didja ever fuck a Chinaman?'

"So I tell him, 'No. Did you?'

" 'No,' he says, 'but I fucked a coupla Chinese women! Ha ha ha!'

"Those guys were unbelievable. And man, they loved their cars. My brother lent me this old '39 Hollywood Graham. Big V-8. Doors that opened back to front. Big fenders. They really didn't like to ride in anything so funky. They all had Pontiacs or something. So, anyway, one day we're blasting out to work, and the linkage goes on her. We went through a couple of fences out onto a field. But we got her going again. Just tied up the linkage with some barbed wire and a couple of old sixteen-penny nails we found on the floor, and got her back to the garage."

John writes a letter to his father in Texas about what's going on in Paradise Valley in his present life:

For a week now we have been living in the valley. The move was very time-consuming and tiring. Five solid days of packing, hauling, sweeping, dumping, raking, selling, losing, discarding, and head scratching. All that accumulation. All that dirt, memories, and reminders. I was apprehensive: It meant giving up of habits (my daily hot shower, TV, cold milk, telephone, oven, etc.). But my fears seem to have been, as usual, groundless. We love it and are adjusting. Even the cats love it. I believe it is good.

There are difficulties ahead (apprehensions again). Interfamily (we who plan to live in the valley think of ourselves as a family) relationships need work and the potential conflicts with the bureaucracies. So far the internal problems pivot around the garden. The garden is central, as agriculture is our aim, and it requires a great deal of effort just now. And we are all very busy working, building, moving, and so forth. We have weekly meetings where we discuss communal chores, responsibilities, complaints, and plans. We are a very diverse group. This causes problems, but is, I'm sure, ultimately healthy.

The external pitfalls are something I should use some ribbon on because I know our stand must worry and interest you. Me too. What we are doing is civil disobedience. I feel like neither a criminal or a revolutionary. Our county (by no means uniquely) has been (is being) massively despoiled by developers. Many acres of delicate and beautiful land is cut, divided, and rendered useless (in any real way, by our lights) by greed. We (mankind) *must* learn to use our land more wisely and sensitively. And this is exactly what we want to learn to do with this valley, for ourselves and as an example.

Our disobedience will be directed mostly toward the building codes. I see (we see) building codes as a mass of legislation developed to protect buyers from dishonourable sellers, builders, realtors etc., to fatten manufacturers of materials and lastly to protect those who live in buildings. Our motive is not profit, and we believe in our honour anyway. Our charter makes it impossible for us to realize profit from our buildings. We will live in our valley and farm it, so who is better qualified to establish standards for that life than us?

We will do things differently, hopefully better, and you know how institutions discourage change. For instance, septic tanks (which the county would approve) along this creek are polluting it. Fortunately, there are only a few, the water is potable. The valley floor is sandy and gets very wet in the winter. We will use composting privies. Our excrement will be completely contained (also, we will probably try to generate methane from it) until it is safe to return to the soil, and useful. We are renting chemical toilets until we get them built. This is a new idea for officialdom and they will need convincing. Nobody makes a profit from this method of waste disposal . . . except for our garden and conscience.

Part of our responsibility is to do things demonstrably better than code. We intend to welcome their positive advice, but we will reject those things which we judge to be inapplicable to our needs. Also there are financial considerations: if we did it by the books we would need much more money (and time) than we have. We would need surveyors, grading contractors, more expensive materials than we want or need, and on and on. . . . Having just sold a house, I am perhaps the most affluent member, and I couldn't afford it. I don't want to be in debt, I don't believe in it. Why should only the rich be able to afford to have land and to build homes?

Another aspect of all this is my (our) growing uneasiness about this huge insecure political/economic/cultural structure hanging over all our heads. Just look at it: Watergate, Cambodia, fuel shortages, inflation, decadence and all those myriad symptoms of sicknesses nobody really recognizes such as drugs, corruptions, perversions, cruelties, inequities etc. Madness. Danger. We see independence, self-sufficiency as insurance. It may sound melodramatic to speak of simple survival, but it might prove to be realistic.

At any rate, these are some disorganized sketches of my motives for trying this. I recognize the gamble. I want more and more for it to work. We can, with work, luck and time, develop a very good life here. It does involve disobedience, yes, but on that Higher Level . . . how revoltingly noble!

Love, J

THE Department of Highways announces that, for reasons of "safety and easier maintenance," they still intend to widen and straighten the highway.

"Why not just put a sign up which says, 'BEAUTIFUL LAND, DRIVE SLOW!'?" suggests Libby.

The battle of the highway continues. People riled up. Writing letters. Making phone calls to various politicians. Trying to contact people in the neighboring towns. Concern is great. But in this struggle, as in all others, it again becomes obvious that we have not effectively solved the problem of keeping people plugged-in and informed.

The first thing they go after during a revolution is the radio station.

PROBLEMS of Organizing a Community:

It's like ordering a meal. You give the waiter your order. Don't want to see the kitchen, feel the heat, or deal with the dirty dishes.

Gimme the meal!

Even in a town as active and educated as this, most people are passive participants in the political process. They're good people. But they'd rather find someone to do it *for* them if he or she can be found.

Last year when we were still fighting the old Kennedy sewer, Future Studies organized a big feast down by the dock on Wharf Road. We dragged out a giant twenty-foot slab of redwood for a table. Everyone was dressed up in pretty clothes. Sunset. Confusion. Dogs scarfing up unattended paper plates full of the potluck dinner. Kids yelling.

After the food dwindled, we tried to have a meeting on the dock so that everyone could say what was on his/her mind about the sewer. But no one wanted to play chairman, get people quieted down and focused.

Finally, Betty piped up, "Hey! We need someone to lead us!"

The problem is to find individuals who are willing to lead, who are not just "civic-minded" power freaks.

Not so many people like the idea of being a leader and getting stuck with all the shitwork. People are so deeply into their own lives. Who has time to spare to lead and be responsible for others?

MORE and more people have begun working on the Plan. The Planning Group has been given a workroom at the PUD Building.

Good news today.

The Planning Group gets a grant from some guy who stayed here a while and became "enchanted" with the town. Confusingly enough, he is a developer himself. He is a rather short, nervous man with worried eyes who has his hair done and wears flowered shirts.

Who can explain it? Bad conscience? Heart of gold? His way to work off karma? Anyway, he has given several thousand dollars on a matching basis to hire Steve and Patrick to do map work, plan writing, and community organizing.

People agree at our weekly meeting to raise the rest of the money needed by going door to door and through benefits. All issues about this town's future seem to be glued together and connected.

Can you plan an economy for a town like this which will not whore after tourists? Is agriculture possible? Is there any way to break the dependency on the city and the endless commute . . . even in some small measure? Are we stuck with the automobile?

"Even if we get a great plan, how are we going to make it happen?" asks Nancy.

"Regular planning misses the point," says Don. "LA has planners. And look at it! It isn't just a question of putting classier houses in the right place. There's something else. Briones magically seems to have qualities which make us want to live here. What are they? Can we plan for them? Will the law allow them?"

"Sure. That's it right there," says someone else. "Will the law allow them? Seems like all this other development is legal . . . the stuff that's making the world so horrible."

"A town is like a house," says Don. "It must be designed to be lived in in a human sense, and not just for efficiency or people's financial convenience."

SITTING on the ridge above the highway, watching the sun slide behind the ocean. The commuters speed home around the Lagoon. The night herons continue concentrating on pecking fish out of the shallow water. The town is laid out below like a relief map.

For a moment I fantasize about what this coastline must have been like before the first Spaniard rode over the mountains from the Mission. Dark. Quiet. Awesome.

A helicopter rattles overhead. An intruding airborne chain saw. Thousands of people on land break concentration, look up, wonder why. Maybe utter a curse or a sigh of resignation.

This morning, too, we were awakened by a Navy helicopter which came down the cliffs at about two hundred feet. Then he stopped and hovered over the reef.

The birds went up.

The harbor seals began thrashing and flopping around trying to get into the water.

Snarling machine.

Write a letter to the Navy: "Why is the Navy bothering seals? Aren't you guys a little overcommitted?"

We cannot escape what men are doing to each other, because they are doing it to the earth and all its creatures as well.

This recognition will someday make revolutionaries and fanatics who will die for the earth, rather than for communism or democracy.

The sun disappears. A family of five deer appears. Two bucks, two does, and a fawn.

FOUR of us sit in the PUD meeting room waiting for the coffee to perk, and scheming on the best ways to campaign for passage of $385,000 worth of bonded indebtedness for our new and improved sewer.

Start putting out another issue of the *BEEPUD Pipeline*, the official PUD propaganda organ.

"Even this little sewer is going to cost a lot," says Greg as we finally leave. "What we've got to do is help redistribute the lack of wealth."

We are legally bound to build a sewer. The state has taken us to court and may, at its discretion, levy a $6,000 per diem fine on our Lilliputian utilities district with a budget of $117,000 this year. Our new sewer will use organic treatment processes and will recycle sewage and spray-irrigate it for agricultural use instead of "disposing" it into the ocean all dosed-up with chlorine. Chlorine kills "germs." But what do they think it will do to marine life?

What a ridiculous, unhealthy, inefficient, wasteful, expensive device the flush toilet is. Why do we flush our shit away in pure drinking water for which we spend billions to collect, pipe, filter, chlorinate, test, and deliver?

It takes from five to seven gallons for one flush of the average toilet. Toilets account for approximately 40 percent of household water consumption. This means that almost half our dams, reservoirs, treatment facilities, and pipes are built to provide water to handle shit.

Some people have suggested that we use water from baths and sinks to flush toilets. But even this is madness. What does water have to do with human waste in the first place? Water actually complicates the process of using or disposing of human waste because it adds bulk and gives the waste mobility, so that it becomes hard to contain. If one looks at the history of man, one finds that only for the tiniest fraction of time has he "flushed away" his excrement. The flush toilet is a relatively new (and probably passing) fad.

Before the sit-down water closet, people shat in a hole and composted their shit with ashes, lime, and vegetable matter. For thousands of years, other civilizations have cherished shit of all kinds as fertilizer and fuel. In China, any tenant, worker, or family member who shat in another man's privy was severely chastised, so valuable was (is) the waste considered. Horses and oxen which haul carts in the street have burlap contraptions fastened behind them, lest their shit fall on the street, be wasted, and make a mess.

Excrement is a valuable natural resource, part of the cycle through which soil is replenished with the residues of what men have taken from it for themselves. But so scared have we become of shit that we have forgotten there was any logic to the way our forefathers, or less "developed" fellow men, handled it. In our rush to turn toilets into hospital-like fixtures, we have debunked without investigation many of the simpler methods of the past which actually worked, or which, with minor technological changes, could have been made infinitely sounder than present-day practices.

It is now 1973. In 1870, *Scientific American* took a stand. The debate is old:

> MAY, 1870: "We have, as our readers are well aware, taken strong ground in favor of the earth closet as a substitute for the water closet, and have based our opinion upon both sanitary and economic considerations. It appears to us, however, that the immense importance of this subject has not seized upon the public mind, and that it fails to be appreciated except by such as have given special attention to the subject of the disposal of sewage. We find this subject fully discussed in all its bearings in the technical journals, and numerous plans—some of them of the most impracticable character—are proposed, but the popular press in this country has been content to drop the subject after a brief discussion and leave the matter to whatever issue destiny has reserved for it. In our opinion no current topic is freighted with such import as the question of cutting off the enormous drain of fertilizing matter now permitted to wash away into the sea, and the purification of the waters that surround large cities from the pollutions now permitted to contaminate them and the atmosphere that sweeps over them."

The outhouse works on the elementary principle that all dead organic matter very quickly undergoes a process of biological breakdown. The matter is literally consumed, or digested, by the bacteria present in and around it. The process works slower or faster depending on variables like temperature, moisture level, bacteria content, and the nature of the organic matter.

Shit, in the bottom of an outhouse hole, breaks down either by an aerobic process (in which oxygen-feeding bacteria digest the nitrogen and phosphate in shit and give off carbon dioxide and water) or by an anaerobic process (in which non-oxygen-feeding bacteria digest the shit and give off methane gas— more commonly referred to as farts).

In an outhouse, the process is mainly anaerobic, since little oxygen can penetrate into the center of the pile. This is why people often aerate their compost piles with perforated pipe. It allows the air to reach the center of the stack. Aerobic action goes slightly faster, and does not cause the methane odor given off through the fermenting process of the more slowly digesting anaerobic pile of matter.

One can view this whole procedure of organic breakdown in an outhouse as a pile of shit being devoured by an army of very small but hungry (and reproducing) bacteria. By the time they have finished eating, they will have reduced the bulk of the original matter to about one-twentieth of its original size. The shit literally gets re-eaten by the bacteria. They merely continue the process of our stomachs. They consume nutrients as energy and "crap" out the residue. The bacteria in the outhouse complete another stage of the biological process which breaks down our waste into its component parts.

If you talk to a health inspector (a real treat!), he will gravely inform you that the bogeymen in the outhouse are the parasites and "bad germs," or pathogenic bacteria which bear disease. He will terrorize you with tales of pestilence and paranoia that put shit well up there on the Public Enemies List.

However, normally, if a person is healthy, there is no problem. Pathogens in the body will show up in one's shit and end up at the bottom of the outhouse. This is where all the lights start blinking and the alarms start ringing in health circles. But then again, a person may sneeze on you. Kiss you. Touch you. Eat off the same plate. So it is not the case that people can become diseased only through contact with shit.

Those pathogens in the bottom of a privy will die rapidly, since most survive only at body temperature. Viruses are more of a problem. But then, they are also a problem in sewage treatment plants since they do not respond to chlorine treatment with any reliability, and since they are not yet adequately understood.

Neither harmful bacteria nor viruses pose any problem with an outhouse, unless they manage to get out. If an outhouse is unscreened, flies, which are notorious shit-gourmets, may fly them out, or plant their larvae on shit in the outhouse and leave it to their sons and daughters to fly them out. Or a poorly situated privy may leak contaminants into underground water-bearing strata which might carry the bacteria to a well, stream, or lake.

One must, of course, choose an outhouse site with care, making sure that the area is well drained, with good percolation. Or, one can seal the chamber of the outhouse with fiber-glass or concrete, guaranteeing that nothing gets out until it is well composted and has undergone some prescribed period of detention. This method is called the compost privy.

Finally, neo-outhouse enthusiasts are encouraged to install seals on their privies which prevent insects from entering (under the seat, through the back) and spreading bacteria. But under normal conditions, any evil germs will die a natural death looking up at the hole wondering why rural health inspectors are making such a big deal out of them.

So, what's wrong with an outhouse?

Nothing, if it works right.

It needs no water. Provides good fertilizer. Is cheap. Does not require expensive sewers and collection systems. Does not need costly septic tanks and leaching fields (about sixteen hundred to two thousand dollars a shot), which are really nothing more than liquid anaerobic digesters allowing all the methane to escape through the small vents on your roof.

Most of the problem seems to come from backlash against the simple, the tried, and the old-fashioned.

Why do people have electric knives? Why are they spraying everything in the house with aerosol poison? Who knows?

Perhaps it is because we have all been taught a kind of TV vision of health which threatens of killer germs behind every toilet. Staph, strep, salmonella lurking in the unclean toilet bowl!

I mean, would an astronaut have an outhouse in his rocket ship?

Even as far back as 1860, Victor Hugo complained in *Les Misérables* that by disposing of its wastes through an elaborate underground sewer system into the Seine, and ultimately the ocean, "Paris casts 25 million francs annually into the sea . . ."

I have spent five years in this town.

Major milestones seem as elusive as ever. It is hard to judge our accomplishments.

Is the sewer done yet? Is the Plan finished? Is Paradise Valley on the cusp of resolving its outlaw status? Has anyone started a dairy or bakery, blocked off a road, got an answer to the weekend tourist madness?

The answer is often no.

And yet, something unusually hopeful is transpiring here. Often I see it more clearly in the small daily details of life than in the large earth-shaking issues—in the almost unnoticeable moments of gladness, in people walking and talking together, in the absence of fear in people's faces, in their enthusiasm for the future. But people here too are plagued with the problems of loving and living with one another. Briones clearly offers no panacea for the seeker of total salvation.

The town is not a cult.

Almost every week someone moves out on someone else. Long marriages dissolve. Quickie affairs end, leaving people unsure for the moment how to approach the former partners. Then there are the times when the phone rings: "Please! Can you come over?" Arguments, fights.

The process of breakup and recombination is unending. Each incident is noticeable for anyone who cares to pay attention. The recognitions are unavoidable among our friends. There appears to be no real escape or antidote anywhere for this anguish.

But perhaps these cases are only the lancing of the boil, the pain before the healing. The town allows these changes, even encourages them.

No stigma is attached to failing in marriage, or in an affair which ends after a month or ten years. These are commonly shared and acknowledged experiences. There is comfort in being in some context when one's personal life goes to hell.

Briones is tolerant. Perhaps too tolerant. Friends tend to be almost too accepting of each other's oddity and pain. People make an effort to see the good or creative side of almost everyone, even those who might need help or even hospitalization.

Nervous breakdowns.

Alcoholics.

Suicidal people.

Drugs.

We might sometimes take a sterner hand with our friends. Help each other get set straight, rather than watching so long in fascinated tolerance.

It is not easy to become a pariah in Briones if you live here.

HITCH back under the stars from our neighboring town.

Campaign meeting. A young guy is running for the Community College District Board, which spends millions of dollars a year over-the-hill.

Four people show up.

For most people, the college board is just another maze of bureaucrats, more paper, more meetings.

The county is not a community. Too big. Who could organize a whole county effectively? Who could even find the pieces, much less put them all back together again? Most of the communities have long since dissolved into regional schools, regional sewers, regional government, county sheriffs.

So, here's this young cat trying to run for this board way out in this hick town on the coast. Trying to let people know what he believes in, and four people show.

The other candidates didn't even bother coming out here.

We couldn't possibly have drunk all the coffee and eaten all the Oreos ourselves.

Politics should not be so lonely.

GOOD news arrives.

Our state senator has convinced the Department of Highways' regional chief to come out here for another town meeting on the fate of the highway.

Someone suggests inviting the highwayman to dinner. Peter suggests cooking him a mushroom dish. "If he widens our road, we'll widen his mind."

In honor of the upcoming town meeting, the highway sign is painted over in black.

For several months now, the large green sign with white

iridescent letters which stands on the highway and marks the turnoff to town has been periodically painted over, bent, and removed in toto by various night phantoms. Sooner or later the Department of Highways maintenance crews reerect it. And sooner or later it again meets its demise.

Some people in town are furious at what they consider pranks by irresponsible elements.

"Well, jeez, I'll tell you," says one man, a retired mayor of a suburban city, "we had these friends who went right past here trying to come and visit us. I mean, they went all the way up twelve miles to the trailer camp before they figured it out!"

Other people see the disappearance of the sign as a blessing.

"Does anyone want all those goddamn cars in town?" asks one of the phantoms.

The war of the Briones sign has become an event of such global importance that the Associated Press has run an entire story about it on the wire.

"This windswept town," the article begins, "would like the rest of the world to think it has disappeared."

Noting that our town is "isolated in picturesque territory just perfect for a Sunday drive," the article quotes Dan down at the Store.

"The people in this town want to feel it's a town," he says, "not a tourist trap. Taking down signs is one solution, and it works. We close down on Sundays because of the tourists. They dirty the place up and they only buy potato chips and little things."

"People come in and say that they have been looking for the town for hours," says Mary at the Bar, noting that sometimes they go "twenty miles north before they realize they have missed the turnoff."

A little more publicity like this, and signs will begin disappearing all over the country.

THE election approaches. Our new sewer hangs in the balance, as does the purchase of ninety federally funded acres right in the middle of town on which it will be situated.

Good planning. Get sewers and reservoirs to pay for open space.

I'd rather have a tastefully designed sewer than a high-rise for a neighbor, any day.

Meetings, mailers, phone calls.

We think people understand.

THE lore of this special coastal highway grows.

A classified ad in a small paper further up the highway to the north reads:

Personal

To the hitchhiker I picked up near Elk on the Highway:
I am pregnant.

Betsy

GREG returns from jail with little fanfare. He hitches home. He just suddenly reappears. Looks just about the same, long snarled blond hair, baggy pants, beard, nondescript shirt, red and white cardigan letter sweater with a large felt "R" on the left pocket, which was acquired at some thrift shop. Same head-down, bearlike shuffle.

"I'll tell you one thing I learned in jail," he says, somewhat reluctant to discuss the whole matter. "Whew! Compared to the guys on the honor farm, our heads are really way out front of what's happening."

We sit in the Future Studies Office talking about the bond election.

There's a sound of heavy boots on the wooden stairs.

Patrick arrives moaning and groaning about his hangover and something involving "white thighs." Patrick was born in Bismarck, North Dakota. Ended up in the Air Force after high school. Plays the concertina. Arrived in town about five years ago. Started studying Sanskrit. Does odd jobs. Spent some time in Nevada working with Indians and sitting in bars talking to cowboys, trying to organize them to save their land. Now, he has been hired by the Planning Group for two hundred dollars a month to help organize Briones and the town Plan.

He wants to borrow a car to go to a neighboring town which is having a meeting. They are trying to get together. Want to hear our successes and failures.

"They want to save themselves *too!*" says Patrick. "This is the third town which has invited Steve and me to explain the survey."

PATRICK

JACK is dead.

One of our artists and carpenters disappears overnight from our midst.

He has fallen in the night from the hand-hewn frame of his half-finished house.

Before he died, he told the highway engineers something they did not understand.

"Hey!" he said, standing up in the middle of their presentation to the town. "Don't you know that you are fooling with a road around a sacred mountain?"

The sacred mountain of the Tamal and Miwok Indians stands between us and what the county planners call the "Eastern Urban Corridor."

We call it "over-the-hill."

Services will be held for Jack on his sacred mountain.

THE election results are in and tallied.

The PUD bond for that part of our new sewer which will not be funded by federal grants ($385,000) is passed in the election by townspeople, winning 83 percent of the vote.

Gary wins the supervisorial seat for our county district in a tight race. Briones delivers the highest town-wide percentage of votes to him. He replaces Louis H. "Bud" Baar, a real estate man. A good trade for Briones.

Nixon wins.

Locally, things seem to be working out well. Nationally, they seem demonstrably out of control.

COLD, clear nights. Frost in the valleys. Beautiful early-morning curls of fog hang over the mountains and the redwood canyons.

The ocean is quiet and sparkling in the sunlight.

These are precious days in town.

Small knots of people standing in front of the Store and post office chatting.

One small child nags his mother to go home. "You know what it's like going downtown," Nancy says. "And I asked you if you wanted to come, and you said yes!"

In the laundromat is a guy who has just hit town. He describes himself as "a trucker."

He is standing in front of the clothes drier in a loincloth, watching his pants, parka, shirt, and sneakers revolve around inside.

Ka-thump, ka-thump, ka-thump!

He asks for a dime.

I give him one.

He starts bebopping off around the laundromat. He takes someone's soap powder, and lays a rap down on how groovy communal living is, and how all soap powder belongs to the cosmos.

He asks for another dime.

"No!" I say.

He boogies off to the magazine rack in an unaffected manner. But he is back in no time, asking, "Hey, man! Ya know where I can get something psychedelic?"

"No!"

He counterattacks by pulling a small flute out from under his loincloth and playing an annoying Chinese-Schönberg melody to the washing machines.

I watch this guy and find myself feeling most ungracious.

"Where do you come from?" I ask.

"Oh, yeah. Well, see, like I'm just spacing around. I find a good place and hit it up for a while and then split," he replies, and then does a little dance over to the soap-vending machine.

This guy bothers me. Not because he is a hippie (even a *clean* hippie), or because he takes drugs or wears a loincloth, but, I think, because he speaks of a kind of disturbing rootlessness which my intuition tells me is a dangerous disease. He is a counterculture tourist, a perennial voyeur of other people's lives and communities. A parasite who lives and enjoys off the host.

There is a small sign above the check-in desk at the local medical clinic just north of here. It reports that the clinic was burned for $9,558.07 in unpaid bills last year. Of the 346 unpaid bills, 173 were from people who were making their first visit to the clinic.

"Mostly just people who came and stayed awhile and then split," says the woman who handles the office work. "Most of them probably knew they were leaving and just never intended to pay up."

Mr. Lauff lives on Horseshoe Hill Road near Paradise Valley. His old red barn tips badly to the east. Behind it are a few old sheds and a bathtub once used for watering cattle.

His house is an ungainly conglomeration of shacks and additions which were joined and merged over the years into one clump of buildings. A milk cow and a donkey are tethered in the adjacent field.

A sign on a cypress tree bordering the road says, "FOR SALE 6½ ACRES," remnants of one of the oldest family holdings in town.

Charles Lauff, his grandfather, was a big blond Alsatian who built Casa Briones for Don Gregorio Briones in 1840.

Charles arrived before the vast Spanish land grant ranchos were lost or divided as gold fever brought an onrush of people to California from Europe and the East Coast. He and Briones built the town's first house on the banks of Pine Gulch Creek using Miwok Indians as laborers.

Mr. Lauff is sixty-seven.

He drives back from town in his pickup, as Burr and I are hauling used lumber into his barn.

He waves. Meticulously backs his truck into the barn. Sits absolutely still for several minutes looking out of dim sleepy eyes. Then slowly, very slowly, he rolls a cigarette. He moves with his age, with a clear conviction that there is little to hurry for now.

His life lies behind him, a life which could no longer happen on this land. His farm has been gradually divided into five-acre parcels and yearly sprouts another new, tastefully designed, custom-built house.

JACK LAUFF

He sits in the cab for twenty minutes before getting out. In slow motion, he opens his wallet and one by one counts the bills inside.

All around him are the remnants of his life. Old ropes, blocks and tackles hang on rusted nails.

I watch and wonder when was the last time, the last day, that they were used? Did anyone think that this was the end?

Old irrigation pipes are strewn around the floor. Rusty. Dead.

Three bags of cement, long since hardened, are stacked on the floor next to a box of old hardware.

Indescribable objects, all old, are piled in disarray.

Clothes, bottles, wire, clumsy old rusted tools of the past, buckets, cables, bolts, a sledgehammer, a lantern, an old stove, and a decrepit ancient refrigerator with its coil sitting on top like a hat ("No," he said, "I want to keep that one").

A man in his truck sitting quietly in the middle of a barn, a museum of his life.

I stand over the manger and milking stanchions. A hand-poured concrete floor slopes away to the door with a trough so that the manure and urine could run out into the barnyard.

When was the last time Mr. Lauff milked in that barn? How many years has it been since the corroded hand cream-separator in the shed has been turned? What visions and hopes of the future, our now, did some long-deceased Lauff have as he planted fruit trees, put up redwood picket fences, built the barn, turned the land, planted crops, and harvested on this farm?

Mr. Lauff just sits there in his pickup. I stand in the milk stalls and watch.

Wondering.

Is it better now?

It is unusually cold tonight. There is a planning meeting in the PUD Grand Ballroom. Someone lights a fire in the big brick fireplace. We pull our folding chairs up around it in a semicircle.

The meeting gets off to a slow start. One drunk civic personage sits in the back of the room, sniggering and needling the others with the same obtuse question.

Steve and Patrick have prepared a recommendation for the local "commissioners" (who represent the various organizations and areas of town) to vote on. They recommend that much of the downtown area be taken out of commercial zoning to confine the spread of commercial establishments, the creeping meatball.

"Not only should we cut back on the amount of land which can be commercially developed," says Steve, "but we want to preserve as many of the old houses for residences as possible, since we have a housing shortage."

The commissioners nod. Even most merchants agree that the downtown area should be dedicated primarily to serving the local people.

Steve cautions that while zoning (over which the county has jurisdiction) is a tool for limiting growth, it is far from being a panacea. Zoning still cannot compensate for the ill effects of a tax system which taxes all land according to how much money it *could* make as a motel or an office building rather than as an apple orchard, dairy farm, or wildlife preserve.

Whether an owner wants to build a motel or not on his land, if it is zoned commercially, he is assessed and taxed on the basis of commercial possibility.

Steve pulls out a large map he has done showing all the different large parcels of land outside the subdivided area. Each parcel is inked in with a different colored Magic Marker. He and Patrick have checked the assessments with the county assessor, and have figured out how much each is worth. Each year the valuations skyrocket.

The assessed value of all property within the boundaries of the utilities district for the 1965–66 fiscal year was $2,879,600. By 1969–70 it had jumped to $4,016,852; by 1974–75, to $5,700,000.

Assessed valuation has more than doubled in ten years.

Higher taxes are forcing people to do things with and to their land which they would not otherwise do.

Someone in 1965 with a $25,000 house found himself with a $50,000 house in 1974. In 1965, he paid around $700 in taxes. In 1974, he paid around $1,400.

Folks are getting eaten up.

Who can vote for open space bonds when taxes are already so high?

FROM a recent draft of the Briones Community Plan:

Briones was once a thriving agricultural community as well as a fishing port. That the Plan seeks to help reestablish these older relationships, older economics, is not an exercise in nostalgia. Instead, it is an attempt to set forward principles of a community basing itself in longtime harmony with the earth rather than the philosophy of rip-off and run, the philosophy to which we are mostly heirs.

Briones farming and dairying began to fade and move to the rich inland valleys at the end of World War II because of the advent of cheap gasoline and cheap ammonia fertilizer which made farming on a much larger machine-intensive scale temporarily economically advantageous.

That day is about over. We feel that the close proximity of Briones to urban markets, and the natural advantages of our climate and soils for coastal crops will once again make Briones a center of agriculture. Much of the Briones Plan is directed toward that end.

The present-day western economic system is based on central collection and distribution. This structure is based on a cheap and radically wasteful use of nonrenewable resources such as petroleum products for growing and moving food.

Towns such as Briones have the capability of raising a substantial part of their own food. And until we are able to process our own milk, slaughter and sell our own beef and pork, and grow our own vegetables, we will continue to be at the mercy of the distant "middleman" and agri-businessman who poisons the land, the animals, and eventually us, to prop up a system which is collapsing from a lack of cheap resources to make it go.

The Briones Plan suggests (gently) that people may need to be responsible for such things as their own food and energy (e.g., wind, solar, natural gas). The Planning Group urges the BCPUD, the Fire Department, the School, and all other local governing bodies to take cognizance of this need and act on the principle that what we can do for ourselves with local materials and effort will more likely get done.

RIDE up around the mesa, doing slalom among the puddles on the dirt roads. They might be one inch deep. Or, then again, they might be three feet deep and swallow up a bicycle without a trace. No one knows until he hits the bottom.

The variety of dwellings is extraordinary. Many of them have been built or remodeled by the people who occupy them. There is a strong tradition in town of building one's own house. By scrounging secondhand materials and providing one's own labor (with a little help from one's friends), it is possible to be both poor and a "homeowner," a pleasure which is rapidly retreating out of the grasp of most low- or middle-income people.

"Did you know that labor usually accounts for about fifty percent of the cost of a construction job?" asks Ron, foreman on the job where I work as a carpenter. "And it can go higher, too."

The house we are building for a man from the city soaks up $154 a day for three carpenters. Almost $20 an hour. About $.30 a minute. One-half cent a second. And that does not include building materials. On days when there are both an electrician and plumber on the job, labor costs almost double. This is with cheap, nonunion labor.

In Paradise, we estimate the average cost per house will be under $4,000.

A few houses are still going up on the mesa in spite of the water moratorium. People have been scouring the area for lots with old water meters or septic tanks. But building of large

SHACKS ON THE MESA

new houses has definitely slackened. Instead, construction of small shacks next to existing houses has increased.

The county building code does not require permits for ten-by-ten-foot structures without plumbing. So a lot of people are building these, converting garages and renovating chicken coops into small living spaces renting for fifty to seventy-five dollars a month. Tenants usually use the bathroom in the main house. Most have small wood stoves for heating and cooking. Kerosene lamps. On special occasions, they use the central kitchen.

In effect, what has happened is that the moratorium has stopped construction on large, expensive, 1,200-square-foot houses (which cost around $45,000 to have built, minus land). Shacks are multiplying and are providing for a kind of unintentional low-cost housing. They use limited resources (i.e., gas, water, electricity).

BECAUSE of the high cost of water in Briones, it is more expensive to wash clothes at the laundromat than to buy secondhand ones, or scrounge other people's rejects from the Free Box.

Actually, the consumption level of new clothes in this town appears to be extremely low (with the possible exception of new blue jeans).

Sartorially, there are two main groups of people in residence here. The first don't really care what they wear, or perhaps they just enjoy a fashion fetish for funky dress. If they show up at a supervisors' meeting in someone else's old football warmup, baggy pants, and high sneakers with holes, they may catch a look or two from people more conventionally attired. Or if they go to the airport to meet a friend in a DICK AND RALPH'S AUTO PARTS t-shirt, boots, and a Spiro Agnew golf hat, they usually get picked out for the skin search at the hijack inspection. But they become used to this when they are over-the-hill. In town no one notices them.

The second group are more self-conscious, and have made an art out of wearing old clothes. But they are not comfortable in just *any* old clothes. They buy cheap (most of the time), but they must find the "right" seventy-five-cent ensemble, to which they add embroidery, patches and bits of leather, fur, metal, whatever.

Free Box nouveau. If you make them yourself, the price is right.

WHAT this town needs is a home–boarding house–rest home–commune for elderly people and our own parents.

OWNER-BUILT HOUSE. SHAKES ARE
HAND-SPLIT FROM DRIFTWOOD.

There is a place here for more old people, whether as agitators, child-care organizers, teachers, or at dances.

We have talked about the possibility of building a large house on the lower part of the sewer land back up the canyon by the old barn. It could have separate bedrooms, a common dining room, a big garden. Older people could be independent from their children's families, but not isolated and alone in some city apartment or hotel room.

They would be within a five-minute walk of the Store, post office, bus stop, churches, and laundromat.

ELAINE

WINTER

REMEMBER BRIONES!

ALLEGED SIGN HANGING OVER A DESK AT
THE STATE WATER RESOURCES CONTROL
BOARD, WHICH ORIGINALLY CERTIFIED
THE KENNEDY PLAN

California is "a hotbed that brought humanity to a rapid,
monstrous maturity, like the mammoth vegetables for
which it is so celebrated."

THE ANNALS OF SAN FRANCISCO, 1855

LAST NIGHT was one of the coldest nights in anyone's memory. Way below freezing.

Drive up to Ten-Mile Beach this morning to get a truckload of driftwood for the fireplace. There is something about gathering all that useless waste and turning it into free heat which is most satisfying.

Scavenging is a compulsive's dream. It combines cleaning, gathering, and using.

About half the people in town own trucks. A branch hardly hits the ground, or a post hardly floats up on the beach, when it is pounced on and carted away.

Besides the beach, the dump is the other great scavenger's paradise. It's always hard to come home with less than you take. The only trouble is that Elmer charges you going both ways. He charges a buck or two to dump a truck, and then again on the way out depending on how much of other people's garbage catches your fancy.

Elmer's dump is a kind of second-class flea market. A huge self-service rummage sale that smells.

What can one get at the dump? Well, our porch furniture, hundreds of feet of hose needing minor patching and attention, a large snarl of telephone wire, a sink, some wood, a fifty-gallon oil drum, a set of ugly dishes, a book on plumbing, some cactus, a broom, some stove pipe, and a complete set of *Science* magazine from 1968.

Elmer has been around ranching all his life. He remembers when the old train used to come up the coast in the 1920s. He remembers the roads before they were paved.

Now he sits on a discarded patio chair near a small shack he uses as an office. He sits in the middle of the dump surrounded by a quarter-acre of objects selected out of the incoming loads. They are for sale. Old tanks, half a bicycle,

screen windows, an old washing machine, bathtubs, sinks, rusty lawn mower, crippled TV, pipe, a few car seats, used tires.

Elmer sits in this junkyard showcase like a king among his subjects.

He gets up slowly to collect a few bucks from entering trucks. He directs them where to unload. He cocks his straw hat up, leans on the truck cab, chats a bit, and then heads back to his chair.

"No," he says. "It's not like it used to be. Everyone's running around a lot faster and getting ulcers. They're goin' a whole lot faster. But are they getting any more done?"

He pauses. Looks around at the piles of trash and junk.

"Has this place changed?" he asks, making a sweeping gesture with his arm out over the salvage items. "Aw, hell. We're just not getting the quality we used to. Don't know why. I guess people are just hanging onto all their stuff."

THE developers describe Martinelli Farms as a subdivision "with a horsy theme." Expensive lots for expensive houses for weekend people to play with their horses.

Slowly, the subdivision wallows through the county red tape and heads down the track for a final hearing before the supervisors. They want to build 68 houses on 200 acres which stand in the middle of miles of open pasture just up the coast.

"Not as dense as Pittsburgh," points out one observer.

What will the impact of 68 new houses be on the neighboring town of fewer than 200 houses? Where will the new people get gas, buy food, mail letters, cash checks, buy suntan oil?

Petitions are circulating through all the adjacent towns in opposition to this development.

Piero takes a rump circus up on a flatbed truck with leaflets and belly dancers to fan the opposition.

Some people are outraged by the belly dancers. Others are outraged by the development.

"WHAT we ought to do," says Richie from the back of the room, "is forget about these money problems for a while, and just put together an ideal school . . . exactly what we want. Do that first. And then see if we can afford it!"

"Why should it cost any more than what we don't want?" asks someone else.

People nod their heads.

The school board is meeting amidst the usual financial problems and confusion about how much money the School will get from taxes. People are pondering the eternal question of why the School isn't exactly what they want.

The five-man board, which is publicly elected, manages the School's $338,000 annual budget for the 210 elementary students. They meet in one of the windowless prefab buildings which were installed as an economy measure behind the old white wooden school building with the bell tower which sits astride the road next to Pine Gulch Creek.

In 1963, the student population was barely 100. In one year's time the figure will have risen again to 245.

The School is growing. There is constant pressure on the board to come up with more money to expand facilities.

Since I have been in Briones, every school bond issue has been defeated by the electorate. Already the tax rate for education per assessed $100 is $5.40. This comprises one-half of our total property tax. It raises $654,100 a year. The School gets approximately half this sum back from the county. The rest goes over-the-hill for high schools and the Community College.

People are reluctant to vote for higher taxes for *anything*. But a sizable group of people in town, like Richie, believe the School's main problem is not money.

"Why should the School be hiring all these teachers from over-the-hill with high salaries, when they could get two people from right here for half the price?" asks Bill. "I mean, god! This community has more intelligent creative people per square inch than any other place I can think of."

There is tension between the more professionally inclined members of the school board and community who stress credentials and qualifications, and those who see the School as an extension of the community learning process.

"What is all this crap about not being able to hire people without credentials?" asks Greg. "Why don't they just *do* it! The hell with the law! They're all so afraid of the law!"

"The community has a lot to give these kids," says Bill. "And equally as important, the School could return some of our tax money to the community by hiring local teachers. You know as well as I, people who live here work for one-third of what over-the-hill people go for."

Similar questions are in constant counterpoint over the buildings. Codes for school structures are some of the most strict in the country. Right now, the kids are crammed into classrooms without windows. Their redeeming features are their inexpensiveness and legality. Several illegal buildings have been constructed by various crews of parents and carpenters in town. They are used.

"Why don't we all just go out there and do a few new buildings," says Rex. "We'll just put some classrooms up, make them safe, and use them. What are the inspectors going to do about it?"

"The School's not used to being an outlaw . . . yet," says Greg.

DRIVE over-the-hill to Berkeley to the First (Annual?) Building Exchange and Energy Fair. A conference on outlaw building, land use, alternative ways of living, and performing political gymnastics, organized by some maverick architects and eco-buffs.

The room is full of bearded be-overalled enthusiasts. Talk tends to be in the "life-style" vein, as though our compost piles were not connected to events in Washington and Saigon.

SATURDAY MEETING IN PARADISE VALLEY

"Waste has its own imperialism," says Peter, our Briones town biologist. "We rip off our own resources in a careless manner. Then, in order to keep the growth monster stoked with natural resources, we head overseas."

There are about twenty people from Briones. Most of the others seem to have come as individuals, or as representatives of some group or commune.

We come as a town. There is a noticeable difference. Other people speak of isolated problems. We speak of a process, of the long haul.

"If you find that you do not appreciate what lives in an area where you want to build a structure," says Sterling, "then you are bound to disturb it. Maybe you should not build in that place after all. Better find a place that you do appreciate."

Sterling is a naturalist. Owns with a friend a large piece of land in Briones upon which he does not even want cows. Wants to allow the natural wild grasses, flowers, and plants to come back. Wants to leave it as a preserve.

As he talks, one senses the satisfaction he has derived from paying attention to plants, animals, and life cycles that exist everywhere around us, even in cities.

He proposes that we build natural corridors into urban areas so that wildlife can circulate into areas where people normally never experience them. He envisions the corridors as natural arteries from the country into city parks, so that animals can make it back and forth across freeways, through housing tracts and industrial parks.

"When you build anything, or disturb something," he says, "try not to make too many waves. Remember, you are invading a natural habitat. Others were there before you."

Both in Paradise Valley and in the town, there are several schools of thought on meetings.

The first school sees them as important, and attends them dutifully regardless of how uninspired any given meeting threatens to be.

The second school is often quite responsible and punctual. But just as often it decides not to come, or to come drunk, stoned, or delinquent in some other unimaginable way.

A third school sees meetings as an unnecessary drag and trusts that all things under heaven will be taken care of by the cosmic banana or some other karmic mumbo jumbo.

A fourth fringe group is hardly aware that there are any meetings going on at all. They may attend when the issue directly touches them, i.e., nude swimming, hippie vans, day-care.

Ilka and I walk up to the PUD for a Planning Group meeting on a bitter cold, dark, rainy night.

Lewis is lighting a fire in the Grand Ballroom for a poetry reading. Candles flicker around the room.

In the PUD office, Steve is putting up some maps. People sit quietly and chat.

The door flies open. A guy with a bushy black beard bursts in out of the darkness. He is breathless.

"Fire! There's a fire! Huge fire! Get the fire department!" He can hardly talk through his panting.

Someone calls the volunteer fire department. Almost before we hang up, we hear the siren go off at the firehouse, tripped off by Alice, Fire Chief Joe's wife, who is faithfully at her post.

People start running out of the PUD into the dark parking lot. Across the street down Nymph Road a huge orange ball of flame billows up under some tall cypress trees. Swirling flame is reflected in every puddle.

We run down the muddy road to the house. Several dark shapes, lit up by occasional flashes of flame like strobe lights, are trying to hook up a garden hose. There's no pressure.

The roof explodes into flame and burns like newspaper, casting shadows on the trees and the gathering crowd. Someone finally gets a hose hooked up to the house next door. The thin column of water disappears into the inferno.

You can hear the sirens on the fire trucks, now, as they speed down Elm.

"Watch out for the propane tank!" someone yells. "It might explode!"

A wall collapses. Someone runs out to intercept Joe in the pumper truck.

"Watch out for the mud, Joe! Don't get stuck in the mud! Get a good run on it going in!"

Joe races the engine in reverse. Truck skids. He tries again. No luck. Ten or twenty people run down to the truck and try to push.

No time.

Joe climbs out and starts ordering people to lay out hose and hook up to the adjacent hydrant. Several people start dragging the hose down the muddy road. The other truck comes in from the other side where the road is drier.

People are running about, now. The revolving red lights occasionally illuminate a familiar face. There is an indescribable terror in the fire.

"God! They sure got here fast," says a voice behind us.

"Shit! If this had been the dry season," someone else replies as sheets of sparks ride up on the heat into the black sky.

FIRE CHIEF
JOSÉ AND
HIS WIFE ALICE

Ambrose runs up to a window with a hose. He wears a fire-man's hat. He smashes in the window and starts pouring water on the flames. Burr grabs a pumper hose and moves in around the back of the house. Joe is yelling orders. He wears a fire hat and a slicker.

A strange collection of young, old, dressed, half-dressed people stand transfixed in the mud.

Water pours into the house. Gradually the sense of awe that one feels before unopposed natural disaster diminishes.

People slowly start to ignore the house and recognize those around them in the half-light. Friends, neighbors, acquaintances, adversaries. One town figure has rushed from his living room after an unfathomable number of martinis. He slips and falls in the mud.

Firefighters and bystanders are indistinguishable.

The fire is almost out. No one was in the house, which belongs to weekenders. People start wandering back to their houses, the poetry reading, the planning meeting. Bunches and groups. Chatting. Holding hands. All somehow enervated by the connection to the fire. It was everybody's fire, each person sensing that next time it might be his or her house. Or, if the brush were dry, perhaps the town itself.

There is something about a crisis which reveals the shapes and contours of a community. The way it responds tells whether or not it has any structure, whether or not there is glue inside holding it all together.

Little by little, people settle back down into the planning meeting. There are mostly older people tonight. Steve has written an agenda. Wants to finalize a smaller commercially zoned area, decide on slope policy (what is the steepest slope people should be allowed to build on), and work out a new road plan making most roads dead ends.

JUDITH (*Judith has more energy than anyone else in town. She is a mother of three. Late thirties. Writes for the local paper. She is a forceful woman, talks loudly, and can seem*

JUDITH

PETER

grimly efficient to those not close enough to her to see her concern and good humor. She plays the banjo and guitar in a square dance band. Her husband Peter is an electrician. They live in the old Briones house. Judith has been summed up by one local observer as the "Empress Dowager of Briones, dressed like a Transylvanian Navajo."): Listen! I just want to say that I think it's a real drag to have to sit in a tiny room at a public meeting with half the people smoking it up, and the other half gagging to death. So, what do you say? Let's everyone stop smoking. *(Her appeal is followed by some bitching and grumbling from smokers.)*

STEVE *(Steve is a planner, an architect who has been hired by the town to oversee the putting together of the Plan. He is mid-thirties, trimmed beard, slightly balding. He has huge powerful arms and chest from having spent the last nine years*

on crutches, the result of a near-fatal dive from a cliff which left his legs severely shattered and without sensation. Steve is otherwise famous for floating down in the cold water of Pine Gulch Creek in the middle of one winter night after a few libations, for being able to maneuver his BMW anyplace short of deep water, and for being one of California's finest racing skippers.): OK. One of the things we should cover tonight is slope policy for the Plan. What do we want? I am recommending that we prohibit building on slopes of 25 percent or greater.

DON *(Don is an old pol who got his wings in the smoke-filled rooms of California state politics working for Pat Brown. Chain smokes. Gray hair. Rather sad, disappointed eyes. Has dabbled in various real estate ventures. Doesn't spend much time in town. Gives the annual Fourth of July party with plenty of good whiskey.):* Listen. I don't think that you can just tell a guy who owns a piece of property on a hill that all of a sudden it's not worth anything! He paid for it. Maybe he wants to build a house or something. What are you going to do to repay him?

STEVE: OK. The point is that these areas are geologically unstable. Documented photographic slides exist. All we're saying is that it's unsafe to build on such slopes. And I think that we also have to protect the elevated backdrops to the town and prevent that feeling of visual claustrophobia that building on hillsides can give.

DON: All right. So, what you're saying here is that unless they can find competent authority to prove they can build safely, it is the policy of the Plan to keep these areas open. You just can't confiscate these lots, you know.

ORVILLE: You know, it's the same old problem. We're taking all this time and trouble to draw up our own plan because we believe this town will never survive if we stay in the old planning ruts. We have to start insisting that there are some new considerations which should be taken note of. I mean, what we're really trying to do is prevent Briones from getting too large. So we may be saying that some people are going to take a loss. It happens every day on the real estate market. Usually a guy's land value zooms up. But there is no god-given guarantee of that. Like, one guy owns land in the suburbs, and by the time the city gets out there, he is a millionaire, and the city zones it so he can rip off a stack!

Well, is there any reason why the system can't work in reverse? There is no legal guarantee that a man should get more for his land when he sells it. That's just habit. And the habit is devouring us.

So, maybe what we should start doing is deciding where houses should go, if at all, and then start trying to make it happen whether through slope policy, zoning, bond issues, water projects, sewers, or means not yet invented. Face it! We're outlaws. If we obey all the present rules we'll end up just like Los Angeles. LA was built by following the rules!

Let's try and think up some new rules. Do we even know what rules we would want if we could have a clean sweep?

A long discussion follows about what we should do about land that people own but may not be able to develop. Everyone agrees it would be nice to buy it all up . . . somehow. But many of the older people are apprehensive about the Plan having the effect of arbitrarily confiscating the worth of someone's property.

The argument cools, when someone points out that our Plan will have no legal status anyway, unless passed by the supervisors.

Someone laughs, and says, "Oh, sure! When pigs can fly."

CONVERSATION overheard at the Store:
Voice A: "Whew! That sure was some fire last night!"
Voice B: "Yeah! Really! Burned that place up like leaves."
Voice A: "Yuh know, if we could have a fire like that once a month, we could keep all the carpenters employed and still have a building moratorium."

THE ruminations of a poet on "town."
Bob writes a letter home to Steve while on a trip back East.

LETTER TO A TOWN PLANNER
By Robert Creeley

Dear Steve,

I've thought about "community" a lot, like they say, since our conversation in Scowley's. In any case I hadn't wanted you to feel it was forgotten.

Quick persistent senses keep emphasizing the *local*, what you can walk around in, locate as simple (however complex) *physical* place.

Conditions in suburbs relate to generalized use of dwellings etc. Can't easily alter walls, plumbing—all emphasizing resale and generalized "value"! "Idea" dominates possible literal experience of living in such houses. Although people thus housed are surely all living in the "same" house they paradoxically feel more "singular" than before, more paranoid, more "alone"—possibly because the situation doesn't permit them to localize their dwellings, thus having specific sense of really *being* there. Same problem as being in hospital, motel, jail, etc. Hard to make it the place specific to your own experience of yourself.

City/neighborhood
Country/town

Again what happens in the suburbs (and why cities humanly somehow do survive despite physical dereliction), is that this local term gets lost—there's no "place" specific to being "there." It's "everywhere"—interchangeable, but never somehow felt to be literal to oneself in being there. The supermarket as opposed to Briones Store. In Coal Hill, Ark., realizing car would momentarily stop because of no gas, drove off freeway about 10 miles in fading light, rain, to arrive at town, one store, gas pump, open-faced people, much talk as they came and went from store, civil, friendly to strangers, *local*. As opposed to kids minding EXXON gas station off ramp in Little Rock. Spooked, didn't know where anything was, e.g., which way to St. Louis; seemingly living only in word of $$$ got from meager job, adolescent "in" talk, pimples . . .

The simple, and I think literally absolute point seems to be: what lives there has to be taken as primary.

Habits and haunts—what Charles Olson spoke of as the real study and persistence required to enable persons to experience true "habits" and "haunts"—a situation of and in experience, permitting us to feel truly "at home" in a place; to know it in the complex of its information and our ways of having that information, words, smells, feels, recurrences, changes, others. Why I was really bugged at getting cut off from bar was the loss of information therefrom: body tones, words, the way people came on, the action, how they responded to weekend scenes etc.; it was one of the town's information centers, quite apart from gossip etc. The street, beach, post office, water board bldg., laundermat, etc., all likewise. Talking with Orville who's flipping eucalyptus pips in pleasant arcs onto hoods etc. of Strange Cars in town for the day. A *local* possibility.

"Absentee ownership"—hard and distorting trip. (I specifically feel it apropos house we have in small New Mexican town north of Albuquerque, predominantly Mexican, or used to be, like they say, which we rent—"rentiers"—and town continues to feel us local to it, i.e., the "Creeley house," but we ain't of course.) Again, when that absence gets more respect and power of qualification than what's literally there, it's a bleak drag. As a kid I lived for a time in Northeast Harbor, Me., where my mother was the Red Cross nurse etc.—community is absolutely staticized for convenience of absent summer people, a weird wiped out "service" group. I went back last spring briefly, drove around, found town markedly "unchanged"—with very few exceptions—this after almost 30 years: town frozen in attitude which the absentee owners found "attractive." Too much. Many parallels as you'd know all through New England—where the organic communal experience is stultified by non-participant qualifications, e.g., again in Northeast Harbor, local fishermen not permitted by town ordinance (or Rockefeller fiat) to sell fish, lobster, from pier. (What they apparently did was to raise old sunken granite pier and get it close enough to shore, so they could hand the fish over to customer— but that sure is a sad "getting even.") Case of: *here's* where I live— not just "passing through." Hippies get localized in Briones as much as businessmen. It ain't "magic"—it's *home*. Old Indian in pueblo a little north of us in N.M. could walk roughly 2 plus miles to daughter's house tho blind— knew the way with his feet, etc. The multiple of that experience is community—its sharing is knowledge, and "tradition"—the handing over. Well, I wish this were talking to you there, like they say. Things are OK here, but god knows it's an abstract situation of "being somewhere." OK. Love to all, and hope things are OK after that deluge. Water sure is wet.

Love,
Bob

P.S. Think of news item I'm now hearing as I write—2 babies, full term, found "Thrown Away" in garbage bags in lake, river— "no one" "knows why"—no community.

No one man or woman has to "know it all" if there is a community—it's a shared possibility and each does what he or she can do—humanly the point.

By a four to one vote, the county supervisors have approved the controversial Martinelli Farms subdivision up the coast from Briones.

Slowly the news seeps back from over-the-hill to town that the supervisors have decided to anoint the land with suburbia.

The two hundred acres upon which the new lots will be carved is part of the old Martinelli Ranch. It sits on a bluff overlooking the Bay. The ruins of the old railroad line snake along its shore. The land has a vast, open, windswept feeling to it. There are no trees on the rolling bluff save for some scrub growth in the canyons. The land lies over a mile outside the last town, just after the houses have thinned and the road breaks out onto the coast again. There is nothing but open pasture, fences, and an occasional old white Victorian ranchhouse.

I walked the road the other day, passed the future subdivision. It was quiet, save for the wind and sound of the distant waves on the Bay. Sun, blue sky, wild flowers encroaching on the road shoulder, few cars. Cattle watched as I walked by feeling gladness, but a gladness tinged with a fear for the perishability of the land around me. It is a feeling I have grown accustomed to.

While going past this ranch, I could not figure out how one might explain such feelings to problem-oriented politicians at a public hearing, beneath fluorescent lights and into a microphone.

And when you are done, the chairman of the Board of Supervisors looks down and politely says, "Thank you, Mr. Schell. Does anyone else wish to address the board?"

The Planning Commission and the supervisors have wrestled with this one for almost a year. There have been months of lobbying, arm-twisting, petitions, letters, newspaper articles, words, hearings, and protests. And they all have culminated

BRIONES PEOPLE AT SUPERVISORS' MEETING

in approval. At least the buck passing, dodging, and endless motions to send the plans back to the planning staff for further review (all of which dulled our sense of just where the matter lay) have ended.

The men and women seemed to lack any real conviction as to whether or not the project *should* actually happen. They bowed and scraped to pressure from both sides. Apologized and self-lacerated themselves, and angered both developers and conservationists. They are all trying to slash their way as officials through the endless jungle of demands, work, meetings, pressure, trivia. Not enough time to deal thoroughly with each problem. Not enough money. Not enough lawyers. They sit in offices. Try to get out into the field. But still, their reality is law books, maps, codes, rules. They speak in lofty generalizations. And then the vision is lost in hundreds of small piecemeal steps of the administrative process. They are forced to treat present conventions of private property as a natural law rather than as just a transitory totem. They try to find a way out using a system which is designed to destroy.

And no one wants to get sued. So few officials are interested in forcing precedents. Peace is more important. So they grade each other on a scale of liberality according to who gives the pieces away the most slowly. So the land disappears one slice at a time, one decision at a time. And no one knows precisely which one marks the terminal stage.

Those opposed to this inexorable process are forced to couch their protest in ways which do not really express their feelings or reveal their real motivation. We may carp on environmental impact statements, administrative errors, recent court cases. We may decry the destruction of the wild flowers or the animals on the land. We grab at any handle available. We may even succeed in stopping the "improvement" the way some environmentalists stopped a trailer park in Santa Cruz, by discovering that the park would have wiped out one of the last ponds giving refuge to a rare salamander.

And yet we know it is not concern for salamanders alone that is in our hearts when a trailer park threatens to move into our neighborhood. It is more an affair of the soul for which we have learned to fight obliquely with salamanders, technicalities, and erosion hazards.

What we feel most acutely, I think, is the threat these intrusions bring to our sense of peace, to our need to live in natural surroundings not always threatened with disruption.

STEP by step, meeting by meeting, paper by paper, our sewer is being born.

"We began with the philosophical assumption that this sewer is really going to belong to the town," says one of the PUD directors at our weekly meeting. "As many people from town as possible should be employed on each stage of conception and construction. And I think we ought to grab onto this septic tank survey as a blessing rather than a curse and do it. We'll just learn more about septic tanks, do the survey ourselves, write the report, figure out the management program, and take over the whole bloody mess of septic tank inspection and care from the county. What we don't know, we can learn, just as we did when we started off and defeated the Kennedy sewer." There are a few nods of assent from the audience.

Phylo is an enigmatic genius inventor who has lived in town for several years. He has five kids and a wife all crammed chaotically into a very small house.

Peter, a biologist, has been involved from the oil spill onwards in town affairs.

The state is requiring that the PUD do a $20,000 septic tank survey of private waste disposal systems which will not be hooked up to the sewer. They will pay $87 (½%) of the cost. Peter and Phylo have drafted a proposal to become consultants, perform the survey, and write the report.

"Sure we can do it," says Peter, squatting on top of a folding chair in moccasins, blue jeans, and a sweater. "If we need some help for skills that people in town can't perform themselves, well then, OK, we'll go over-the-hill and pay someone."

Several people are apprehensive about giving such a large and official contract to local people who are not "experts."

The PUD board votes to go with Peter and Phylo. Take a chance. "By trusting in experts for a hundred dollars a day we teach people to distrust themselves. Stunt their ability to learn. Intimidate people with the complexity of a problem, and then bring in outsiders with suits and ties to soothe their impotence. People lacking in self-confidence find refuge in the professional consultant," says a PUD director.

You never quite get what you want when you have someone else do it for you. You can't have a vision, and leave its realization in the hands of hired help.

A cold snap has frozen all the flowers. Today is gray and warm with constipated showers.

Steve calls. Ask how we are. Listens to the answer, and then announces he has just badly burned both feet over a heater. The nerve endings are dead below the knees from his old accident, so he did not feel his feet burning while he talked on the telephone. It was not until he went to put his shoes on later that he saw large blisters on the soles of his feet.

We call a local doctor. Not in. Call a nurse up at the clinic. She says she will bring down some penicillin. Steve's lymph glands are already aching.

Russ arrives from cutting wood and bandages Steve's feet.

"Well," says Steve, looking down at the bandages, "It looks like the Planning Office will have to move over here for a while."

ENDLESS rain. Put on boots and slog up to the PUD office.

Robbie, the administrator, has left a note on the bulletin board: *Tuesday, 2:00 p.m. Expansion of Highway comes up before Supervisors.*

Call Gary, who takes office in three weeks to represent this district. It's the first he's heard of it.

He's pissed.

Call Judith. She agrees it's the moment of reckoning.

"Can you imagine those supervisors putting this on the agenda before Gary takes office?" she half screams. "Christ!

And these guys are supposed to be the best supervisors in the state!"

We start a phone chain. Got to get the warm bodies out and over-the-hill to the meeting. Cram the room. Clog the works. Let the supes know that while there may be two possible different decisions, only one is acceptable.

So much energy. So many people rearranging their lives to stop this highway. All spent to *stop* something, not to build something.

STILL calling people for the supervisors' meeting. The first three numbers of everyone's phone number are the same. This makes it conceivable to memorize most of your friends' numbers. Since there are no numbers higher than 2,000 (868-2,000) there is a small area of possibility. People carry complete phonebooks in their heads.

Many numbers silent. Six days before Christmas. Lots of crusaders are away in such mythological places as Palm Springs, New York, Miami; parents taking children to see grandparents.

Sign up at the Store:

JOIN THE BRIONES ARMY
ATTEND THE SUPERVISORS' MEETING, TUES., 2 P.M.
PROTEST THE HIGHWAY

Spend the afternoon at Steve's changing bandages and vacuuming before his six-year-old daughter arrives. Friends showing up all day long. Bringing things, doing things, helping out. Steve working stoically on a critique of the building code for Paradise Valley confrontation with the county over building permits for non-code houses.

AGAIN the Briones sign on the state highway has been dealt a blow.

Unknown phantoms.

Bent right down into the grass.

Says BRIONES 2, and the arrow points right into a ditch.

A duel is going on. So far the sign has been sawed down at least five times, bent twice, painted over once, and epoxied once.

The Department of Highways has escalated from wooden posts, to wooden posts enclosed in chain link, to metal posts.

Now, a bending contest. Up, down, up, down. It's almost undignified! Like this bridge near a village I remember in Vietnam. Each day the Americans would build it back up, and each night the National Liberation Front would blow it apart.

The sign goes up and down almost every week. It is doing pushups. But even when it is down, the people of this town know exactly where they live and where they must turn to get home. The sign is for the others, those who come to watch the town like a zoo or to enjoy it in their cars on the weekends. The sign is a symbol for those who understand it as the hallmark of a possibility they do not want to live in. They see it as the big come-on for tourist dollars, the antithesis of a community which survives from its relation to the land rather than to motels, short-order restaurants, souvenir shops, boutiques, and gas stations.

Farms, dairies, feedstores, bakeries, orchards, hardware stores. The dream.

The motto of the Holiday Inn is "World Peace Through Tourism."

THE supervisors' chambers. Again.

No open windows.

The room is almost filled. People in the audience wait quietly. The county counsel comes into the chambers holding a stack of yellow legal-sized pads. He looks at the crowd. Seems somewhat startled.

"Are all these people here for the highway deal?" I hear him ask another county employee.

The group is a strange pastiche of people wearing almost every conceivable mode of dress. It's not the kind of group at which you could look and even begin to guess what it is that they share in common. In this case, it is a highway.

People troop out to the coffee machine in the hall. Many have skipped breakfast in hurried late attempts to get out the door at home. Coffee is the only available relief for their hunger.

I drink two cups, and feel my Civic Center stomachache coming on.

The War of the Highway moves into another theater.

Today the Department of Highways is represented by Jerry O'Shea. Gray hair. Red nose. Middle-fifties. Neatly dressed in a suit. Small beads of sweat appearing on his brow. Looks like a career man, and obviously not too high in the department command.

He gives his presentation. He speaks without rancor or fervor about "safety," "hazards," "accidents per thousands of miles," and "the one hundred-year flood threat." He speaks of "improving" the highway, but his tone suggests more that he is just doing his job and does not really care what happens.

O'SHEA: Well, that about concludes what I have to say. But I have a picture here which shows you what our concern is. *(He puts up a large blowup of a severe flood on the highway. There is a long pause as people digest it.)*

VOICE *(from the audience):* Oh boy! Terror tactics! *(Laughter, whistling, and clapping from the audience)*

VOICE: For Chrissakes! I live there, and I don't know what that is!

SUP. ARRIGONI *(sternly):* All right! I'll remind you that Mr. O'Shea has the floor. You'll get your chance later. *(More loud hoots and guffaws)*

VOICE: When was that photo taken?

VOICE: Nineteen-twenty! *(Laughter)*

O'SHEA *(continuing without expression):* The black line on the photo is the center of the roadway. *(Howls of laughter)* And, uh, these pictures were taken from a grader. A high-wheeled vehicle, you know. Anyway, this is the situation which occurs.

VOICE: When? How often?

VOICE: Is this the famous fifty-year flood?

O'SHEA: Uh. This has occurred three times during the year. It did not occur last year. It occurred two years ago. I don't know what is going on over there this year. But we are carefully recording just what the floods are.

VOICE: They don't know what is going on over there, but they are carefully recording. Oh, wow!

SUP. ARRIGONI: Mr. O'Shea, thank you very much. We request that you stay around awhile. I am sure there are some people in the audience who would like to comment. But (looking at the audience the way a teacher looks at a class of unruly students), we have a lengthy afternoon. So, I would request that you make your statements brief either supporting or opposing the project.

VOICE (an older man, portly, outraged, in a blue blazer. Lives in the neighboring town through which the highway runs.): Our community is a village, Mr. O'Shea. It's not a recreation center or an amusement park! It is a natural setting. It does have the healing power of fresh air. And importing the character of Market Street to it will finish off one of the few natural communities in California. Your highway plan will lay the foundation for this mistake. We don't want it!

Now, I invited Mr. Lammers [Head of the regional Department of Highways office] to get in touch with me. I said that we would provide a house for him to live in for three or four days so he could get some sort of feeling for how people live on the coast. I have not heard from Mr. Lammers in regard to this. (Whistling, applause)

SUP. ARRIGONI: We're really short of time. And the longer you applaud, the less time we're going to have.

VOICE: In two days we accumulated 222 signatures on this petition of people who are totally opposed to this highway project. (He hands the petitions to the supervisors, who do not appear impressed.)

Now, the Department of Highways, by filing a negative declaration of environmental impact on this first phase [claiming that the project would have no "substantial impact" on the environment] has gotten around the fact that this is actually a three-part project. Phases two and three are all integral parts of the same project. But by splitting them up into three projects, or phases, and declaring a negative declaration on the first, they are hiding the effect of all of the three parts together.

The first part will necessitate the second part, which will then necessitate the third part. This is the way these kinds of projects work. No one part is significant. But put them all together, and you have a mess.

So, I hope you will ask the Department of Highways to do an environmental impact report on the entire project before they begin any small part of it.

SUP. ARRIGONI: How many of you are opposed to this project? (About a hundred hands go up.) How many of you oppose just the first section? (One hand is raised.)

SUP. BAAR (Louis H. "Bud" Baar, the lame-duck supervisor for our district and a real estate man): Now, I think I'm going to speak for a different concern than all you people who are against whatever might happen. I want to speak for the people in that area who are not here, for whatever reason. Whether they're working, or whatever . . .

VOICE (from the back, loud): Yeah, selling real estate!

SUP. BAAR: Yeah. Some of them are selling real estate. It's very easy for you people, and most of you are newcomers here . . . (Hoots of derision) Now, I don't hold that against you, but. . . .

VOICE: I've never seen you out in our town! (Applause)

SUP. ARRIGONI: All right! That's enough! (To the audience) We have listened to you patiently. And you'll have an opportunity again when Gary Giacomini is on the board.

SUP. BAAR: This highway is just a cow trail that they paved over and made into a road. Now, we have two national parks which we fought hard to get, and now we are going to have to provide access for that area. All I can say to people who are so adamant against the highway is that you have to consider that other people have a right to have safe travel on the roadways. (*People start chattering.*) This is one roadway which is not safe. And I don't think that it is fair for you or myself, however long we may have been around the county, to say for someone else, "You can't participate or enjoy this."

VOICE: Whom do you represent? Us, or everyone outside the county?

VOICE: If they're so god-fearing afraid that the road is dangerous, why don't they put up signs and rails?

SUP. BAAR: All I'm saying to many of you who have found this area recently, it's not for your exclusive use. And I hope that in the future . . .

VOICE (*loud*): Your two minutes are up!

SUP. BAAR (*mad now*): Listen, I've seen better heads on boils than yours! So, don't give me any of that! (*The whole audience goes bananas clapping for Baar's joke. He tries to continue talking through the clapping, but finally gives up.*)

SUP. WORNUM (*smiling*): Well, I don't want to follow this, which is a difficult act to follow.

He goes on to suggest that the board defer action until Gary takes office three weeks hence. Some people are relieved. Others are angry that today was not the end of it, and that the whole circus may have to be rounded up once again for a future hearing. Slowly, people clear the room, chatting, joking, cursing, and head back home over-the-hill.

TODAY is one of those days which leaves me tired and divided somewhere between Vietnam and the California Coast.

"God! There's more demonstrating in Poland than in this country!" says Barbara B. on the phone. She is calling a meeting at her place over-the-hill to try to organize something against Nixon's Christmas bombing of North Vietnam.

A friend sends three telegrams to the Florida White House: STOP THE BOMBING. STOP THE WAR. STOP THE LIES. He charges them to the telephone number of the Army recruiting office in the city.

It's one of those days when the walls just fall over in your mind, and you lose the ability to define some things as more important than others. Priorities break down. The highway? The Ho Chi Minh Trail?

I have a hunch, though, that when this murderous war and all its corruption ends, there is going to be a tidal wave in domestic politics which is going to drive Dick Nixon and his corporate zombies right off the Continental Shelf.

THERE is a protest vigil at Hamilton Air Force Base.

Two other people from Briones go over-the-hill and spend the night standing around in the cold. Although it saddens me and confuses me when people from town seem not to feel the necessity to try to do something about this war, I also know that maybe it is better for now. Rather than dissipate all our energy outward, perhaps it is better that people direct themselves toward their home where their efforts will have some real impact. Build blocks at the bottom, and perhaps the top will not be so debased.

THE sun has appeared for our Christmas.

The air is filled with thousands of bright orange monarch butterflies.

A warm east wind blows the air out of the inland valleys to San Francisco Bay. A layer of brown smog leaks out under the Golden Gate Bridge and hangs over the ocean like a false horizon. The final indignity for an ocean.

The oil industry's present to us all.

STEVE'S feet have been burned seriously a second time, by being washed in scalding water by a careless friend.

Everyone trying to help.

Much talk about self-sufficiency and independence. People reluctant to call the doctor.

Our illusions of grandeur.

Steve will be in bed for months. He will need reconstructive surgery and skin grafting. The Plan has bogged down without Steve.

We are learning. But we are far from the self-reliance which we brag and joke about in our cockier moments. Independence will be a hollow promise until we are truly our own experts, and can do what we need in order to live.

Farmers must really know how to farm. Sewage managers must understand sewage. Medics and doctors must be able to deliver help when it is needed. Storekeepers must be able to provide people with what they need in a reliable manner.

Rebels never quite seem to believe that they are for real. So used are we to being in opposition to the authorities who keep the system running that we forget that a real victory will put the burden squarely on our own backs. And if it is not assumed, we will suffer.

TODAY is a beautiful day.

There is a birthday party for Landon and Dick on a remote stretch of beach with no access by road.

I walk out over the meadows and canyons rather than go along the shore.

The grass is green. Eucalyptus trees are turning brown from the week of frost. Cows with their newborn calves stand and stare intently.

I walk out across two different vast, open, quiet pieces of land wishing that I did not know so much about them—about the property lines, the price paid, the taxes, the development plans, and the wheeling and dealing that goes on in distant offices over their fate.

I cross Rolf's land and try to conjure up some image of the other faceless, nameless investors in his consortium to develop it.

"Reasonable profit." The words are stuck in my mind like some singing commercial.

We have had many meetings with Rolf, and talked with Steve and Patrick as they worked on the Plan. They were cordial meetings, but underlaid with a tension born from the mutual recognition that our purposes are different. Rolf is a developer with his rationalizations. We are conservationists and protectionists with ours. We are both riddled with contradictions. But one thing is crystal-clear in the minds of most people in town: There should never be condominiums on this piece of the coast, not only because they would mar its beauty, but because the new people, cars, attention, and need for services would drastically alter the town's whole metabolism.

Rolf understands this, but does not agree as to the qualitative effect. It is strange to be so unalterably opposed to someone who is otherwise so likable.

Giant storm surf rolls in on the beach below me at the foot of the cliff. Heaps of wood are stacked like pickup sticks just above the high-tide line.

A cluster of people surround a driftwood fire.

I walk down a half-caved-in dirt road cut into the cliff during the oil spill to get the clean-up trucks down to the beach, noisy lumbering machines speeding down this inaccessible beach as though it were a freeway. The beach was sliced with tire tracks. Helicopters landed bringing men with clipboards and bullhorns who stood and assessed the situation as volunteers covered with pitch-black oil wrestled the two-hundred-pound blobs of goo into dump trucks.

A very special, private, isolated oasis, to which none of us had ever before gone in a vehicle, had been invaded by an army with a job to do, a job which had nothing to do with anything that had ever naturally happened there before.

The beach was covered with oil and littered with the tar encased carcasses of birds and seals. The rocks and tidal pools were smothered in oil. And the only antidote to it all was the machines for which the oil was destined in the first place.

Today, the beach feels much as it had before the oil spill.

IT is a weekend, and the city has emptied into the countryside like a scourge of locusts.

A steady stream of cars is on the roads. As I walk back from Paradise Valley they speed past. There's an abundance of well-polished sports cars with megaphone mufflers. The snarling echoes off the wooded hills behind the School.

People out for a Sunday drive. Five minutes later, before I have even gotten up Finney Hill, they return, coming back out of town.

Did they find what they wanted? Is their fascination with the countryside or with their cars?

Our town has acquired a much criticized reputation for our unwillingness to embrace the tourists (and their money) who come to visit us from the city. They come here for relief. Many people here see their search for relief as disruption. There have been numerous cases of outright hostility exhibited against tourists. Sometimes it is unprovoked, as when children taunt tourists downtown. Other times, it has followed accidents or near-accidents where an animal or a child has been run over.

At times, the hostility which parts of this town displays toward cars and tourists has worried and angered people. Even some local residents find it unfriendly and distasteful. Accusations that Briones is a group of elitists trying to keep everyone else out of their own special preserve have not been infrequent. In particular, people who live in the city and share in the hope that urban residents can gain easy access to the country feel Briones' protectionist sentiments to be selfish. And indeed, they are. But I sometimes wonder if the urge to protect and to make secure one's home is not a healthy form of selfishness.

There is a feeling shared by many in town that it is time for people in the cities *and* the countryside to make some sort of a stand in the place in which they have chosen to live. If it's in the city, do it in the city. If it's in the country, do it in the country. What people seem to react against so strongly here is the escapist mentality, that of people using the city to make money and then abandoning it and coming to someone else's home for recreation and relaxation with little regard to the impact they are having.

Perhaps we should all stay home a little more and see if we

can't get things together. Then we might not be so desperate for that weekend house and a fast car with which to make our getaway.

Anyway, our battles are here. We would be foolish to think that we could solve the problems of the city, even if we were to offer ourselves up as a full-time playground.

DAWN. It is so clear that the distant coast looks twice as close as it really is across the Bay.

Judith, Burr, and I rendezvous at the PUD to work on a highway information packet for the next hearing. Draft is written. Judith has some classy binders. Burr has sent letters to all the TV stations. Have a lead on a highway engineer who might be able to come and testify on the side of the Lord.

We start trying to think up a name for the group opposed to the highway project. The Amalgamated Association of the Enemies of Asphalt? Briones New People's Army? Concerned Citizens for Narrow, Unsafe, Slow Roads? Finally decided on something really flamboyant, Friends of the Highway. We call our info packet the *Highway Bedside Reader*.

HEAD up to the vet and Ten-Mile Beach.

The beach is empty. Just the giant frothing surf churning in. Then suddenly out past the surf I see the whales shooting steam above the horizon line. Magical geysers at sea. And then occasionally a huge glistening body encrusted with barnacles arches slowly out of the water and plunges back in with a strange rolling motion.

The California gray whales are heading south to calve.

WALKING home.

The sun just setting in a raging orange scramble of clouds and colors out over the ocean.

Ilka stands silhouetted against the sky on the cliff edge, yelling and gesticulating.

Below on the reef is a pack of dogs. Strangely out of place at the end of the bare reef, now exposed by a minus low tide, is a doe. The dogs stand between her and the shore, barking and dancing. They have stopped at a channel of water between the rocks which slowly widens as the tide rises. The doe is trapped.

We yell down at them and whistle. But our voices are drowned out by the surf.

I bound down the steep cliff, sliding ten feet at a time in the loose snow-like earth. My mind is pierced with a memory from last year of a doe stuck in the mud of the Lagoon. Up to her stomach. Head twisted down as though to lick her haunch. Dead. Chased out by dogs or a car. Helpless in the mud while the tide slowly rose and filled her lungs.

I hit the beach. Run out through the seaweed and shallow water onto the reef. Without noticing it, I find myself running past a colony of surprised seals. They panic, flop, and slither into the water.

Seabirds protest the intrusions overhead.

I reach the dogs. Throw some rocks at them. They retreat.

Finally the doe starts moving back toward the land, splashing across the filling tidal pools.

Such a graceful creature. Inappropriately exposed on the reef. She moves hesitatingly toward the beach, and then dives up a canyon filled with brush.

AWAKE just after dawn to go over-the-hill to Gary's supervisorial coronation.

The wind has turned to the south. The reef is roaring with huge rollers surging in over the rocks.

Rain; warm, wet air. A strong wind blasts the trees littering the road with eucalyptus nuts and shredded bark.

Stop in blinding rain to pick up Patrick, who is still asleep.

We head out to the highway, relying heavily on the promise that after the ceremony there will be free coffee and doughnuts.

The ceremony is quite plain. Gary nervous. He's been stoking away coffee all morning. He gives a nice short spiel which puts the other supes on notice that he stands for something new, but he is not antagonistic. Talks about accessibility and the need to preserve the integrity of rural communities and farming.

The ceremony ends with a little flatulence from some other supervisors.

Finally, get some coffee. Manage to garner a Danish and half a doughnut in a highly competitive "feast."

We split for home through misty green rolling hills covered with cows all facing the same direction.

Make home in time for a consultation with our sewer engineer.

AN old stock car is parked in the muddy driveway. Painted purple. Bears the inscriptions MCCOY'S POULTRY SERVICE and STATE DRY CLEANERS on the fenders. It's missing a few tires and lights. Next to it stands an old buckboard.

Ben's trailer is up on cinder blocks across the driveway near a fruit tree. He stands at the door next to two garbage cans wearing a pair of blue coveralls which have the word *NESTLÉ* embroidered in script on the breast pocket.

A cigarette is drooping out of his mouth, shaded by a cowboy hat. He is instructing three teenage girls. They are busy roping a sawhorse which has a pair of taxidermist's cow horns nailed on the front.

Ben is in his early fifties. He leases forty-five acres of pasture just before town, and runs a horse-boarding operation for kids. They pay twenty dollars a month, and groom and feed their own horses. It is one of the few places where children who live on small lots on the mesa can keep their horses and ponies inexpensively.

"Now, for me, I wouldn't care if I hadda lotta money, you know what I mean," says Ben, leaning on his blue pickup with a bale of hay in the back. Kids are everywhere. In the trailer, out front, in the barn, in the pasture, and riding around on horses.

"This lawyer sends me this letter. Well, it says my rent is gonna go up from $150 to $350.

"Now I got this letter from the lawyer right here." He gets

BEN

into his truck and rummages around through some papers on the dashboard.

"This here's my A-1 filing service," he says, finally coming up with a certified envelope with an impressive embossed return address in the city on the upper left-hand corner.

"So, now, like I tell the kids, I got four hundred bucks. I can pay one more month. And then, that's it. Hell, I cain't do nothin' here! I'd be just plain ole silly to go ahead and fix up these barns. 'Cause any day they can tell me to git out. Kinda wanted to put a ring down there for the kids. But what's the point?"

Some people bring in a pony and ask if they can board it in Ben's pasture.

"OK. Let's try it," he says. "But them ponies gits out of almost anything."

He makes a cigarette jump out of his pack and offers it to me. "You know, I just like givin' these here kids somethin'. Like, maybe have a little rodeo or somethin'. Git the hardware store and other places in town to put up a few prizes. You'd git a lot of folks down here. Ya know. Maybe bring a six-pack of beer, have a picnic, and have some fun.

"If I gotta go, OK. Sure. They can do it. It's the land. If you ain't got the land, you cain't do it. I figure, what's the use of havin' money anyhow, if you cain't do what ya want?

"Hell, I can just pick up my trailer and drag it down the road. But then the kids ain't got nothin'."

Q: What did you do before you came to Briones?
A: If I told you everything, it would be embarrassing! I've been here seven years in Briones. I was born and raised in Sonoma. Then I moved to Colorado after I quit rodeoing. I was a ranch manager. Worked in Colorado as a ranch manager. Runnin' horse ranches there and trading horses for a big construction outfit. You can use that for, I guess, a write-off or something. The horses were comin' in and goin' out all the time—it's hard to say how many. There was always twenty, thirty, forty, or

fifty head. We trained them for everything imaginable: for show, for ridin'—you name it and we done it. That's how I come over here. Most all my life I've been on my own. I had a ranch of my own in the Sonoma Valley. I had horses—I had a dairy ranch for a long time. Also I had beef. I've always trained horses, too. Then I rodeoed for years. But I also had a business, too. My vintage wasn't like now. Now they're up in the forty to fifty thousand dollar racket. I was maybe— what—four, five thousand dollars. 'Cause I never rodeoed like now, they're goin' twelve months a year. A lot of 'em are makin' three rodeos at one time. You know, flyin'. Flyin' in airplanes. In my vintage when I stopped rodeoing they were just beginnin' to start that. I made two rodeos in one day— done that a few times. That was in the late forties, early fifties. Rodeoin' is a business.

Sure it's a sport, but it's also a real business. When you are rodeoing, you're a businessman and it's a business that you're in. Not as an entertainer—you're in it as a business makin' a dollar. When you get cold you back off and stay away from it a little bit until you start hittin' a hot streak again.

Roping. I roped. I done all of it at one time or another but ropin' was my speciality. I rode bulls, too. First thing is to get him rode and the second is to get away from him so you don't get worked over, stepped on. Take a rodeo like the cow palace—young Balzan is down there now. In some places ten seconds is damn near out of the money. They're gettin' 'em down to eight or nine. It's all passé to me now. I used to enjoy it. But if a young person would like to do it, I'd help 'em.
Q: How many horses do you have here now?
A: I guess it must be twenty. And here, what I was tryin' to do is do something for a bunch of kids. Different ones have asked me, "Hell, why don't you raise the rent?" but I ain't into the horse business. All I'm lookin' for is a place to live and have these kids—do something for them.
Q: What's happening with you now you're not working at school as janitor?
A: I got a lot of enjoyment out of that school. I don't know

BEN AND CHILDREN

what I'm gonna do now. With this damn leg I've got, I don't know what I can do. I can't go back into trainin' horses.

Q: It would be great if you could teach something about horse training at school for the activities program.

A: Sure I'd be interested. I had a little deal like that goin', but I did it free. Maybe it sounds screwy to you, but I get a big thrill out of it—helpin' kids. 'Cause I like kids. 'Cause money ain't all the greatest thing in the world either, far as I'm concerned.

Like the other night there when I quit workin' at the school, and they had that little deal for me. The kids sang "Don't Fence Me In" and gave me a bottle of Kentucky bourbon. You couldn't buy that for money.   INTERVIEW BY JUDITH WESTON

FOR several days the rain has fallen relentlessly. High winds have whipped the ocean to a constant roar. Power lines are down. Huge branches of trees have come crashing down on roads all over town. Streams are all swollen.

The weather report predicts no letup.

IT's still raining.

The PUD meets for the third time in two days. We declare ourselves a "disaster area." Our whole water system has been knocked out by mud slides. We are left with only a three-day supply in our tanks on Shoefly Hill.

Four inches of rain in four days. Whole sides of hills are pulling loose. One house in town is hit by a slide so sudden and so strong that it sweeps the first floor right out from under the roof, which lands behind the house as in a Roadrunner cartoon. The people are in bed and miraculously escape by coasting to safety on their mattress with their young child.

Everything awash. Roads flooded. Downtown is a lake. Service road to the water system catchment dams is blocked in twenty-seven places by downed trees, slides, and swollen streams. The transmission mains have been broken.

"Hell! They's nothin' but rust holding most of 'em together anyway," says Bill, the PUD maintenance man, with gruff resignation in his voice. "If them tanks goes dry, then the pipes will drain out. And if we put 'em back under pressure, shit, we'd blow 'em out like soaker hoses. And then what are you gonna do for water?" he says, giving a big laugh.

The San Francisco *Chronicle* runs pictures of Briones on the front page which makes it look like Hiroshima. Actually things aren't that bad. (Are they ever?) But it does set the stage nicely for a little "disaster" theatrics. Americans love disasters. Politicians excel in aiding disaster. No controversies. No enemies. The supervisors are being extremely helpful. Gary has come out and helped us work on some requests for relief equipment and disaster funds.

UP at 6:30. Hardly slept. All night long gale winds shake the house and drive sheets of rain against the bulging windows. Big chunks of the cliff are sloughing off with the weight of the water. Waves roaring on the reef.

Rubber boots, slicker, hat. Black Navy coat. Slosh up the hill to the truck. The whole mesa looks like a rice paddy. Drive over to Bill's house. It's blowing like crazy.

He comes running down the hill, coat flapping. Wades through a river at the roadside.

"Oh, shit!" he yells. "What the hell is this?"

Can barely see his face in the colorless gray of the first light. It is the kind of rainy day when one's imagination loses the power to summon up recollection of the sun.

Bill: "Think we can get past the School? Pine Gulch Creek is really cooking."

Me: "I dunno. Maybe we better take your truck with high axles."

Bill: "Can't. It's not here. Left it over-the-hill last Sunday when we hauled in those emergency pumps and chlorinators."

Me: "OK. Let's have a try in this."

Bill: "OK. Let's hope we can get those supes to make us a disaster."

We hit two bad floods. Almost snuff out the truck. Nothing

worse than being up to your floorboards in a river flowing across the road and not being sure whether it's getting deeper or shallower.

Hit Big Pink at 8:15.

"Man, I sure could suck on a cup of coffee!" says Bill.

"Yeah. I got my heart set on some Civic Center Danish," says me.

The meeting is called to order.

Seems like the whole county is flooded.

The supes look a little puffy from working too hard and getting up too early.

Finally our agenda item comes up.

We give our little rap on the situation in town. I screw up on the numbers for costs of emergency repairs. Can't make all our estimates add up. Get too rattled.

Embarrassing.

But the supes are friendly.

Basically, the biggest favor you can do for them is to keep it short so they can move on to the next agenda item.

They finally declare Briones a disaster area, an "emergency."

We head back home.

Still raining.

We hit home and meet the PUD maintenance crew. They are all in slickers. Covered with mud. Wet.

They are trying to set up disaster relief pumps and canvas settling tanks in Arroyo Hondo for the emergency town water supply.

They have been working around the clock.

THE PUD office is full of people this morning in soggy clothes, boots, and slickers. Meeting, talking, drinking coffee.

The state sends word that we are required to post signs telling people to boil their water which is pumped by an emergency system from a muddy pond covered with weeds. The water is nuked with twenty times the normal amount of chlorine.

But the state says, *"Boil!"*

State terrorism! The health bogeyman! We may die of chlorine before the amoebas get us.

People in town not sure what this order means. Many "disaster rumors" are beginning to circulate.

One lady who is fond of gin calls and asks if it is true that there is "a band of primitive people camped on the banks of our water supply and putting their sewage into the drinking water?"

Poetic sense of paranoia. Somewhere in the back of her mind, no doubt, lurk half-digested tales of Paradise Valley.

The coffee drinking is interrupted by two gents in suits and trenchcoats who step out of a car marked OFFICIAL BUSINESS.

The driver opens the trunk. Extracts a pair of galoshes. They both come into the office. Everyone stops talking, and looks up.

The men are from the state disaster center. They want to see our disaster, to see if the state wants to "accredit" it.

Mark and I agree to take them up the canyon to see what's left of our water system.

We arrive at the emergency pump site, which looks like a combat LZ in Vietnam. Pumps, canvas, tanks, chlorinators, engines, gas cans, trucks, generators, pipe, and mud. Much of the equipment has already broken down and been cannibalized to keep other equipment running.

Bill, Chuck, and Bobby are on shifts twenty-four hours a day to watch the pumps.

We head up the canyon with the two bureaucrats.

The one with the galoshes and clipboard manages to get one galosh stuck in the mud. He tries to pull it out, and instead pulls his foot out of the galosh, which stays stuck in the deep jelly-like mud. He dances around on one foot trying not to lose his balance while he tries to reinsert his foot back into his stuck galosh. Then, with a lot of slurping and sucking, he pulls out both foot and galosh, and moves on to the next tenuous step.

We hit the first slide, and he suggests we have seen enough. The other one wants to go on.

Up we go.

Me: "Well, how long will it take to get some of this disaster money?"

Him: "Well, first we have to decide what kind of a disaster it is. State or federal. Which one."

Me: "And then what?"

Him: "Well, under the state disaster you can get money only for 'restoration of plant.' For the federal-type disaster you can get money for everything. One hundred percent reimbursable."

Me: "You mean like for labor, gas, trucks, equipment?"

Him: "Yes, that's something like it."

Me: "Who decides?"

Him: "Well, it's all politics, see. First, it goes to the county. Then it goes to Reagan and then to Nixon, and it all depends on politics, like whether they need to do some favors out here or not."

Me: "Well, when could we get some money?"

Him: "Well, the thing of it is, we don't give you any money until you have your system completely repaired."

Me: "You mean, after the disaster is over you give disaster relief?"

Him: "Yes. Hell, we got guys down at the '69 LA earthquake that haven't gotten a cent yet."

Me: "So, we can't expect anything now when we need it?"

Him: "No. We're just out here looking at the whole area to see if the county qualifies to be called a disaster."

Me: "So what are we supposed to do? How can we fix our disaster if we can't get any money until after it's all repaired?"

Him: "Well, you got to start tapping other sources. Sometimes it takes two years."

Me: "So there's no real point in us talking too much now, huh? Nothing you can do for us for a couple of years?"

Mark: "Well, there is one thing that I learned today, and that's that a disaster is something you can live with for two years."

THE disaster has taxed us all. The PUD has been forced to hire extra people and spend thousands of dollars in emergency funds. The directors are all pretty much worked to a frazzle. All this has come on top of regular work on the new sewer.

For the first time in the district's history, we are considering small salaries to be paid to directors.

We are at odds with one of our own most vaunted ideals: the volunteer ethic.

Ideally, the whole job should stay volunteer. But the PUD board has come to more and more serve the role of a town council (which we do not have, because we are not incorporated), while performing various sewer, water, and other utilities functions.

The job has grown. Several directors find it difficult to put in the requisite amount of time without any pay.

Some people in town resent any suggestion that we, the great selfless moralistic critics, should now vote ourselves part of the spoils.

Others feel that pay is essential to free directors to do a thorough job, and to make it possible for those who are not retired or independently wealthy to consider running for office.

While neither side accepts the state public utilities code as gospel, it does stipulate that directors can be paid up to $3,600 a year.

The debate begins at our weekly PUD meeting.

(D)* BILL: Well, in all honesty, I should say that we have talked about the subject of salaries for directors informally an awful lot. It's gotten to the point where I am spending, where everybody is spending, full days dealing with utilities matters. I know that personally I can't afford to do that. If I'm going to work full-time on the sewer and long-range water plans, I'm going to have to draw some money.

PHIL (*very hostile local real estate salesman*): Why don't you all resign? (*Laughter*)

*(D) before a name connotes a PUD Director.

[79   ]

(D) BILL: Well, if we all resigned, I wonder who would come in and take over?

PHIL: I think you could find a group!

(D) MARK (*smiling impishly*): Yes. I think you could find a group. (*He looks at Phil.*)

JOE (*fire chief, ex-PUD director*): Now, at the time when you members ran for the board, you knew what the conditions were. You had to donate your time. This was a volunteer service. The past boards in this district donated their time. They got only mileage and so much pay for certain meetings.

Now, was it your intention when you ran for the board that you was going to be paid someday? 'Cause here we are. Just a small, very small district. This is not a big district. How many people are you going to hire in this district?

(D) BILL: Well, we are facing an emergency now. And all of a sudden we had a sewer to plan in a year. And we got that accomplished. And the reason why our water system is in trouble is because it was neglected for many years . . . and the time has come where a lot of full-time . . .

JACK (*from an old-time family, and ex-owner of the Store*): That's a lie!

JOE: It was not neglected!

JACK (*with anger*): That's a goddamn lie!

(D) BILL: The time has come when a lot of work must be done, and it has to be full-time. The town has grown.

(D) MIMI: Wait! Wait! I had my hand up. I want to ask a question! Please! It's related to this. Is the grant money for the sewer. . . . can we get grant money back from the federal government if we pay everyone salaries?

(D) GREG: I would think that we could get . . .

BOB: What does Paul say about that? He's a lawyer.

(D) PAUL: Yes, any work that the district does toward the sewer is eligible.

CLARENCE: You know, the chairman of the board long before you, Burt Waldorf, welded all the pipe going up into the canyon for nothing.

JOE: That's right!

CLARENCE: And another fella volunteered . . .

(D) BILL: Do you know how much work we have done for nothing?

CLARENCE: I know ya have! With Future Studies and all. And I don't think anybody worked harder than you all to defeat the old sewer plan. And I think anyone who lives within the area which would have been sewered by the Kennedy Plan owes you a big debt. We would have had our taxes raised from five to fifteen dollars per one hundred dollars assessed value. You took a terrible load off our shoulders. . . . But I still don't think that anyone who sits behind that table (*points to the directors' table*) should ask for payment from the community. If he has to have the money, I think he should go out and work and let someone else take his job. Because in the past everyone volunteered. Not only the people on the board, but the people in the community. They did everything for themselves!

(D) ORVILLE: Clarence, let me try to respond. You know, I have been really opposed to any of us taking a salary in the past. Money always alters people's relationships to work. And the job has been one where people worked as hard as they could when they could. Of course, it just feels better not to take money. It removes a lot of problems from the public mind, and issues are easier to deal with when people are not getting paid. But still people have to live.

Now, in my own case, I know that I left my job in the city when I realized that I really could not be here and there at the same time. Someone was getting shortchanged. And this job meant more to me.

I think that over the next few years this job will be sufficiently time-consuming that it will automatically rule out ninety percent of the people from taking it. I mean, who could afford to do it now? I don't think there are many people who can handle emergencies, design a new water system, and build a sewer in their spare time.

(D) GREG: I think we should be conscious that in previous years when work got intense, engineers and consultants were paid to do what we are now doing. I think you have to remember that. Personally, I have every bit as much ambivalence as Orville about receiving a salary. And I really respect Clarence's comments, because he is speaking from a place of being the epitome of a volunteer.

CLARENCE: Well, I think that if you decide to pay yourselves, you'll be turning the community against you.

(D) GREG: I think that you are right in some respects. But I am not sure. . . . I mean, I have had a lot of people come up to me, as have others, and say, "Why don't you pay yourselves? It is so apparent that the work you are doing is saving the community money and taking up a lot of time!"

THE salary issue hangs like an albatross around our necks. Our ideals run headlong into our needs. There seems to be no total escape out either end of the issue. The last meeting has left us drained from self-justification. The money issue has somehow tarnished even our expectations of ourselves.

Guilt is our copilot. Today we give up and decide not to take salaries.

The opposition is limited but vocal. They come to meetings and holler. Have to admire them for that. Most people probably would like to see us be paid a small amount. But they are elsewhere. There is no doubt about it: publicly elected officials feel the effect of those who come to their meetings.

DENNIS, Greg, Patrick, and I take Raggedy Ann (Dennis' truck) around the Lagoon to see what lumber treasures have floated in on the storms.

The storm south wind blows all kinds of big pressure-treated dock timbers and pilings up our way from San Francisco Bay.

We need a gatepost, but cannot resist other pieces.

Lumber fever sweeps Paradise Valley as people get ready to build houses, barns, chicken sheds.

Our spirits are always high at the prospects of free wood. Particularly five-hundred-pound pilings delivered to our door

by Mother Nature. Some are so heavy we cannot load them onto the truck. We have to float one down to the truck. Another falls on my foot while being coaxed up a bank. Misses bones. Leaves ache.

And it's all "waste"!

A friend who taught in Santa Cruz reports having had one student who graduated and became a garbage man. When asked what he does, he says he is a "garbologist."

PHYLO and the septic tank survey crew are bunched in a small area out back, of Bob and Sabine's, hot on the trail of a leach field. Jeff is stabbing the ground with a curtain rod, teaching them how to locate septic tanks by following sewer pipes under ground. The crew has been undergoing a series of lectures. They keep turning up endless yards of clay pipe that lead nowhere. Finally, they find a septic tank, but it is out of service. People getting cold. Phylo lectures on the meaning of the black surface sludge. Some take notes.

There is still some flack around town about the crews not being "experts" or "qualified."

Mil opines that the contract has been given to "hippies."

Mark doubts that the crew can turn out a first-rate report which will satisfy the state.

Others from the ranks of the Property Owners Association express disapprobation and harbor doubts about our local inspection crew.

"Excuse me, ma'am. My name is Susan, and I'm here to look down your septic tank."

"Oh, my god, Fern! It's *them*! Run for your life!"

THE road to Petaluma winds through miles of hilly open pasture. There is an occasional ranch house tucked back in one of the folds of the hills. Then the road winds down into the Sonoma Valley and runs smack into the housing tracts surrounding this old and once small city.

Past this outer buffer zone of "new homes" are several blocks of sovereign old Victorian houses with turrets, wide porches, gingerbread, and grand old trees arching over spacious lawns. Then comes the center of the city: old brick buildings with faded advertisements for feed and chewing tobacco painted on the outer walls, and with names and dates embossed in brickwork under their ornate front parapets. They form a backdrop for the more recent gas stations and hamburger drive-ins as though they were discarded sets from some long since closed play.

The city's downtown movie theater went porno a year or so ago.

A canal divides the old city, and used to be the artery connecting Petaluma to San Francisco and the Bay before the time of the freeway. A few old fishing boats and barges still linger as historical reminders of an era when men found it easier to move on the water than on the land.

Captain Bill still survives, although people say his recent illness may do him in. He's an old man. Gray hair. Short. Runs one of the finest junkyards in Petaluma. Has everything. Lumber, windows, plumbing, steel. He claims he used to be a millionaire.

"Hell! You know, when I was building my studio," says Rob, a local carpenter and potter, "I got everything from Captain Bill. The whole studio only cost me fifty bucks!"

Captain Bill used to run the garbage barge between Petaluma and San Francisco. He claims that one day during World War II he saw a periscope of a Japanese sub sticking up out of the waters of San Francisco Bay as he made his run. Well, by god, if Captain Bill didn't just turn his barge around and ram it. He says he made a mess out of it. Some people doubted it. But then the bodies of three Japanese sailors floated up on Ten-Mile Beach a few days later and Captain Bill got a citation and a lot of commendations from the military.

When barging garbage became passé, Captain Bill moved onto the next logical calling and went into salvage.

Some of the best salvage yards, like Maselli & Sons, lie across the drawbridge over the canal, near the railroad tracks, the feedstores, and the cattle auction. They used to be at the outskirts of the city. Then the freeway pushed the boundaries further out, bringing with it a cordon of spoliation and ugliness encrusted around it: Fast-food chain restaurants, trailer parks, used car lots, and vast open industrial lots for rent or sale.

And then, before the damage fades back into farmland, there is one last subdivision with the houses so crowded in on each other that from the highway it appears as an endless sea of roofs. It is unrelieved by any trees or grass. A board fence has been erected around the entire development like a girth attempting to contain the houses from sprawling any further out.

If one turns right at the Fast Gas, and heads out past the high-tension lines and a booster station surrounded by chain-link fence, the land begins to return to normal. One gets a sense of what it must have looked like before the first Spanish settlers arrived. And there on a lovely bluff overlooking the valley is the Petaluma adobe ranch house built by General Mariano Guadalupe Vallejo, one of California's most powerful hidalgos in the 1830s. Rancho Petaluma was 66,000 acres, only part of Vallejo's holdings of 175,000 acres granted by the Mexican governor José Figueroa.

At one time, some two thousand Indians worked on the ranch, which sold tallow and hides.

Today the grand old building, with adobe walls that are three feet thick and spacious cool verandas, sits on the bluff waiting, as the housing tracts advance outward from the city.

THE new Petaluma Civic Center is a linoleum and cement block structure. It is clean, but cheerless. I find Charlotte Teeples of the Planning Department. She is busy, and slightly fatigued from talking with visiting firemen.

She reports that, since 1970, Petaluma's stock of existing housing has almost doubled. Petaluma's growth rate is almost twice the county average. In 1960, the population was fourteen thousand. It is now well over thirty thousand. Petaluma is on the freeway and is becoming a bedroom community for commuters to San Francisco, about thirty-five miles away. Most of the growth has come from large developments rather than from single-family dwellings.

In response, the Petaluma planning staff came up with an environmental design plan which sets an annual growth rate of five hundred units of subdivision a year over the next five years. The purpose of the growth limit, the report says, is "to analyze the course it [the City] had been following, to investigate forces affecting its development trends, and most important, to search out the basic dissatisfactions of many citizens with recent development, as well as their needs and desires for the future."

The design plan goes on: "As logical as it seems, the formulation of a five-year strategy and the setting of a target for annual growth is new. It has not been tried elsewhere in California, where, for many decades, cities have equated growth with progress, or accepted unlimited growth as inevitable. Now, a different philosophy which emphasizes quality over quantity is emerging in the US. Petaluma has embarked on an innovative course to implement this philosophy." The voters backed up the growth-limit concept by an overwhelming margin of four to one in a special election.

So, Petaluma, once the self-proclaimed Chicken Capital of California (Russ "The Moose" Syracuse, a disk jockey from San Francisco, used to give away free one-way Greyhound tickets to Petaluma as a joke), puts a foot down on growth.

The developers, of course, immediately sue. Five hundred units a year are not enough.

"Five hundred units a year?" says a secretary at the city hall with a quizzical look on her face. "Not enough? Hell! It's too much! This city's still gonna die."

How did it all happen?

"Well, there was just an awful lot of pressure from residents," says Charlotte Teeples. "And it passed the city council by quite a wide majority."

Do they think that they will win the suit?

"The city attorney's not too pleased," says Charlotte. "But, I guess he'll have to defend us."

THE PUD board reverses itself and votes four to one to approve salaries of $175 a month for each director.

I find myself feeling good, not just about the advent of some money, but for having slashed our way to some final conclusion on this issue.

Our own ambivalence and indecision were driving us crazy. The money will provide welcome relief for almost all of us who find ourselves in a monthly scramble to keep our bills paid. This, too, can sap a lot of energy.

It feels good, almost forbidden, to receive money for something we all enjoy doing, in the past have always worked at for nothing, and in the future would continue to work at for nothing if the money were not there.

OUR famous nonexistent sign continues to startle, intrigue, and irritate. The top-flight international staff of the Los Angeles *Times* picks another key story of global impact off the wire.

"A lot of people in this rustic coast town don't like visitors," the article begins. "At least one of them feels so strongly about it, he's cutting down road signs that tell strangers how to get there."

"They take a chain saw and whack them off," says the county road superintendent.

"And steel signs haven't stopped efforts to hide the town," notes the article. "Vandals just spray the signs with paint."

Some nameless United Press International correspondent has spent a morning trying to interview people in town. He seems to have trouble finding anyone to talk to. He plaintively notes at the end of his article: "As for the younger people, they don't want to talk much. One man, who said he was a 'struggling painter,' refused to be interviewed, saying it would only bring more tourists."

Several disgruntled people from the Property Owners

Association do air their minds. They see the repeated demise of the signs as connected with "newcomers." One leader of the Property Owners says something about "fascism" and complains that the town has "been taken over by the new left in a quiet revolution."

There is talk of "people on welfare," "unwed mothers," "nude swimmers," also of vandals and burglars. "We have a big dog that keeps them away," says one woman.

The headline mentions vanishing signs and the "rustic" little town which "used to be there." Two members of the State Division of Highways are reported as "convinced the person or persons wrecking the signs want to keep tourists and new settlers away." The county road superintendent estimates that he has had to replace twenty signs in the past six months.

It is strange to read about our town as seen through the eyes of a hurried reporter.

AT times, it is hard to believe that this puny town and all its efforts are going anywhere.

Sometimes it feels as though we are trying to bail out the ocean. We win some lesser battle on a practical level, but lose the larger one. We win a point at a hearing, and then so often our small symbolic victories seem to lull people back into a false sense of confidence that all is well, and that none of their effort is further required.

Most people want to remain either undisturbed, or confident that someone else will work things out.

Is it realistic to hope that an ever wider group of people can be infused with a sense that their lives, their town, their land, and their world depend on what they do?

Endless struggle?

And then Richie says, "Yeah, sure, man. But you only got one life. You better get some livin' in around all this work."

It is hard to pinpoint the wellspring of this periodic pessimism and uncertainty. It doubtless has something to do with the endless process of keeping the dragon at bay. But equally important, our sense of strength and well-being in this town revolves around our camaraderie as we work. That is a delicate and perishable thing, and so vulnerable to our private craziness.

Our politics suffer when we do.

WE begin the first structure in Paradise Valley.

It's a toolshed, and it's built completely out of wood we found in the valley from old fallen-down sheds.

There will be development and growth.

But, there is more. There is a vision of trying to reestablish family agriculture, food, jobs, enjoyment in producing the essentials. Self-sufficiency, although it may never become a total reality, is our direction.

Growth is good and bad.

There is a difference between a second-home weekend subdivision and a producing farm.

"Progress," "growth," "development" need redefinition. They need to be rescued as words from the destroyers.

OUR police are the county sheriffs. Ever since they phased out the resident deputies who lived in each town, the sheriffs have patrolled several towns at once in cars. Some of the men are pleasant, others are downright ugly. Most are rendered remote and faceless by the cars and their immense beats. There is rarely time for them to get out of their cars.

In the past few months antagonism has been building to a crescendo against Sheriff Joe Kelly. He never gets out of his car unless he is giving a ticket. He never smiles. He speeds arrogantly around town and triumphantly arrests people for minor infractions like parking on the wrong side of the street, swimming naked on the beach, or for stopping and talking with someone in the middle of the street. He once caught Luigi, age eight, peeing in the street. He threatened to send him to reform school and made him cry.

Kelly is a gray fellow. People have been complaining and writing letters about him for a long time.

KREEEEEEEGAAAAAAAH!!!

The supervisors vote unanimously against widening and straightening the highway. The state gives up present plans.

Why did they vote this way? No one really can figure out why some of the votes switched against the project. It is still unclear how at least three of the five supervisors actually feel about wider and straighter roads. The final vote is one of those strange about-faces which occur in politics and seems to stem from confusion and inconsistency rather than from new insight or conversion to a new understanding.

Everyone is so glad that we have given up trying to analyze the inner workings of the heads of the five men. We feel as mighty as King Kong.

Sometimes the confluence of events comes together without warning to dispel the gloom.

MR. Sawdek's profession is to float cameras with strobe lights through underground sewer pipes to photograph the insides and get an evaluation of the shape they are in. We are hiring Mr. Sawdek to photograph our sewer collection main to see if it is worth hooking into our new treatment ponds.

We stand at the intersection of Wharf Road and Brighton Avenue with the cars whizzing around the corner past us. Mr. Sawdek pulls out a little hand viewer with some slides of someone else's sewer in it. He hands it over to us, announcing that we can have videotape if we do not like the slides.

The slides are definitely another universe. You can see a river of sewage flowing through a round pipe. In places, roots from trees have grown down through the cracked pipe and caused cave-ins.

"It may surprise you," says Mr. Sawdek, "but we never had a camera trapped inside a sewer for more than a week."

He shows us more pictures of several large rats staring into the strobe light from their perches on sewer laterals coming in from houses and buildings. The rats look surprised.

"You know," says Mr. Sawdek, "they have it better than we do. They just sit in there and wait for whatever they want to come floating by. No sweat! Most of the stuff is even ground up for them by disposals. Sure beats working!"

He is curious about our town. "It's a pretty little town you've got here," he says. "My wife is on the planning commission where we live out in Vacaville. But, Jesus, we're being eaten alive by those subdivisions." He shakes his head and pauses.

I tell him that the only success we have had in controlling growth is through taking advantage of our utilities shortages and system inadequacies. We talk about the building moratorium, the water shortage, and the ban on new sewer hookups downtown until we finish the new sewer. He listens with a kind of faraway look in his eyes.

"Ah, well," he sighs dubiously. "We got all those water projects out in the San Joaquin Valley. I don't know. I guess you just can't stop progress." He gives me a friendly open smile of finality.

Mr. Sawdek wants to stop progress. But he doesn't believe that it is either permissible or possible.

I leave Mr. Sawdek looking down a manhole and head for the Store. There are lots of kids mauling ice cream in the freezer. Two little boys are stealing candy. Sue and Mike are behind the butcher counter. Francine and Gwen are at the checkout counter. About ten people are standing around with arms full of groceries, talking, reading papers, or waiting to be checked out.

Warm words. Free bones for the dog.

I buy a few things. Hitch a ride up the hill. Walk the rest of the way along the cliff. The sun is setting. The hills turn red on green.

Suddenly, near home, there is a huge explosion. The gulls and birds on the reef rise in a white cloud over the rocks now exposed by low tide. Look across the field. See a man on a porch lower a rifle with a telescopic sight. I run down the hill. Slog across the soggy field to the house. Out of breath. Suddenly get a flash of fear.

Guns?

Who is he?

Visitor? New tenant?

Land of strangers.

Start up the steps. Hear him eject a spent 30-30 shell from the gun. Get to the top. Can hardly talk. He is standing there. Young guy. Droopy mustache. Basic dope dealer getup.

"Did you just shoot that gun down on the reef?" I ask.

He puts the gun on the couch.

"Well, yeah, man. See I was just trying out this new rifle here and . . ."

He rambles on about being a conscientious objector. None of it makes any sense. Looks stoned. Frightening. Not because he is hostile, but because he is so casual, so apparently unaffected by having just shot a high-powered rifle over his neighbor's roof out onto a wildlife preserve where people often walk.

"What the hell do you have a gun like that for, anyway?" I ask.

"Why not?" he replies, vaguely, without malice.

I tell him that I do not like cops, but that I like rifles less. At the mention of cops he gets quite upset.

When I leave, he jumps in his car and drives off. Dope dealers hate to attract attention.

This town has it's share of dealers: one way of making a living.

DENNIS pulls up in front of the Store in Raggedy Ann.

He wears the grin of a man who has just swallowed a goldfish.

He has just been arrested by military police for illegal trespass and entry onto Army property.

Dennis went to the lot where the Army Corps of Engineers piles all the wood that they haul out of the Bay, so ships

will not run into it. It's mostly large posts and beams from old docks.

The Army Corps pulls them out of the water, stacks them, then moves them to another fort where they are burned, bulldozed, and buried.

Dennis thought he would take some to build his house.

He is now scheduled to have a military trial.

JOE Kelly does it again.

Today Ben is found guilty of operating a stable without a license. He is fined $250, sentenced to one year's probation, and ordered to build new fences immediately or his horses will be removed by sheriffs.

An article in the *Paper* describes the sequence of events:

Several weeks ago on a cold black night, Nebo, a pony, got out of the pasture. Nebo is black and he was hit by a white car. His leg was cut and bleeding, but otherwise he was OK. The owner of the pony was notified; she in turn called the vet, who appeared at the scene. Nebo, the vet, the owner, the driver and Ben were all on the scene and were all on friendly terms. The "problem" was taken care of in a friendly, neighborly fashion.

Then a car drove in the driveway and would not dim its lights. Drives right up to the nervous pony and makes him more nervous. Upon demand, he will not turn his lights off. Finally, much later, at the request of Ben, he dims his lights. Joe Kelly, your neighborly peace officer, is at the scene of the crime. For it is now a crime, not an accident of nature. First thing good Joe does is call the Humane Society and report a violation—negligence. A misdemeanor—five hundred dollars and/or six months in jail. The Humane Society writes Ben up for not having a license and negligence.

They actually tried to convict Ben of negligence. The district attorney subpoenaed several witnesses: the cop, the Humane Society, the driver, the owner, the pony? Ben had a lawyer who had to show the court that if an animal wants out he is going to get out. That this is just nature in action and not negligence. The charge was dropped and the taxpayers dropped a goodly sum for the hour-and-a-half proceedings.

The district attorney wanted to close Ben down. Ben will build the fence as the court ordered and will buy a license. The Humane Society will then have the power of inspection and the power to close the operation down. The pressure is on to close it. Why? What has anybody really done wrong? Why close it down?

Should we invite the DA to a town meeting and ask him why a legitimate operation should be shut down? An operation that is a direct service to the community and one that provides a lot of happiness to a lot of people? Ben gives free classes in horsemanship to the kids once a week. What does Joe Kelly do that is free and fun? Is Joe an asset to the community as a peace officer should be? Or is he an outside mercenary causing trouble around here?

America: the land of the free—maybe the court should come out here and explain their actions to the kids.

The judge, kind soul, suspended the fine and it remains to be seen whether the Humane Society will close the place down.

WE plant sixty-four fruit trees in Paradise Valley. Apples, pears, peaches, plums, cherries, figs. Light, sunny, warm day. Patrick arrives with some ale and his concertina. Plays for us in the garden. Brings word of Washington's Birthday traffic jams downtown.

OVER-the-hill again today at Big Pink to a planning commission hearing on the county-wide master plan.

Today's subject is: Village Expansion Zones.

What is a village? Should villages stay villages? Is it possible to take a small community off the assembly line of development?

All of this is going to be decided by people who do not live in villages.

VOICE A (*a young man in his middle thirties. He wears coveralls, boots, longish hair. Looks strangely out of place in the hearing room. He speaks in gentle manner*): You know, when people look at things like population growth or development, their arrogance usually makes them think that it only relates to their condition. But if you were an animal looking at the situation, you would feel differently. And you would see that as man's numbers increase (*he points to a Planning Staff chart on the wall estimating county population in 1990*), your own population decreases.

People don't seem to see this play-off. There should be maps where people vote, showing where the deer live and where the different birds, bobcats, and foxes live. There should be census figures so people could see their decline. Perhaps people would see how their votes affect creatures other than themselves.

VOICE B (*young man, early thirties. Beard. Slightly strident tone of voice*): Doesn't everyone understand that sooner or later we've got to stop feeding this growth monster? The county plan talks about twenty years. But what about fifty years, or a hundred years from now?

(C)* GEORGE LEONARD: Mr. Chairman, can I ask a question?

(C) JACK NIXON (*chairman*): Yes.

(C) GEORGE LEONARD: Where do you live? In Briones?

VOICE B: Yes.

(C) GEORGE LEONARD: How long have you lived there?

VOICE B: About four-and-a-half to five years.

(C) GEORGE LEONARD: Aren't you really the problem rather than the solution?

VOICE B: Mr. Leonard, I was born on this earth (*laughter*), and you were born on this earth. We all need someplace to live. And I live in Briones. I wouldn't feel like an interloper if I had arrived yesterday. I feel as entitled to speak as someone who has been there a hundred years. No one is saying that people cannot move from one place to another. But when they move, they must bear in mind the effect they are having. And if a town has reached a point where it feels the quality of its life is affected by more people, then I think those people have a right to defend themselves against the ill consequences of more and more people. Isn't self-protection a right? Some people leave, and some people come. It's a question of numbers, not freedom to move. Sooner or later we're going to hit the top.

*(C) before a name denotes county planning commissioners, who are appointed by the five elected supervisors.

(C) GEORGE LEONARD: Aren't there a lot of people like you who would like to move to Briones? And should they be stopped? I think that this is unfair.

VOICE B (*louder*): When you invite six people to dinner, do you want to have to serve twenty? I mean, there is a finite number . . .

(C) JOHN WEST: I object!

(C) JACK NIXON (*yelling*): Now wait a minute! (*Pounds gavel furiously*) Now, I'll let this one go one more round, and that's it. But this is really not a debate. It's a public hearing!

VOICE B: Well, my comment is . . . I mean, I have repeatedly heard people raise the specter of the old gangplank theory. You know, get on board yourself, and then pull up the gangplank.

But, when Noah built his ark, he didn't just say, "OK. Everybody and anybody get on board." He would have sunk his ark. So, he had the good sense to take two kinds of each animal.

I think what we are saying is that sooner or later you reach a point when your ark or your town gets supersaturated with people it simply cannot sustain any more. Stopping at this point may be pulling up the gangplank, but it's no different from getting out of the water when you're drowning. I mean, no one in his right mind would propose that you drown . . . even if you could make some money.

Now, if you project our own recent growth rate out over the next thirty years, it spells disaster. At least, it will mean a real qualitative change in the life of people. We will cease to be a "town." We will start to be something else. It has happened in area after area. And it breeds a very obvious kind of disenchantment and rootlessness.

There were some very interesting figures in a Field poll a couple of months ago on crime. It showed that the rural areas and small towns had the lowest crime rate. The rate climbed progressively as they sampled larger and larger communities, or what I would call "non-communities."

So, I think what we have to try to do is *stop*, or we will be looking toward a time when there will be no villages or small

towns in this country. What's this place going to look like by the time our kids get grown up?

It's not like we are talking about making it better. We're talking about how fast it's going to get worse. We'll never live in paradise. It'll only get worse. So let's stop it from getting worse too fast. That's probably the best we can do.

SEVERAL people have commented on it.

There have been a lot more strange faces around town lately.

One is more conscious of noticing strangers when one is not looking at them in great numbers all day long.

Remember the westerns where the newly arrived stranger in town sticks out like a sore thumb?

Why was he such an upsetting and obvious intrusion?

Why do dogs bark at people they do not know?

FRANCES is a slight woman. Almost birdlike. Graying hair. Twinkling, impish eyes. Lives alone with her daughter. Her husband is five years dead.

She was raised in New Orleans. The daughter of the West Texas Military Academy president. Her long odyssey somehow brought her to her house on a hill overlooking the Lagoon, for which she has spent the last eight years of her life fighting.

"Do I feel lonely now, alone? Oh, no! I can't keep up with all the meetings!" she says with a kind of squeal of protest.

And there is always some kind of meeting at her house. A pizza party for someone running for Congress, a hearing on the town plan, a fund raising for the Butterfly Grove purchase, a candidates' night for the PUD election. Her house is like a community hall for good causes. And as though there were not enough meetings right in her own house, Frances is an inveterate ombudsman at the county hearings. She rises out of her seat, follows some bearded conservationist to the microphone, "My name is Frances Stewart of the Conservation League, and I'd just like to say that I think it would be devastating if . . ."

People look around to see who is speaking. It is not just the words, but the fact that they are being said by this small sovereign woman in a dress and a neat cardigan that gets people.

Tonight is Frances' sixty-fifth birthday. There is a party at Barbara's house in celebration. Judith brings two large decorated cakes. Everyone brings a dish for a midnight potluck feast.

Dancing. Drinking. Talking. Peter waltzing around the room shaking a can full of coffee beans, pretending he is Joe Cuba. Greg transformed into the town fool after countless beers. And beautiful Frances, in a long gown, dancing, laughing, and hugging people who are giving her birthday greetings.

FRANCES

A gray, lusterless day. A very convincing rain doesn't look like it intends to stop. Everyone in rubber boots and raincoats. Dogs all wet and smelly. Fifty inches of rain so far, compared with twenty-seven for last year.

Big community jam session tonight on the sewer. An indescribable cross-section of people show up. PUD directors, people who are angling for jobs on the sewer, and various other sewer-crazed individuals. Bill O., who is the guru of this kind of land retention system, is out from Berkeley for the evening.

Greg stands up near a map of the sewer ponds and starts explaining.

GREG: OK. Let me just quickly run through the basics again of how this system works here on this map. And then maybe Bill can tell us what goes on in the ponds.

Here's downtown. (*He points on the map. Everyone strains to see.*) And the raw sewage will be pumped up the hill past Hurford's barn to the big meadow in front of the firehouse. Here it will go into one of the two primary treatment ponds which will be used alternately. Each of these ponds will be just a little over an acre and will be surrounded by berms about eight or nine feet high. These ponds are going to be quite deep, so most of the solids will settle out to the bottom. Then the water will pass in turn through the two or three other ponds. And in each one it will get purer and purer.

DON: How does the water get to each pond?

PETER: Pumps. You have to leave them either dry or full or they won't work right. If you leave them only partially full, then they won't biologically digest right and they will smell.

ORVILLE: Maybe Bill could explain how this treatment process works.

BILL: Sure. OK. The raw sewage comes into the primary or facultative ponds, and, like Greg said, it settles out and the natural digestion processes go to work. It's like a double-decker sandwich. The anaerobic bacteria work at the bottom where

[89]

there is no air. The sewage ferments and makes methane. Any smell coming up from the bottom level through the water at the top ought to be reduced by the high Ph level at the top of the pond.

Then the top layer will digest aerobically. So all this happens naturally without any kind of machines except standby aerators we will put in to speed the process up if we have to.

It's a low-energy, low-maintenance system which turns out good water at the last pond for irrigation.

In fact, there are lots of other things you can do with these ponds. You can install floating baffles and catch some of the methane gas.

CHILDREN ALONG THE SEWER PONDS

PETER: Or couldn't we do some kinds of fish aquaculture or algae farming?

BILL: Yes. Some kinds of fish thrive in these sorts of ponds. At least, you will probably want some kind of mosquito fish for insect control. You could also algae farm in the last ponds. Protein algae is getting to be a popular livestock food. Yes, the possibilities are unlimited.

PETER: I would *love* to get into being an algae farmer! (*Grins*)

THE PUD engineer is a soft-spoken retiring man. He arrives at work on time every day after a two-and-a-half-hour commute from a suburban apartment. He works in isolation above the PUD kitchen. His former employer was a huge international engineering firm.

The office in which he works is plain and uninviting. Although free to do so, he has never made it either comfortable or pleasant. No potted plants, no posters or pictures. The slide rules, blueprints, and his talk of feeding our town's statistics into a computer to figure out needed pipe sizes and pressures seem somehow almost comically professional in this context.

"What do you work for?" I asked him one day, curious.

"To be a good engineer," he replied, smiling with amazement that I should ask.

He is unmoved by our obsession with growth.

A gentle, good person. An engineer with no third eye. Not all the words and explanation could bridge the gap between our world and his.

Today the PUD board fired him.

WE are now surrounded on all sides by the National Park Service and the ocean.

The town is a kind of small reservation in the midst of this instantly created public domain.

National parks; American land reform. But like all else, these fine parks cut us two ways.

There is Park Service rumbling about making a southern entrance to the National Seashore just north of town.

Access would be through town on a road which is essentially the main nerve of this community.

Impalement by asphalt, running Detroit's progeny right up a channel to our heart and brain.

Rolf is keen on the idea. Would put his condos and lodge right on the beaten track.

One automobile driving one block uses up as much oxygen as one hundred people breathing an entire month.

THE Farmer's Home Administration of the US Government has told our bond counsel that they will buy $385,000 worth of bonds at 5 percent over forty years for our new sewer.

What would happen if, after they sent us the check, and after our sewer were built, we told them, "Sorry, you guys. But we ain't gonna pay these back! We're takin' em on account for misspent taxes."

Would they repossess our sewer?

BULLETIN BOARD MENU FOR MARCH 2

We'd be *mulch* obliged if you would give us your:

Sawdust
Woodchips/shavings
Piles of leaves
Straw or hay

For our garden. Call . . . .

Ivory whale's teeth for sale. Call John . . . .

I desperately need $1,000,000 for a worthwhile project. Good references. Call, Fred . . . .

Horseshoeing.
Call . . . .

Hatha Yoga (with a picture of a holy man)
Call . . . .

Wanted: ROOSTER
Please Call . . . .

THIS town has three restaurants.

Vernon has begun to remodel the upstairs of the Bar, which he owns, to convert it into a new forty-seat restaurant.

Vernon is a young lawyer and lives over-the-hill. "Pugnacious" would best describe him. He was a former Golden Gloves champ before getting into law and blue pin-striped suits which seem strangely out of place in the small city of San Rafael, in which he works. Over the past few years he has become rather portly.

No grass is growing under Vernon's feet. He has his eye on business, and his courage for a new restaurant is bolstered by the only hard-liquor license in town.

Vernon tells me over the phone that he does not believe that a new restaurant will add to more tourist congestion downtown. Nor is it his legal opinion that it would violate the state's cease-and-desist order against putting more raw sewage into the Lagoon while the sewer is being built.

The PUD board disagrees.

NEWS gets around Briones fast without wires.

Good circuits.

In the city, people get the word over the TV like cows browsing at an electronic hay rack.

Here in town, it comes over the organic network for which there is no schematic or repairman.

Grapevine News Service.

"Hell!" says Patrick. "The FBI guys, when they were in town looking for some of those big dope dealers . . . well, everybody knew who they were right off, and just said, 'Howya doin'?' when they passed them in the street. No secret there."

The town's sense of itself is held together by many things. For one thing, people talking and gossiping. Some feel that gossip is bad. They feel a dishonesty in anyone talking behind anyone else's back. But the gossip one hears also functions as a kind of binding agent, feeding people's need to stay in touch. News travels like lightning. Intimate details are revealed about everybody. A collective sense of relief is derived by seeing the fallibility of others almost as clearly as one's own.

Gossip reduces us all to mortal levels.

Gossip centers:

Running into people on the road
The laundromat
The Bar
Scowley's
The Store
Bobby's
Renée's
Liz's
Joanne and Peter's

Gossip is our endless interoffice memo.

SPRING

The main point is that a modern city, no less than a medieval town, must be planned to human scale, and must have a definite size, form, and boundary.

LEWIS MUMFORD

"You want to know what this town wishes it was? This town wishes it were an island."

GREG

THE RAINS ARE gone for now, and are replaced by late-night frosts. Clear white moon. Wind. Puddles drying. The grass is shooting up green in the sun. The poppies have started to bloom; orange on green.

The land begins to take color back on.

The town drifts. A welcome peaceful interlude. There are many things in the works, but no crises except for the stirrings downtown over the new restaurant and expanded commercial area.

Dear Warren and Marion:

I thought that I would just dive in and write you both about various things around town since you were out here last and we talked.

The town is perking along. Paradise Valley is gearing up for spring.

Both the town and the valley feel good and hopeful at this point, although both are not without their wrinkles. Our visions attain perfection, while we as actors leave something more to be desired. But our sewer appears on schedule even though Richard Nixon has impounded much of the money from which our Clean Water Grant was to come. We have twenty or so local people salaried up with government grant money doing a septic tank, soils, and drainage study to try and reinstate the good name of the septic tank. We know a lot more now than when we began, and there have been no insurmountable fuck-ups to date. It's a humble beginning in our attempt to try and work out some kind of local economy which will not require tourist traps and restaurants. This is the crux; We can't preach decentralization and not be able to give people a way to make a living.

I think we all are beginning to see in a myriad of inexpressible ways that "smallness" is the key to a town's sanity. There is something about the possibility of communication on a close personal level which seems to keep most of the bones out of our throats. There is a growing recognition that political paralysis grows out of bigness just as death comes from age. Bigness is a kind of unlabeled poison.

It is not yet clear whether or not we have it under control out here. But I know that we are lost if we cannot do so. Steve and many others are working away on the Community Plan, and have been providing some inspiration for other local planning groups. The secret ingredient of the Plan will be a 1 percent annual growth rate. Lawyers on both sides will have a field day. That failing, we still have our hands on utilities. But in the meanwhile our rents skyrocket. Will we end up saving this turf for the rich?

We are all thinking. The low-cost housing continues to go up in people's backyards. There is talk about working out some low-cost housing on PUD land. And, as ever, the great hope: to somehow get people settled on the land on multifamily farms.

The center of town is as vulnerable as ever. Could a town actually get together a co-op type commercial center with the buildings community-owned and used for community-needed services? Sounds almost like communism!

The garage is for sale. What about a town garage? Patronage refund, free air, mechanics classes, no big blinking Exxon sign harpooning in the thirsty Sunday drivers. Let people come in, but "encourage" them to get out of their cars and walk or ride bikes.

Another small weekend delicatessen, Snarley's, is for sale. How about a community bakery?

When did towns stop having bakeries? Isn't it all of our dreams to get rid of the truck with the red, blue, and yellow polka dots destroying our bodily juices with Ho-Hums and Yo-Yos? And what about a brewery? Pine Gulch Lager. (You'd probably take a lot of crap from the Alcoholic Beverages Control Board on that one.)

Anyway, part of the vision lies in securing the soft commercial underbelly of the community, the town's center, *for* the community. I don't think that it has ever been pulled off so that a town serves itself; can survive from itself rather than orienting itself toward the big-city bucks.

Why must every town be decimated for the alleged benefit of those who spend least time there?

And then, the old dream, a nonprofit real estate office, perhaps run by something like the New Land Fund, to match people with land uses.

It would sure be nice if at least one town could get things

screwed around right. And it sure would be nice to live there. People outside might also take hope. It might blow a few clouds away from people's brains just to see that it could be done.

The vision! Sometimes it feels so good. At other times it seems so far. But for now things seem to fit together in a rudimentary way. Two pieces: the town and the valley. It is good to have an asparagus patch to retreat to after talking to bureaucrats on the phone all day about sewers. Feels like you can learn something from the man in front of you. But I'm not sure the telephone has done much to elevate human consciousness.

Take care,

Orville

FULL moon. Nina says it never rains during a full moon. Sunday. Clear. Warm. Sunny.

The salmon fleet is way off the reef on still morning water waiting for the noon wind to drive it back to Fisherman's Wharf.

Boats. So quiet on the distant sea.

WE work all day in Paradise Valley.

Our new hand tractor is fixed. We work in teams wrestling the tractor through the thick spring sod. His-and-her teams like tag-team wrestling.

We plant asparagus and artichokes.

Spring has brought new energy to both us and the plants.

Walk back down the creek to town looking for spawning salmon.

I see none.

BIG night. Two hundred people jam the PUD hall for a town meeting on Sheriff Kelly. The head county sheriff, Gary, head of police-community relations, and sundry other brass and notables come over-the-hill for the meeting.

Judith, Perry, and several others play some bluegrass music to get the gathering off to a mellow start. They fail. Tremendous antagonism in the room. You can feel it. Some people mad at Kelly for his nastiness and lack of helpfulness. Some weekend and older people fear that the meeting is an attack on all cops and an assault on law and order.

Discussion opens with several long and boring speeches by the over-the-hill dignitaries.

Floor is opened for discussion.

No one speaks. No one wants to spit it out.

Meeting starts floundering. People start raising small and insignificant points. They start hacking and slashing at each other rather than at the problem. The meeting turns in on itself dividing people in town rather than bringing them together.

Feels like three years ago when the town was more divided; each side fearful of the other and reveling in stereotypes.

DEPUTY SHERIFF (*Mike, who lives in Briones but covers the whole coastal beat*): OK. Well, I was a resident deputy here for a year. And I averaged fourteen hours a day. And then when I went home, some local nut would come by the house, see the car there, and say, "Beautiful, time to rip off the town." (*Scattered clapping*)

VOICE (*Young man*): We could set up our own force and at least issue some speeding tickets. I mean, it's about time we started slowing people down before someone gets killed.

VOICE (*woman with baby*): Why do we have to pay for sheriffs who end up spending a lot of their time helping tourists and other people who are just passing through, and whom we don't even want here?

VOICE: The sheriffs are never sticklers on speed. Kelly speeds all the time on his big macho trip. But when it comes to a kid who might be smoking a cigarette that might be thought of as marijuana, they grab him out of school and give him the third degree in the back room. It's that kind of difference between attitudes of police officers that we are talking about. We want someone who understands that the world is changing and who will be more reasonable inside the context of the law.

[95]

VOICE (*PUD director*): I have been around this community quite a while. And I think that most people are here for one reason, to deal with the one man who is responsible for officers being called pigs in this town. Now, why can't we get some action? (*To the chief sheriff*) Why can't you get Kelly out of here? He's a bad apple, and he is the one responsible for bad police-community relations. (*Cheering, hissing*)

CHIEF SHERIFF: OK. Yes. We will take grievances. But we will not take any action against an officer who is unpopular. My door is always open. But it would be unhealthy if anyone could go out and say, "If you don't do this, I'll have your job." I'm proud of the men who go into law enforcement. We do make mistakes, and we'll try to correct them.

VOICE: Well, I appreciate what you say. But I heard you say that two years ago. You guys should be doing something within your department, because guys like Kelly are making it difficult for you. I think that there are very few people in this room who are not grateful that there are police around. The point is that we *want* a good policeman, one who can serve the community.

Now, if you're going to figure out what kind of a cop can serve the community well, you'll have to look at the community. I think we are a town . . . at least trying to stay a town as we grow. And I've goddamn near been run over by Kelly. He never comes into the bar like Mike. Kelly never chats with anyone. Hell, I remember one night when we had a big potluck dinner out in the street by the Wharf when we were trying to stop the old sewer, and goddamn if Kelly didn't drive right through everyone. For no reason. Twice! To get to the end of a dead-end road!

The point is, this is a community. People feel safe with Mike. He doesn't harass them. I don't agree with him on everything. But he lives here and is on the school board.

So, lemme just say, I think we gotta look at the general problem of how police fit together with people in a small town. And I think that we are getting the picture that there is one officer who doesn't fit in well at all. And I think that you,

Chief, oughtta start listening when people say that they want cops, need cops . . . but for god's sake give us a good cop!

The meeting ends inconclusively. Many people leave feeling more upset about the apparent schisms in the town than about Kelly.

"What we need," says Greg, "is a good dentist who can sharpen teeth."

THE last storms of winter have passed. The land is turning green. Wild flowers are everywhere. And the real harbingers of spring, the campers and trailers with out-of-state plates, have begun to miraculously arrive in droves, as though released from winter bondage. It seems that every year the town falls prey to people moving through it earlier and earlier.

Perhaps it is my imagination. But with a strange 1984 logic, many residents of Briones are glad for the wet weather, just as they are glad for the junk cars and other eyesores. They know that we pay for every ounce of quaintness and beauty that can be seen from a moving car.

The town still seems to be in somewhat of a funk, a kind of disenchantment with our own possibility. There is less enthusiasm to work, attend meetings, get involved—almost as though some dim warning mechanism had been sounded against the despair that can follow impossible hopes.

There are squabbles on the septic tank survey which give the feeling that the grind has obscured the greater purpose. Or perhaps money has obscured the meaning of the work, for some.

The PUD board seems limp. We have not seen much of each other, or worked together since our last crisis. Even our engineers in the city seem to be treading water waiting for some magical deadline to bludgeon them to the post.

Saturday, Greg fell off a barn which we have been dismantling. He broke some bones. It was almost as though some physical justification for whatever dispiritedness he felt had been delivered.

We need a new transfusion of zeal . . . or perhaps a huge kick in the ass.

BUBBLING out of the tar pits of Christmas past comes the news that the Martinelli Farms subdivision has just folded.

Just up and caved in!

Died a natural death.

Was it hassled to the point of no return?

Should we take any credit?

Well . . . we win, even if by default.

THE cycle has come full circle around.

It is difficult to describe just why spirits rise and fall in this town. But, in this case, relief comes from a new design for our sewer. (You get relief where you can!)

Don and Steve showed up tonight at the PUD meeting with a new sewer layout plan all drawn up in lurid Magic Markers, which gave us an alternative to the rather grim, lifeless plan proposed by our city engineering consultant.

"That plan's dull," says Don, comparing it with the one he and Steve have concocted. A smile turns up one corner of his mouth under his gray beard. "What we've tried to do is to draw up an arrangement of the treatment ponds which fit into the land better and provide better access for people."

In the engineer's drawings, the oxidation ponds (where the sewage brews to pure water) are all bunched up in an artless clump on a flat piece of land. Don and Steve's plan calls for them to be spread out in a pleasing irregular pattern in which they are form-fitted into the contours of the hill. One is drawn above the other so that there will be cascades of "treated effluent" flowing into each successive pond. There are bike paths, bridle paths, a monitoring and swimming pond, and an orchard.

Will we end up with a prize-winning sewer featured on the cover of *Better Homes and Gardens* or *Public Works* magazine?

A woman's group has formed out of the carpentry class.

They meet tonight at Lizzie's. Each woman is taking a night to tell the story of her life. Almost all the women have children and are separated from their original husbands.

The women enjoy the meetings immensely, and seem to derive a sense of relief from this world of friends outside their own homes.

Other women in town, some facetiously, some humorously, call the new group the Better Women of Briones.

EASTER weekend has come and gone.

The garden in the valley is tilled, planted, and standing neatly in row upon row of motionless vegetables and fruit.

Greg, Harriet, and Renée kill and pluck twelve chickens for a feast. John is chef with his world-renowned barbecue sauce.

The chicken is tough as garden hose. But the feast is exquisite.

Fire, drums, music.

The children put on plays in the grass for the adults. Then they demand that the adults do a play for the children.

Adults at a loss.

The wine bottle goes around, followed by a joint.

The adults decide to perform *The Three Little Pigs*, the melodrama of three little pigs who build illegal houses—one out of sticks, one out of mud, one out of bricks.

Harriet, Leah, and Wilma play pigs. John, Orville, and Greg play Herb W. (Building Inspector), Rae C. (Zoning Administrator, and Bill D. (Health Officer).

The play is performed. The children say, "Awww. That was no fun. We didn't understand that play."

The adults say, "That's the story of our lives."

SOME fanatic has painted BRIONES in huge white letters on the asphalt at the highway turnoff. The paint job includes a giant curved arrow aimed at the town like a weapon.

The road sign is still down.

The war of the signs escalates with a technological innovation.

SEWER PONDS AND IRRIGATION FIELDS

Someone does not want our town forgotten.

Perhaps it is one of the people who reports having had friends drive clear to the Oregon border before realizing that they missed the turnoff.

FLOCKS of Canadian geese land on the reef and swim to and fro in the tide pools. Then they take off northward, bodies straining forward as though they are turning into one elongated neck with wings flapping behind. They go out across the ocean in a lazy, undulating V-formation.

Be careful, geese.

THE roads grow narrower and more winding. Towns turn to villages, then to ranches, then to open meadows with redwood groves in the canyons.

MICHAEL, DEBBIE, CELIA, AND KIT IN PARADISE VALLEY

We head north to get redwood stumps for the foundation of the Paradise Valley barn.

We pass from one world into another.

We buy some groceries. Leave the last stores. Pass the mill at Cazadero, spewing sawdust out one end and boards out the other. Up into the mountains where the road tapers into little more than a path for vehicles.

For most of the day we work in a canyon which was logged two years ago. The scorched remains of huge toppled giants lie along a creek bank; the final end for redwoods which were alive during the Renaissance.

Signs of man's rapaciousness hang heavy over the canyon. The recognition is only slightly dimmed by our enthusiasm to join in the spoils and turn the loggers' waste into our bounty.

Except for our own intruding chain saws, no noise is out of place. There are sunlight, clear air, the creek, and ourselves.

We load redwood bolts cut from abandoned stumps onto the truck. Thousands of board-feet of lumber have been inexplicably left behind by the lumbermen in chaotic bulldozed heaps. The lumbermen apparently tried to burn their mess of slash, stumps, and abandoned trees back into neatness when they left. But it looks as though someone dropped a bomb.

The sun starts to sink behind the mountain.

We strip off our clothes and jump into a pool in the creek. Cold!

Flail around. Dunk once. Clamber out. Hop around in the last rays of the sun's warmth. Sit on a fallen redwood and slowly dry off.

Tired.

We light a fire downstream where two creeks converge under bay and redwood trees. A doe appears in the meadow across the creek. She occasionally looks our way with her antenna-like ears rotating for unfriendly sounds, and then continues her grazing.

We cook a chicken over the fire, drink some ale, roll out our sleeping bags, fall silent, and then sleep beneath the night sky.

SAN JOSE, the fastest-growing city in northern California, terminal case of suburban sprawl, sitting beside a ten-lane freeway like a grease trap on a sewer pipe, passes an anti-growth ballot initiative.

The initiative stops further development until schools are enlarged, or until developers provide new school facilities for new people. People are angered by the way their schools are being overloaded with new kids from the tract houses.

The developers opposed the initiative. Did everything they could to defeat it.

But actually, San Jose is beyond the point of no return.

Right, Norm Minetta?

All they can do now is slow down and give people a few more years to convert to smog.

Tonight the PUD passes a motion setting guidelines for any new water system. It will be designed so as to adequately provide for the existing community plus a 1 percent growth rate.

No larger.

EACH week, on Saturday mornings, members of Paradise Valley hold a meeting, usually in Russ's tent or John's house. If the weather is fine, we all sit out in the grassy circle which is set at the middle of the garden. We try to discuss the week's jobs and problems: What are we going to plant? Why hasn't anyone been weeding? When are we going to fence the horses? Who's going to get the big red truck fixed? On which side of the creek are we going to build the chicken house? How many people need to go to the next hearing about our outlaw status at the county?

Some Saturdays, only half the people show up for the meeting. Sometimes our meetings are satisfying and feelings between most members are in good repair. Other times our meetings are frayed and incriminating.

Today, it is raining and gray. The meeting is in Russ's tent. Susan has a pot of coffee on the wood stove. But there is a kind nastiness in the air between us as we sit and wait to see who else will show.

The county seems on the verge of doing something about our absence of permits.

How should we approach the county as we begin to violate their codes, laws, and customs? Defiance? Evasion? Hostility? Spirit of cooperation? Contempt?

We disagree. Much bravado and machismo characterize the meeting, as though the county were a completely pitiful and helpless creature. So often this attitude reflects our own laziness and dereliction. The county is not worthy of worship; neither does it warrant our spite.

As we work together more and more in Paradise Valley, it is easy to see how threatened we all become by each other's weaknesses and irresponsibilities. Someone is sloppy, careless, doesn't work enough, is uptight, angry, drunk, and it all goes into a reservoir of feelings—strong feelings, which remain snarled up and unspoken because of some deep taboo within each one of us against being a complainer or becoming too personally critical of those around us.

Some people in the valley find it easy to talk, and even complain, to one another. Others remain locked in some tense interior silence. A deep conspiracy from the past makes it hard for us to get right with each other. Gripes fester and come out obliquely or behind each other's backs. Sometimes they degenerate into fights or someone's threatening to leave the group.

Today, we resolve nothing, and leave feeling bad about each other.

FOUR out of the five school board seats are up for grabs during the election today. Mailers began arriving in everyone's postbox last week. Several candidates' nights are held at different houses with the usual bottles of jug wine and coffee. But they are listless and without excitement. No one seems able to pinpoint the deeper issues in a way which succeeds in en-livening public consciousness. One of the problems seems to have been that none of the candidates has run on a slate, and thus there is no apparent overarching purpose tying any group of them together.

Looking back on it, I think running on a slate with three other people for the PUD was not only what got us elected, but what animated us and helped clear our heads about a lot of problems. Tremendous mutual support was given. We talked a lot. And above all, running together was good fun. That really got us cooking and thinking. The voters had an easy time distinguishing us from the other candidates. If you knew what one person stood for, you had a pretty good fix on the other three.

The biggest issue in the school board election is the latest proposed tax increase. Most candidates seem wary of it because they do not want to give low-income people another shove out the door. On the other hand, the School is tempted by the thought of more money. It now has a budget of over a quarter of a million dollars. And that seems like a lot of money to many people.

The School is a mass of contradictions. Some educators see it as one of the most exciting innovative schools in California. Others see it as barely organized chaos. Some parents, mindful of their own overdisciplined school days, like the freedom it gives their children. Others send their kids over-the-hill to learn to read, or to go to "good schools." A few families have even left town because they felt the School left their kids intellectually unchallenged.

There is the usual pack of troublemakers. Ten-year-olds smoking dope, stealing (a big favorite is to steal bicycles and cannibalize them into parts, and one teacher even had her paycheck lifted). Of late, the more precocious kids have started drinking.

On the other hand, the School has some fine dedicated teachers and numerous special programs which are largely run by volunteer or poorly paid local people. Piero has done

MR. MOHN

theater and puppet shows. Harriet and Pat run the shop. Peter has led a series of nature walks around the area. O'Brien has started a music program and school chorus. David works with the kids on jewelry in the new workshop built with scrounged wood and local volunteer labor.

But people of all persuasions have been known to criticize the School for being a little lightweight in the three R's, in serious intellectual inquiry, and in sports (although there is a controversial motorcycle shop run by Dave, a saintly man, who drives the school bus).

The general rule of thumb seems to be that slow kids like the School, while the fast ones get bored.

We have no high school. Kids must get up at 5:30 in the morning and commute in a school bus, or hitch.

The school situation is one of our town's permanently unsolved dilemmas.

THE usual group of older ladies is sitting at folding tables in the PUD Grand Ballroom administering the election. You give your name, and they hand you your ballot, treating you at once both in friendly fashion and as a Russian spy.

Old George wanders in. He wears a green shirt and workpants. Suspenders. Felt hat.

He gets his ballot and stands there pondering it with a puzzled smile.

Mr. Mohn, considerably his senior, has just arrived on a bike, wearing his usual, a plastic Albert Schweitzer hat and a windbreaker. He walks over and starts explaining to George how to punch out the ballot. They both disappear into a voting booth.

There are screeches and squawks from the official ladies at the folding table.

"Mr. Mohn must sign an affidavit to help Mr. Rodriguez!"

Mr. Mohn reappears from the voting booth with his hands up.

"OK, OK, OK," he says. "Take it easy. Take it easy."

FOUR people are elected to the school board. The measure to raise the tax rate for the School from $1.20 per $100 assessed valuation to $1.70 is voted down.

HOME today, after a long meeting. Find the dog, panting, motionless, dull eyes, dried blood on his legs. Sharp fractured ribs protrude chaotically from his chest. There is something about the way he lies which makes it clear, even from a distance, that he's been hit hard.

Ilka and I put him in the truck between us and race to the vet through bumper-to-bumper weekend traffic, the "recreation" crush. I can see any one of these shiny overbuilt leviathans running him down. Suddenly, as though I am in a dream, it is a child that is being hit. A mother hysterical with grief. And I find myself almost wishing it would hurry up and happen so that the symbol of the automobile would become clearer and unavoidable.

The dog is on the operating table, his chest cavity hastily torn open by the vet. Lung collapsed. The vet pumps air in while he tries to make some sort of order out of the tangled, scrambled dog muscles, bones, organs.

We go home to wait by the phone. My mind is trying to find explanations. I see myself in some sort of a courtroom arguing a case against cars and man's insane devotion to them for travel, sexual reinforcement, recreation, prestige. The judge is stern. I can tell quickly that I must discard any soft-core arguments about the sanctity of life, about how people become attached to living creatures and how the automobile puts all these attachments in unnecessary jeopardy. I find myself formulating an argument against cars on the basis that they cost me too much in vet's bills. The judge understands my reasoning. I want to stop talking, and just say I hate the cars and don't care about the vet's bills. Somewhere I have learned that money is the issue, not life.

Planning, utilities, school boards, elections, open space, community services, local economy, agriculture—all are efforts which confess our ignorance or unwillingness to confront more basic issues. The whole underground conspiracy of oil spills, smog, and what Americans hear referred to on TV as "death on the highways" has become a routine, a way of life so entrenched that there may be no question of withdrawal.

And when I allow myself to think clearly, it occurs to me that the most sensible reasonable solution is to blow up the bridge over the creek coming into town and turn this small part of the world back to creatures on foot.

But this is clearly a juvenile and impractical thought? Isn't it?

7:15.

We talk to the vet. The dog has died.

We both cry.

Up early on a bright and beautiful day.

Put a spade and the dog's sheepskin in the back of the truck.

We drive up to the vet. No words, except a few to bridge the sadness.

We bury the dog in Paradise Valley thinking of Lame Deer's words, "Today is a good day to die."

We fill in the hole and go to Scowley's for breakfast.

A kind of a dog wake.

George, the County Counsel, comes out to advise us on our new septic tank ordinance.

Will our attempt to assume county powers over our excrement meet with success?

Does the State Public Utilities Code mandate us such broad powers?

Would George defend us if the county (his employer) sued us?

George gives us his answer.

He says, "You have a choice to pioneer or to play it safe. The law doesn't say you can take over the management and maintenance of septic tank systems, but neither does it say that you can't."

Thank you, George.

Back from the city late, 2:30 in the morning. Spent all day at a conference on land reform.

"Well, I uster have me a cornfield over there. Now hit's gone got buried by some of the property of them strip miners. They calls hit slag. . . . Has hit got uglier? Well, jes look for yerself."

Film on strip mining for English television. Straight, simple, unideological mountain people talking. Sitting on old porches, in family homesteads against a backdrop of men and machines reorganizing entire mountains.

The banquet room of the hotel is absolutely quiet. The second film comes on: agro-corporations and automation taking over food production.

Food with no taste. Raised indoors. Fed by computers. No bugs. Picked by a machine. Farm workers on welfare. Small farms being gobbled up into 18,000-acre tracts by Tenneco as tax write-offs. Their progeny: tomatoes with pulpy, juiceless flesh, devoid of flavor, but extolled by the Department of Agriculture because they have thick skin and can be picked by a machine without bruising.

Small farms as a way of life, as a social unit, as a family livelihood, as a place to grow edible food and raise children . . . it's all disappearing. The farmer is being replaced by agro-managers in neckties, drip-dry white shirts, with breast pockets full of ball-point pens. There are half as many farms in the US today as there were in 1945.

One such manager sits in his office and announces without passion, "Yes, sir. No doubt about it. The family farm is on its way out." He walks over to a graph. "That's right," he says. "These indoor plants produce three times as much as the outdoor ones."

Thousands of cattle munching unknowingly away on diethylstilbestrol-treated grain. Cancer.

In the next feedlot some weird ungainly cattle, who can hardly walk because they have been bred with two sets of muscles, stare into the camera. Genetic manipulations. More meat: more profits. There are even chickens with feathers colored differently by genetic meddling to indicate sex.

"Saves us about one cent a bird in identification," a balding poultry executive announces gravely. Fascist food.

My thoughts turn from the Grand Ballroom of the San Francisco Hotel to Paradise Valley. It's clear. We are running right upstream against the corporate madness. We're heading in the wrong direction, but the right direction.

And then a vice-president of the Bank of America starts talking on film from his cool, quiet, dignified office on the thirty-sixth floor of the B. of A. Building. He's in charge of "agricultural loans," and he's sitting there in a hand-stitched continental suit saying that you need fifty-thousand dollars to start a farm. "And that's a minimum." Banks don't even deal with loans for someone that small. You got to get up into the hundreds of thousands of dollars before the banks get interested.

A real live person gets up. A Tennessee miner. Clear eyes. Strong arms. Short-sleeved shirt. Short hair. Upright look about him.

J. W. Bradley talks in a slow Tennessee drawl.

"Now, I don't have any words of my own. I don't have any words that's not been said. 'Fact, I'm gonna read a quotation to start with. 'Will future generations say of us that we were the richest nation and the ugliest land in all of history? Are we doomed by some inexorable thing called progress to give our children land devoid of beauty, empty of scenic . . . scenes of nature's grandeur, filled with gadgets and gimmicks, but lost forever to the wondrous, ah . . . and inspiration of nature?'

"See, I can't even read. And yet, y'all know who said that quote? It was the President of the *U*-nited States.

"I'm satisfied that he might of picked this out of a group of sayin's that someone wrote for him. But if that was his sayin', then why isn't more bein' done about it?

"We got this group in Tennessee called SOCM (sockem). Everything has to have a zing to it these days if its gonna git anywhere. We got zing, and they calls us 'Ole Soc'! . . . the strip miners do. 'Course, they calls us other things, too." (He laughs.) "But we don't care. 'Cause we been there for years. 'Fact, my mother's people, according to history (if you can believe a thing that's in it), were the first white settlers in Tennessee. So, we been there ever since we tried to show the red man that he didn't know what he was doin'. And the more we tried to show him, the more we found out that he was right, and that we didn't know what we is doing."

The room is completely quiet. Focused on this man.

"We know there are people who own the land. But that don't give 'em the right to destroy it. So, the best thing to do is band up together, 'cause there's unity in numbers. It's gettin' the people together and showing them that we're gonna stay with 'em, and showing 'em that money's not what's gonna rule their community and their lives, and that you're gonna be opposed to it even if it costs you your job, your home, or your life. 'Cause eventually, that's just what it's gonna come to anyway. 'Cause this is the only place we got to live."

The next speaker is a red-faced woodcutter from Mississippi. He is stout, strong, middle-aged, wears baggy pants. He comes to the dais with a certain dis-ease.

"First off, I'm not used to speaking in purdy places like this with all them purdy lights. I'm use to speaking in Alabama and Mississippi where there's one light hanging on a string off the ceiling. I'm use to having a group of people with a bottle o' whiskey in one pocket and a pistol in the other.

"Now, there's alot of talking 'bout land what needs ta be taken out o' the hands of the companies. And naturally we don't know what to do. That's why we are so glad to have a chance to come here this weekend and talk 'bout these things.

"It's gonna be a long fight. But one thing's for sure: we can't set down in the South, or anywhere else, and let these out-of-state companies take land out of production.

"When I say out of production . . . well, the cost of meat is talked about a whole lot now. In our section of the country there is a whole lot of cattle on the small farms. But when the farmer dies or sells out, the paper companies gets it, lookin' after pulp. And they sets pine trees out. And in the South they's several black people's houses on one farm. And they takes bulldozers and pushes the houses down, or tears 'em down. An that's why a lot of blacks has had to leave the farms and the farms is just going; because they's gettin' pushed off by the companies."

A young, brash, dark, mustachioed Chicano from the Southwest gets up.

"This system's just as good as any other system if you happen to own it.

"You know about the real power structure? It's very simple. One person is getting screwed, and the other is doing the screwing. OK? And the person doing the screwing is only able to do that if the other guy lets himself be screwed. So it all begins with how disorganized we are."

WE visit the herons and egrets today. From a high knoll we look down on their nests in the tops of tall redwood and fir trees. The young are just hatching. Incredible leggy creatures. So graceful in the air. So awkward on the ground on their toothpick legs. As we peer down at them, they sit in the stick nests primping, squabbling, and tending their young.

On our way home around the Lagoon we spot fish moving about in the shallow water. We stop. Tails and fins wallowing slowly around in lazy circles.

Salmon!

Dennis appears in Raggedy Ann. "We gotta catch some!"

We try to wade into the water and grab one with our hands. The fish are huge. But the mud is too deep. We sink right up to our thighs. Dennis wants to go back and get his wet suit, spear gun, and bow and arrow.

We stop at the bridge over the creek to see if any are running up the creek. Nope. Nothing.

Find Burr, who knows all furry, feathered, and scaled creatures. Head back to the Lagoon. Dennis pulls in with all his gear, a big smile, and some talk about salmon dinners.

Burr takes a close look at the fins.

"Sharks," he says.

Ooops!

Let's catch a few with our hands!

Anyway, we launch Burr's kayak and paddle out right into the middle of the sharks. A mammoth stingray leaps out of the water. Burr says they are spawning or mating. Lots of them. Conk one on the head with a paddle. He makes a large whirlpool with his tail.

There is an outgoing tide, so we decide to paddle back out the channel to town. Beautiful warm evening. The herons and egrets are feeding all around us.

We glide down the channel past black brant geese, godwits, merganser ducks, loons, cormorants, gulls, terns, grebes. We can see the seals on Kent Island. Big round fleshy beached monsters.

They spot us as we paddle toward them. Raise their heads and start flopping and twisting down the beach to the safety of the water. One cow with a small pup stays on the beach. The others slide into the water. Then, all around us, these curious rubbery faces pop up and stare at us. Wonderful pudgy, shiny faces with whiskers appear noiselessly out of the water beside the kayak, study us for a while, and then disappear.

Old bald men with wrinkled brows.

Slowly we approach Briones, paddling against the wind now. Sun setting. Clams shooting miraculous jets of water out of the mud almost everywhere.

THE Septic Tank Survey and Report is finished. It is described by national septic tank guru, Dr. J. T. Winneberger as, "The best septic tank report I have seen."

The report concludes that septic tanks and other individual waste treatment methods work adequately, and are economi-

THE LAGOON

cally far more sensible than sewers. Septic tanks have been maligned as old-fashioned and backward. The big scare has run sewers into many small communities, making them large suburban sprawls.

(Note: If you're going to build a sewer, build it with no margin for growth . . . unless you want growth.)

Report claims that septic tanks in town are efficient and effective if installed right, maintained, and not drowned in bad drainage. They recommend a PUD drainage project.

The report is our first paid community effort, our first term paper. And we got an "A."

Peter and Jeff are working on a septic tank manual to teach everyone simple ways to love and care for his septic tank.

No Drano—kills the digesting bacteria. Clorox is bad. Don't throw down poisons of any kind. Use one-ply toilet paper; creates less solids to digest. Don't flush every time. Put yeast down your toilet for added bacterial action.

I spend the day trying to call the Regional Water Quality Control Board's lawyer to ask him why they approved Vernon's restaurant request. He's out, but finally calls back.

"We usually just allow these kinds of requests if there is no public outcry," he says.

Is he aware that a forty-seat restaurant would add a large amount of raw sewage to the Lagoon, now a wildlife preserve?

"Yes, we are," he says.

Is it not the Regional Board who hit the PUD with a cease-and-desist order, hauled us into court, and then slapped a moratorium on further sewer connections in the area served by the old sewer collection system because of a raw sewage ocean outfall?

"Yes, that is correct," he says.

"Well, then how in god's own name do you justify allowing a new restaurant?" I ask.

He says that Vernon came in and claimed there would be no increased discharge. He says that they don't like to have hearings "unless absolutely necessary," because they are "costly and time-consuming."

"But we would certainly hold one if you request it," he adds without losing his cool lawyer-like dignity. But I hear him thinking, "Listen, buster, what's a two-bit little town like you bothering a guy like me on a big board over a nothing restaurant?"

"We want an appeal!" I say.

The law's a wet noodle. What is important to a bureaucrat is whether or not he's going to get his "board" sued.

"Do you like living in the street, Ikon?"

"No."

"Do you get used to it?"

"No."

Ikon Chanel.

Born in Sayer, Oklahoma. Adopted by his grandparents. Part-Jewish, part-Indian; self-described "gypsy" and street person.

Ikon has long, thick, frizzy black hair, and usually is in bare feet. He is often garbed in strange, colorful robes he has picked up here and there. They suggest old bathrobes, couch covers, and blankets.

"It can get nippy livin' outside in the winter," says Ikon. "Gotta fortify yourself with a little antifreeze." He offers a drink of ruby port.

Ikon waits on table at Scowley's when he is together. He provides the most gracious service of all the waiters. Never gets the orders screwed up. Always there with the ketchup or syrup just bfore you recognize that you need it.

Sometimes Ikon does chores at the Store. Sometimes he just sits downtown on the curb or by the Bar.

In his less together period, Ikon fought in the street with Crazy Patrick, another drifter, and was leader of the Wharf Road dog pack. He would stand in the middle of the street and get the whole pack dancing around him and howling like banshees.

IKON

Saint Francis of the Canines.

This morning, as I drive through the still quiet town past the post office on my way to my carpentry job, I see Ikon, sitting on the bench in front of the real estate office.

He is alone. I wonder where he slept last night. On the beach, in the woods?

He is barefoot. He has a yellow daisy fastened to his brow with a black headband. He wears orange long underwear, and a miniskirt over some long padded cotton pants. There is a lady's pocketbook lying on the bench beside him.

Ikon is going through one of his self-admitted crazy periods.

"Yeah, man," he tells Ilka, "I've been really spaced out lately. And I've been doing a lot of wine, too." In the past these periods have ended with a stay either in jail or in Napa State Hospital.

Each day he appears downtown in a new colorful and outrageous outfit put together from the lost-and-found box at the laundromat or the Free Box at the Community Center. He wears clothes with no regard as to their intended sex, although as far as anyone knows he has no homosexual tendencies. It is simply a matter of Ikon's self-expression with available resources.

IKON

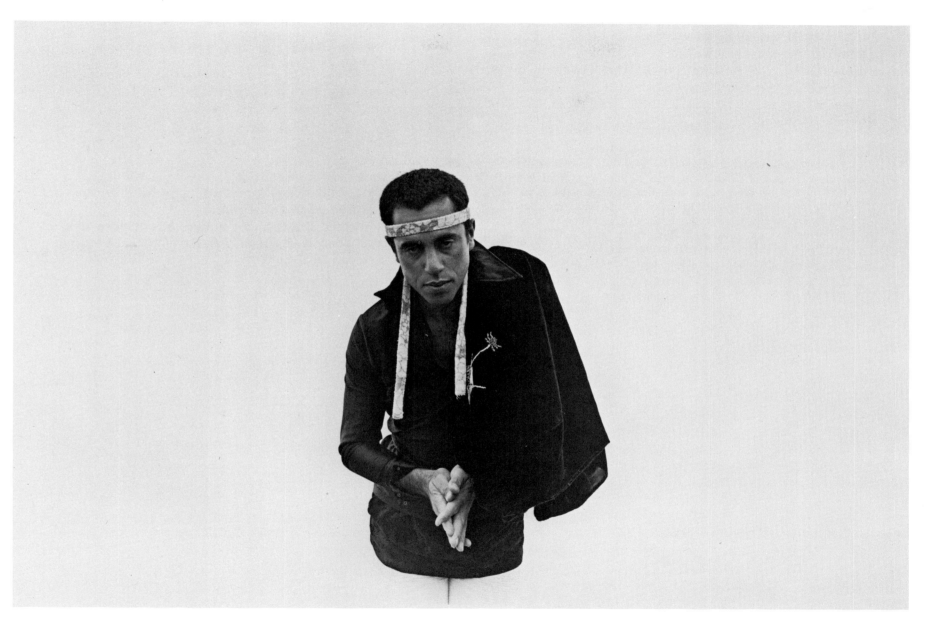

IKON

His hangouts are the front of the Store, Scowley's, around the Bar, at the beach, or the day-care center at the PUD. He is known by everyone in town.

This morning, he just sat on the bench waiting for the town to wake up, and waved as I passed.

This afternoon, an article by him, written in longhand, appears downtown.

Bobby Dylan walking down Wharf Rd. in Briones for his first time. Oh, by the way, this is totally unofficial. For even though he did not identify himself, there were more than one spiritual, psychic, gentle-strong vibrational verifications by many—I myself found him gentle, shy, uncertain how to act properly. But, then, that happens to everybody on their virgin visit to Briones.

He asked for our free press and for old friends who, alas, had moved away. I told him, "Please come back, Bob —y'all are most welcome."

As we shook hands in parting, it seemed we both almost started to cry.

IKON LEE CHANEL BRIONES
MARSHAL 7XR

Madman.
Pest.
Clown.
Saint.
Mendicant.

Ikon often panhandles. But he also gave me fifty cents one day in the Store when I was short.

He has adopted Briones, and Briones has adopted him.

There could only be one Ikon. Two Ikons would be too many. Three would be a freak-out.

SUMMER

"Maybe we should have an earthquake and start all over."
OVERHEARD IN THE BAR

BRIGHT SUN, warm, light wind. City smothered in a great cloud of smog beyond the Golden Gate. Sutro radio and TV tower sticks up through the airborne effluvia like a giant swizzle stick.

Gotta get them TV beams through no matter how thick the smog!

A group of us drive over-the-hill to the Civic Center.

We sit. Watch. Listen.

The supervisors in their "chambers" discuss the growth limitation and open-space element of the County-Wide Master Plan.

Try to digest Gary's new role as supervisor. He is only one among many. But even in losing votes he often succeeds in articulating a point of view formerly heard only from the floor (and often ignored).

Glad he got elected. But "The County," in spite of its reputation as being forward and imaginative, is still all too often a headless zombie. No doubt, most other county governments are worse. But, the county is still the last level of the governmental pig pile which is close enough to people to pose even remote possibilities of real communication with constituents. It's almost too big. A supe can have some effect, but he all too easily becomes consumed by paper, phones, meetings, and politics. Shoving a good man into state or federal politics is like putting a few drops of dye in the ocean.

Even within the Briones Community Public Utilities District, a candidate does not know the name of every person registered.

Nonetheless, the county has cast some benign tentacles over-the-hill. Gary gets the supes to pass $165,000 a year to help dairy farmers pay high interest on loans necessary to stop feedlots from polluting local water courses. The Regional Water Quality Board is threatening them with shutdown, which would virtually halt agriculture in the county.

County gives the Briones Day-Care Center $24,500.

A new county office has been set up which brings social services (food stamps, medi-Cal, welfare, mental health program) closer to people in the rural areas.

MARK is in his sixties. Smallish man. A dedicated nature lover who organizes the annual wild flower show in town. He often has a pipe or cigar in his mouth as he drives around town in his jeep truck with his dog.

Mark quits the PUD board today. "Well, you know, I retired once," he says. "And now I find myself running around like a chicken with his head cut off again."

Keeping this record is a depressing task on those days when enthusiasm vanishes and hope is eclipsed that we may be able to do something different and important in this town.

Vision, energy, and optimism seem at a low point. Meet with the sewer engineers. They hardly seem to know what they are doing. They keep moving the ponds, calling for more soil tests, sending us inflated bills, and telling us things we don't need to know or don't want to know. The sewer seems to be getting whittled down and bullied back to a bare functional minimum.

State guidelines, regulations, health hazards, costs, and people who "just wanna get the job done" are all in there plugging for an uninspired sewer complete with a chain link fence around it and a sign saying: NO TRESPASSING—HUMAN WASTE.

SOMETIMES it feels as though the struggles we are up against are so huge, so all-pervasive and endemic, that one might struggle forever and forget to live the one life we have to enjoy with each other.

One small town. So much to set right. Often the tension, anger, frustration, resignation, and futility of seemingly endless problems get a mighty grip on the soul. Then one is tempted by the promise or illusion that perhaps things are simpler or easier somewhere else.

Our vision so far surpasses our ability to act. Our good ideas come so easily; their execution comes so hard. So many of our plans seem to get snarled in our weaknesses, in our own screwed-up private lives. We are all wrestling with ourselves and the world. Our sewer, the Plan, Paradise Valley are all prey to our idiosyncrasies, which too often leave the vision punctured like a sieve. People running out of money, people drinking too much and smoking too much dope, marriages breaking up, sickness, people cracking up, fights, petty hatreds which go unresolved.

But the meetings go on, the papers continue to be shuffled, the phone keeps ringing. The town is as vulnerable as ever, oblivious to our personal lives.

For me, the moment has come to split for a while. Both my public and private life seem out of control. The need to save myself eclipses all higher callings. I need a purgation; a ceremony to untie the knots which households, jobs, sewers, and small towns can create. Friends left behind understand and fill in. There are enough of us so that the temporary absence of a few people does not bring everything to a halt.

Monday.

Flight. Meetings will be missed. Responsibilities abandoned.

I leave town quietly. Sleeping bag. Guitar. Truck.

As I turn off on the highway to head south along the coast, I notice that the road sign has again vanished. Someone has left an old chair leaning comically up against the bare signposts. I try to envision the marauder standing on its wobbly back in the darkness, unscrewing the sign bolts.

NIGHTTIME on the road.

Coming down into LA.

Air brown under mercury-vapor lamps.

Listening to a Baroque oboe concerto on the radio coming out of the mountains. It keeps being interrupted by blasts of mood music from another station. LA trying to leak in under the door.

Stop at a gas station. Look at a map. Want to get through here and out into the desert while it is still dark. Just don't have it in me to face this in the daylight.

LA below me stewing in smog. A giant malformed pinball machine blinking in the lit-up night.

No shape. Even on the map, the freeways just run into the general area and collide in a snarl.

Do people live here? Do they call it home with gladness and pride?

Freeway exits with names borrowed from the past whiz by. Orange Avenue, Via Verde, Citrus Boulevard, Cherry Avenue. The off-ramps feed from these giant highways into a dense jungle of neon signs which grow out of the asphalt. They are in competition with one another, each trying to crane higher than the one before.

Forest Lawn Cemetery shines down on the freeway. Garish lit-up fountains. Bogus Greek sculptures littering the land. Reminds me of someone's prizewinning bathroom in Miami.

Stop for coffee at a truck stop. Map says that the desert is near. Quiet, dark, open, clear.

Coffee shop has a sign announcing, "No one without shoes and a shirt will be served."

Turquoise counter top. Matching turquoise uniform on the waitress with dyed red hair.

My body craves something healthy. Decide on vanilla ice cream. Waitress asks me how to spell "scoop" for the check.

Pour some non-dairy creamer into my coffee—a sleight-of-hand corporate prank on the coffee drinker. Good stuff! Just read the ingredients: "Corn syrup solids, vegetable fat, sodium caseinate, dipotassium phosphate, emulsifier, sodium silico-aluminate, artificial flavor and artificial color."

Pictures on the wall show a family of chimpanzees dressed up in suits with cigars in their mouths. A sign hangs behind the coffee maker: AROUND HERE COWS MAY COME AND GO, BUT THE BULL STAYS FOREVER.

Truck drivers dressed as cowboys stir their coffee, eat a steak, and chat about their rigs. Bellies, flabby from years in the driver's seat, strain out over large metal belt buckles. Okie accents. Jukebox.

Feel like driving until dawn in this rootless tide of late-night vehicles.

BACK on the freeway. All I can see is chaotic pieces. It's hard to remember that it was not always this way, that it took tremendous energy, time, money, commitment, and initiative (that great American word) to ruin this land.

In 1845, Lansford W. Hastings wrote in *The Emigrant's Guide to Oregon and California* that the time was not distant when "those wild forests, trackless plains, untrodden valleys, and the unbounded ocean, will present one grand scheme of continuous improvements, universal enterprise and unparalleled commerce . . . when the entire country will be everywhere intersected with turnpike roads, rail-roads and canals; and when all the vastly numerous resources of that now almost unknown region will be fully and advantageously developed."

Fearful signs that scream replies to unasked-for requests adorn stores and restaurants:

> WE DO NOT CASH CHECKS.
> WE DO NOT GIVE OUT CHANGE.
> WE RESERVE THE RIGHT TO REFUSE. . .

Pink, turquoise, orange painted cinderblock houses arranged like cars in a parking lot. The bright colors seem an afterthought by someone hoping to disguise the desolation.

The roadside is dotted with large agro-industrial installa-

tions, featuring huge tanks of pesticides and billboards with cartoon insects and worms gagging and reeling on poison.

Heading east now. Clear desert stars overhead. Cold.

Hank Williams—found ODed at the age of twenty-nine in the back of a robin's-egg blue Cadillac outside Oak Hill, West Virginia—comes in over the radio from Gila Bend, Arizona.

> Hear that lonesome whip-poor-will,
> So blue he cannot fly.
> The midnight train is whining low,
> I'm so lonesome I could cry.

The desert glitters in the sunlight from broken glass strewn on the roadside. Animals along the highway lie in different twisted postures of death from the killer automobile. Papers and trash blow with the tumbleweed. Dune buggy tracks disappear off over the horizon in the sand. People safe in large cool cars with the windows rolled up. Prosperity and ugliness.

"To make so much money that you won't—that you don't 'mind,' don't mind anything—that is absolutely, I think, the main American formula."—Henry James, *The American Scene*

TAKE the back road up over the mountain. A ceremony for returning from long trips.

Freeways behind. Narrow winding road. Have not passed a car in five miles.

Stop at my ceremonial spot just over the ridge. Look down once again on the Pacific and our town. I hear the surf. The lights on the dark land beneath mark the points where the town begins and ends. And I know each light.

BACK home again. Completed circles.

The PUD met tonight, and we appointed Paul to serve out the rest of Mark's term of office.

Paul is a lawyer in his early thirties. He is smart, thorough, and ambitious. Except for those cases which he takes to make a living, the entire thrust of his legal career could be summed up in two words: Stop development.

He has defended the PUD against a wild fishing expedition

of a suit which Vernon filed against us for everything from the water moratorium to raising water rates. (The suit just became more and more complicated until it was dropped.) Paul has filed numerous suits himself against housing developments, dams, roads, and the sheriffs for arresting nude sunbathers.

As a director, Paul promises to defend the PUD free.

The board decides to take a strong position against the proposed restaurant at the upcoming public hearing in Oakland.

AM staking tomatoes in Paradise. County and state inspectors (State Water Board) come up Pine Gulch Creek to inspect the headwaters of the PUD's emergency pumping operation. They find Paradise Valley: hippie tents, much evidence of lumber, building, gardening, animals.

What to make of all this?

Pygmies?

Are they clean?

Should Sacramento be notified?

No doubt, repercussions and headlines will follow: TOWN WATER SUPPLY IMPERILED BY UNLAUNDERED OUTLAWS!

It would take a book in itself to chart all the governmental bureaucracies which maintain some sort of jurisdiction over this small, insignificant town.

ALMOST the whole town seems to have sought refuge on the beach. Most people are nude in spite of the fact that Joe Kelly made a raid on the beach yesterday, panicking everyone into their underwear with threats of mass arrest.

"That was the first time I ever saw Joe Kelly out of his patrol car," says one beach veteran. "When I saw him comin' down the beach with his club, gun, and dark glasses, I just ran down and jumped in the water."

It's so hot that most of the surfers are out of their wet suits. Knots of people lie around in the sand, talking, smoking, drinking beer. Young girls are riding around bareback on their horses in the waves. A few men are cruising the beach and drinking in the lithe bodies of several well-appointed women. A pregnant woman sprawls on the beach in the sun, eyes closed, arms outstretched, her enormous abdomen sticking up above the others like the Rock of Gibraltar.

Three old Portuguese fishermen walk past us down the beach toward the reef. They carry bait buckets, poles, and a burlap bag for their catch. Their eyes are riveted to the sand as they pass the groups of nude swimmers and sunbathers. The wife of one of the fishermen walks behind with a wicker picnic basket. She is looking all around, smiling, nodding.

Walk downtown in the balmy evening as the moon rises. As I walk, I hear the hiss and glucker of people watering their plants and lawns; forgotten faucets left on in the dark making huge rivers which run out into the street.

Knock on one or two doors.

"Oh my, yes. We did hear something about a water shortage," says one pleasant woman out for the weekend. She turns off her hose.

Water is taken for granted. But that will change.

Can faintly hear Danny "Wide Load" playing the piano in the Gibson House, allegedly the town whorehouse at the turn of the century.

Round the bend by the Bar. Richard and Danny the Fisherman stand in slickers on the dock. It's high tide and about to ebb. They are getting ready to go out. Their boat, which they built themselves, floats next to the seawall.

Richard and Danny have been around Briones quite a while. Mid-twenties. Have a clear love affair with the water and boats. They caught over a hundred pounds of fish today. Bonnie, Danny's partner, took it around in their pickup, house to house. The price is right. They sold it all. Made over a hundred dollars.

They use a bottom net and jig lines to catch halibut, rock cod, sturgeon, flounder. Scowley's bought a big pile today and served fresh fish dinners. The Store is going to take some Monday. They are the only fishermen in town. Even have a license. But they are not sure how long they will stay now. Rents high. Housing uncertain. Bonnie has a new baby.

Leave them in the moonlight as they take their boat out the channel through the surf. Sails, old long-handled carved oars, small outboard in a side well.

Up on the cliff I see them nearing their small schooner anchored in the Bay, where they will spend the night.

Many coastal California towns do not have even one fisherman.

JANE, LIZZIE, AND JOEY

THE parked cars extend all the way from Art's furniture shop to the turnoff.

Today, the Craftsmen's Guild, which Tom and a group of other furniture makers, weavers, jewelers, and sculptors organized, has its annual show and crafts sale.

Many townspeople, as well as weekend tourists, stop by to see the wares and watch some of Ben's films.

"We just have to have it on weekends, you know," says Nancy, an apprentice weaver, "because nobody here in town can afford what we have to charge to make a living from one piece of work."

Newsweek runs an article on the Guild.

Return of the Guild

During the Middle Ages, European craftsmen who lived and worked in the same quarter of town formed guilds in order to monopolize local production while at the same time insuring good workmanship, fair prices and the continuous training of apprentices to carry on the craft. The craftsmen and their monopolies long ago fell victim to capitalism and mechanization, but now a revival of a modified-guild system has begun in (where else?) California. Just two weeks ago, the Briones Craftsmen's Guild of master jewelers, weavers, a stained-glass maker and—with a nod to the twentieth century—a film maker celebrated its first birthday.

The guild . . . is a nonprofit educational group that includes 21 master artisans and ten apprentices. Like the medieval guildsmen, the Briones craftsmen teach their apprentices not only the skills but the economics of their art. "Everybody here is essentially a businessman, earning a living by the production of his craft," says master furniture maker Tom d'Onofrio. The guild's own economic structure, however, has yielded to modern times; while medieval masters paid their apprentices subsistence wages for a period of some seven years, the Briones craftsmen charge their apprentices from $130 to more than $600 for three months of study. Most of the craftsmen's support, however, comes from sales of their wares. The Briones artisans' housing also differs from the medieval style. While the masters still retain their individual homes and shops, the apprentices are put up in private homes and boarding houses in the area.

The craftsmen are no ordinary street artists of the leather belt-glass flower variety. "We swore this guild was not going to be an incense-and-candles affair," says Alexander Jacopetti, a master weaver and one of the guild's founders. While a few of the masters are self-taught, many hold advanced degrees from U.S. and European universities and teach part-time at several San Francisco Bay area art schools. To be accepted by the guild, each master must have worked in his field for at least five years, had several shows and expertise. The only criteria for apprentices are an interest in the craft and an ability to pay the tuition. The ten current apprentices include teen-agers who have just graduated from high school, a sociologist who is studying jewelry-making and a former political speechwriter who is now learning how to make furniture.

The guild has already begun to attract national attention, and its birthday festival drew hundreds of people from California and several other states. The guild's founders hope to expand the group to about 25 masters and 25 apprentices and, eventually, provide some scholarships from the initiation fee and $15 monthly dues that each member now pays. Furniture maker d'Onofrio even dreams of one day establishing an international guild, a loose organization of independent artisans. While the craftsmen's life-styles and working hours have already been changed by the added responsibility of teaching students, they feel that a larger guild should remain flexible. "I don't want an institution," says Arthur Carpenter, the guild's grandmaster and a furniture designer whose work is exhibited at the Smithsonian Institution. "I want a shop."

TODAY Greg quits the PUD Board. There is an absence now. In so many ways our election and our rather unique brand of water-sewer politics were his creation. We will miss him. His interest was flagging as he got more and more into affairs at Paradise Valley.

We will appoint a new interim director. The idea of constantly replacing people in positions of authority appeals to most of us. It is with a sense of relief that we watch various "town leaders" demote themselves and retire back into the crowd rather than scramble forever onward up the political pig-pile.

Square dance tonight at the PUD Grand Ballroom. Not too rowdy. Lots of women there without their old men. Almost none vice-versa. That's a refreshing switch.

Soft, gentle morning, Bicycle over to Frances' house at 6:00 to drive with her and Judith over-the-hill to Oakland. Today is the hearing before the Regional Water Quality Control Board on permits for the new restaurant.

It's hot as hell on the inland side of the mountain. Thick smog hangs over the East Bay. The freeway moves through condensed ugliness: endless industrial warehouses and plants surrounded by chain link fence. Tract houses baking in the sun. Temperature hits 104 degrees. Heat shimmers up off the pavement and hoods of cars.

Where have all the trees gone? There is no shade. Only air-conditioned franchise restaurants.

Our destination is the Alameda Utilities Building, a huge ugly cement building bearing the pretentious mark of an architect. Even in the hearing room, everything is cement. The only relief is provided by some linoleum. No natural light, although the sun is blazing away outside. The toilets and water fountains are immaculate.

Wait all morning as the agenda crawls toward our item. Men and women on the board sit around a curved table on a dais trying somehow to stop all water from becoming hopelessly polluted.

I Xerox files while I wait. Find record of the whole intrigue.

Who could understand it all? Who cares about the wording, cease-and-desist orders, legal mumbo jumbo, hearings, resolutions?

The point is simply that our town does not need another restaurant (the existing ones barely scrape by). More cars, more noise, more publicity, more tourists.

Finally talk to legal counsel. Why did the board cave in? Not clear. He talks about "staff vacillation," "confusion." I guess they just hoped no one would notice. What's one more restaurant in one small town?

Hearing starts. I march up to the microphone and lectern (always facing the board, never facing the audience). Legal counsel gives confusing "clarification" about why they will allow more sewage to flow into a wildlife preserve already

under their own cease-and-desist order. Board members are looking at their watches, wondering why they cannot move faster. We keep pressing. Explaining.

Suddenly a woman board member perks up and says, "Well, this clearly violates the spirit of our own laws."

Heads on the board slowly turn in her direction. Tired faces. They just want someone to lead them out of this mess, which they don't really appear to understand.

The woman board member explains her understanding. The board votes. The resolution they vote on is too complicated to describe. But, in short, we win.

For most carpenters around town the building moratorium has not been as devastating as we originally feared. Most have found periodic work doing one or more of the additions and remodeling jobs which have increased dramatically. In a way, the moratorium has been good for local tradesmen, because the available jobs are usually small enough to render them unprofitable for larger over-the-hill builders with out-of-town crews.

It is the day after the Fourth of July. The holiday weekend seizure is over.

Ride my bike out to the radio towers to check on a site which we think might work for a new small reservoir. Small road in human proportions beneath me. Cows grazing on either side. Sun. Strong, fresh wind from the Headlands.

Leave my bike by the fence. Climb up the steep hill through the motionless radio poles humming in the wind. On the hilltop are old cement revetments and bunkers; relics of World War II. Tiny slits in the concrete just above ground look out to the Pacific Ocean.

I sit on top of a rusting gun mount looking out across the town to the ocean. I remember a photograph of my mother standing in front of two barrels: one filled with tin cans, the other filled with bullets for the bellies of the Japs.

Nineteen-forties ecology.

It was wartime. Serious business. But I cannot help thinking how beautiful it must have been to be stationed on this bluff in 1943, spending the whole day looking seaward through binoculars for Japanese subs. And at night, sleeping beneath the ground in these cement burrows on this friendly hill, dreaming of small yellow men with knives in their teeth stealthily climbing up from the ocean cliffs to slit our patriotic throats.

The shadow of a hawk sweeps overhead in the wind.

How immediate the enemy was in those days. Japanese in Briones? How else would they have taken our country? A Normandy landing on our beach!

And now the land will play host to an invasion of Americans, not Japanese.

Our enemies change.

THOUSANDS of pelicans are back on the reef. Great, clumsy, comical flocks of them wheeling and diving over schools of anchovies like old-fashioned airplanes. The ornithologists report that DDT is rendering pelican eggshells so thin, that few young are hatching. The DDT flows from the valleys where the agro-corporations spray thousands of acres, down the creeks, into the rivers, to the Bay, and finally the ocean, into the food chain, and out here onto the reef where the pelicans return each year.

I sit reading Sym's plans for a PUD-sponsored "Echotechtural House" which runs on wind and solar power, with a compost toilet and a methane generator.

A car pulls up in front of the PUD with lettering on the gray doors saying, INTERAGENCY MOTOR POOL.

A middle-aged man in a suit and briefcase gets out and walks into the office.

"Hello," he says as he flashes a badge in a small wallet. "I'm from the IRS."

He smiles. I invite him in. Pour two cups of coffee. We sit down at the table.

"Well, we've had some complaints about your increase in water rates," he says.

"From the laundromat?" I ask.

"Well, actually, I'd rather not say," he replies. "But we believe this raise does not conform with the President's Phase Three and a Half, or whatever it's called." He laughs and slaps my shoulder.

"What president?" I ask.

He smiles impishly and goes on to say that we must roll back our rates. Then he starts talking about the price of soybeans, the Russian wheat deal, and inflation. He pauses, reins up a little and says, "Actually, I just came on this job about a month ago." He hauls a thick notebook full of Xeroxed questions and answers on Phase something or other out of his briefcase and starts looking at it.

"But this tells it all," he says, thumbing through it as though mere contact with his fingers would impart the requisite information.

He takes notes about our rising operating costs, leaking pipes, pumps, and long, tenuous, transmission lines.

"Jeez, you guys are really up against it," he says. "But it says in the book here pretty clearly that we can't let you raise rates."

"Should we just close down?" I ask.

"Well, now," he says, "we couldn't just do that. Maybe you should just apply for an exemption."

He opens his briefcase and pulls out a stack of forms.

"We should be able to have an answer for you by December," he says. "The only problem is that it's July and Nixon's freeze ends in a month."

THERE is a new group in town, The Eastern Pacific Transport Company. Consists of several local carpenter-types who have taken over the planning, dead-ending, and repairs of our dirt roads. The county has promised one thousand yards of creek gravel, delivered. Eastern Pacific is organizing a volunteer weekend to get the whole town out in trucks to repair some of the more impassable roads. There is talk of a road party and potluck dinner afterwards.

Briones has more miles of potholed dirt roads with three-foot-deep puddles than the entire country of Laos. But we love them this way.

TODAY, Sheriff Kelly and several assisting officers drive their patrol cars down to the end of Brighton Avenue. They walk out onto the beach wearing clubs, guns, and dark glasses, courageously arrest five nude swimmers, and take them over-the-hill to jail.

One of the criminals is Liz, mother of two small boys and a retarded daughter.

Paul files massive legal brief in defense of the five apprehended nude sunbathers: the Briones Five.

Some fear the publicity a victory might bring.

Others want to turn Sheriff Kelly upside down.

WHILE driving around the mesa looking for Minor, I find that someone has driven a large highway grader down Poplar Road. The road has been widened, the drainage ditches filled in, and the potholes patched with dust. Lo and behold, if it is not Mr. Kraft, who lives elsewhere and who has distinguished himself by building several spec A-frames which he rents to rich dope dealers at astronomical rents.

I follow the widened road down to where he has his grader, a tank truck, a steamroller, and several pickup trucks.

The grader is hard at work gouging a two-track country lane into a wide, plantless scar in the earth. I talk to the guy on the grader.

"Listen, my friend, I don't know anything. The boss sends me out here to do a job. And all I know is that this machine is costing someone a whole lotta bucks everytime I stop moving," he says, then hits the throttle, which sends a big black belch of diesel smoke out the stack. He gouges away another piece of the hillside.

The sense of futility that one feels while standing beside one of these large ominous machines is overwhelming. It occurs to me to just throw myself in front of the machine. The idea of confronting this driver, who has no idea what's going on, leaves me feeling foolish. But something has got to be done. This fellow Kraft has just decided to do what he wants to roads which do not belong to him.

Jump in the truck. Find Bill. We spend an hour calling lawyers and contractors and trying to find Kraft to tell him that we are going to issue a stop-work order.

Both of us are wired, hungry, pissed, and tired. The coffee is getting to us. Bill eats a raw English muffin from my bag of groceries.

We drive back out to the cliff and give the grader driver the stop-work order from the PUD. He accepts it with a mixture of irritation and resignation, like a good soldier bending to the whimsy of the generals.

Get back to the PUD office to find Kraft on the phone. He's fit to be tied.

"I got a lot of money tied up in that equipment!" he says. "And I'm just trying to get a decent road into my houses!" The way he's talking, we know he means business.

We ask him why he didn't ask permission. No answer. Does he know people who live on Poplar are mad as hell? He just gets madder. Says he's going to come out.

Kraft is a contractor over-the-hill. Early forties, medium height. Drives a white "Coop da vill" Cad. Has a brusque "get the job done" manner. He is not at his most genteel when confronting long-haired utilities directors.

He arrives, and he's really got a head of steam up. We show him the deeds giving the PUD title to the dirt roads. He doesn't believe it. Describes himself as "just a small guy with a few extra houses." Clearly has no sympathy for people who love narrow, potholed roads to keep the traffic down. He's likely lost a muffler or two off the Coop da Vill coming in to check out his real estate.

We talk. Vibes are heavy, but slowly cool down. Kraft agrees to reditch the roads and stop widening. We shake hands more out of relief to get out of his way than in the belief that he will clean up his act. Indeed, he never does anything to fix the roads.

Roads: our blood veins. Once widened, they never shrink. It is absolutely essential that our jurisdiction over these roads be clarified and publicized.

UNTIL this century, heart disease, which is directly related to crowding, stress, and anxiety, was virtually unknown anywhere in the world.

In the first two years after Paul Dudley White set up practice in 1912, he saw only three or four coronary patients.

Last year, 700,000 people in the US died from heart disease. Mostly men.

WE have just heard that *Sunset* magazine is carrying another article and map showing people how to get to Briones and wind their way through town to the southern part of the seashore.

Paul has a scheme. The PUD discusses it and agrees to buy and put up two eight-foot signs at the entrance to town. They will be emblazoned with a skull and crossbones and the warning:

> RAW SEWAGE OCEAN OUTFALL
> BEACHES QUARANTINED
> DANGER OF HEPATITIS, TYPHOID, AND SALMONELLA

The chief county health officer finally agrees that people should be warned of our raw sewage ocean outfall, first built in 1906.

THE Colemans have their Model-T truck decked out with racks. They drive around town and sell fruit and vegetables which they buy at the Farmer's Market in the city.

Going to the city to get fruit and vegetables for the country?

Tomorrow Ilka and I leave for a family visit back east.

Martha's Vineyard
August 25, 1973

Dear Gary and Judy:*

I have wanted to write both of you for several days now. The motives have been strange. And I regret to say that they have been mostly ones of gloom and depression over what we have been seeing and sensing around us on this once beautiful island, Martha's Vineyard.

In short, it seems to be doomed to a kind of extinction. It is not that there is any one villain or demonic force at work to destroy it, but rather that all the small forces which seem to make up the country's motion have conspired here to make the process more rapid and the evidence more obvious than in many other places.

Returning for the first time in several years, I hardly recognize the island. The number of ferry boats serving the island has been increased, filling the streets of the small New England towns with bumper-to-bumper traffic. The roads have been repaved and slightly widened. Now there is an almost constant flow of vehicles from one end of the island to the other (some eighteen miles). From this house, on the hill overlooking the ocean, it is difficult to distinguish between the sound of the surf breaking on South Beach and the roar of passing tour buses, cars, and trucks. There is a new jetport.

Today, in one short hour I counted forty aircraft flying overhead. They used to be a rarity. Shops, galleries, boutiques, restaurants, and curio shops have sprung up everywhere. The beaches which are open to the public are crowded. The others are plastered with No Trespassing signs and patrolled by police.

Almost everyone seems saddened by what has happened, although some are making money. No one seems to know quite what to do. The subdivisions are moving in and hundreds of single-family dwellings have gone up during the past few years, all very high-priced, needless to say. The individual towns have almost no resources for planning. The county has been painfully indecisive, commissioning a few studies and reports and then burying them because their conclusions are so full of despair. The only possible refuge is a state bill and Kennedy's federal bill, both trying lamely (as big government does) to come to grips with the eroding situation.

What is both strange and amazing is that the problems are so familiar to the ones we face in Briones and the county. The place is

* Our local county supervisor and his administrative assistant.

growing too fast, and no one knows how to stop it. Few have the courage to even think that it *can* be stopped. There is much talk about land-use planning, and yet one has that sinking feeling that all the planners in the world will be unable to save this island unless they are given the legal tools and electoral support to do it.

In any event, they have hardly even begun the process here, and are thus that much farther away from failure.

But what is most depressing is the fact that the island has little cohesion. The winter people who own most of the land, and vote here, do have a community because they live here all year round. Some are pretty pleased with the boom in land prices and the absence of land controls; others are clearly upset. The summer people (who outnumber the winter people ten to one, but have no vote) are in disarray. They want to "save" the island, but they neither live here year round nor have much of a sense of community which would allow them to convert shared concerns into some sort of organized effort. Most people are busy escaping to their private secluded houses from the vicissitudes of some big city, and do not have the energy on weekends for getting organized. Anarchy and poor communications prevail, and there is no central hub for any organized action to revolve around.

Social discourse occurs either at the beach or through invitations to cocktail parties. These form a kind of seasonal interest group. And while the concern of these people is laudable, it is precisely they and their summer wealth which have brought the problem to where it now stands. This is not to say that it would not be better to stop it now, but that there is a strange unreality about the efforts of these people to save a place which is not even their home and to which they have attached themselves as summer sojourners by virtue of being wealthy. Houses rent for $1,500 to $2,000 a month in July and August.

If I had to put my finger on the most conspicuous absence here among the summer conservationists, it would be the lack of a real sense of community. Of course, this is inevitable when people are spending nine months of the year elsewhere. But still it seems clear that unless people can face the destruction of their towns and the land in groups which derive from some common entity, they will perish from a sense of discouragement and futility. As one middle-aged woman told me at the beach, "Well, I think it's just awful. We came up here to get away from New York. Soon we'll have to go somewhere else."

The contradictions are complete, so that people cannot save themselves. They hope Kennedy can. But I doubt it.

What I see here is a kind of self-protective mechanism going into effect. People become less and less willing to get involved and fight because it appears they would only be signing up for a crash landing. More than anything else, it seems to be this fear that nothing can be done which immobilizes and paralyzes people into accepting what is happening, and makes them stand passively by while what they love disappears.

There is no doubt that public officials have increased rather than lessened this sense here. No one in office has really led a charge against this kind of fatalistic thinking, which can find a million reasons for not doing a million things. There is all the usual distance between what people want and their spokesmen in office. The hearings are just as intimidating and boring here as anywhere else, and they seem to militate against people asking for the kinds of imaginative new solutions that might take the bull by the horns and stop the rampaging destruction. But in the meanwhile, no one even dares suggest that there will come a time in the very near future when to think in terms of more growth of almost any kind will be just like giving another bottle of rum to a cirrhosis victim. . . .

I just don't know if any place in the long run can withstand the pressure of land speculation, taxes, growth, the automobile, and most important, the destruction of community. For it seems to me that it is only *community* which can successfully provide people with human contact and sufficient political strength to take on the onerous job of self-protection. Wherever community is absent, I see chaos, cynicism, and resignation. Once the smallness of human scale is destroyed, people lose touch with each other and become vulnerable.

Well, enough said. We miss you both and home. I feel something really good is happening there. That's just intuition. But you should see people's faces light up with interest here when they hear of any one of our small victories.

All the best, much love,
Orville

FALL

The good life depends on intimacy and small numbers.

ARISTOTLE

How big should a State be? Large cities are never well governed, because a great multitude cannot be orderly. A State ought to be large enough to be more-or-less self-sufficing, but not too large for constitutional government. It ought to be small enough for citizens to know each other's characters, otherwise right will not be done in elections and lawsuits.

The territory should be small enough to be surveyed in its entirety from a hilltop.

ARISTOTLE

THE HOMECOMING. For several days we piece together the events that have taken place during our absence; like catching up on the life of a good friend.

Happened while we were gone:
1. One person stabbed—BAD.
2. One person tried to commit suicide by shooting himself in the chest—BAD.
3. Road Day & Potluck Dinner takes place—GOOD.
4. More static and bullshit over the size, shape, and funding of the new sewer ponds (this may go on forever)—BAD.
5. County issues encouraging report on the viability of agriculture—GOOD.
6. County blows beeg whistle on Paradise from just about every department at once. Followed by alarmist stories in all papers—BAD.
7. PUD election draws closer. No one quite knows what the issues are/should be—UNCLEAR.
8. Rains have started. Grass already turning green—GOOD.
9. Car runs through front window of Store—BAD OMEN.
10. Town still beautiful—GOOD.
11. Town meeting is held with Rolf present to discuss his proposed subdivision—GOOD.
12. Fishing boat wrecks up on reef in fog. Everyone rescued —GOOD.
13. PUD hangs the quarantine signs up at the entrance to town and catches a lot of flak. They take them back down—GOOD OR BAD.
14. Renée performs a citizen's arrest on Officer Kelly for speeding—GOOD.

7-7-1. Not such a bad scorecard for a beleaguered small town.

"You know, I was really the one who got rid of Joe Kelly. It wasn't all those meetings where people just went and then did nothing," says Renée, late thirties, single mother of three who built her own house, and weaving and spinning wizard of the town who dyes her own fleece with natural colors from indigenous plants.

"It was simple. I was driving up Terrace, and Joe Kelly comes speeding past. Really fast. About thirty mph in a fifteen mph zone. So, I really got pissed, 'cause this guy is a menace. So I went down to the laundromat at the bottom of the hill. In no time flat he was back down the hill with some sergeant he had gone to pick up on the mesa!"

"Did you stop him?"

"Yeah. I went right out, stopped him, and said that he had been speeding and I wanted to make a citizen's arrest. We got into this tremendous thing right out in front of the laundromat and post office with everyone watching. Joe Kelly started to defend himself, and the sergeant was trying to cool everything off and get out of there in the patrol car."

"What did Kelly do when you told him he was under arrest?"

"Well, he started arguing. So, I asked him how fast he was going. He said twenty-five mph. So I said, 'OK. But don't you know it's a fifteen mph speed limit? Can't you see the sign?'

"And then I told him he had crossed the center line too. He started to tell me there was no center line. Well, there was. So there was this big flap over that."

"And then what happened?"

"Well, it sort of mellowed out and they left. And then a few days later the DA calls up and asks if I still want to press charges. He said they had docked Kelly two weeks of pay, and that it would cost the county a whole lot of bread to have a jury trial. They were just asking me to, you know, say, 'OK. Let's forget it.'

"But I said, 'No way! I want that man stopped!'

"So, then a whole bunch of sheriffs came down and told me

RENÉE

they would like to talk to me up at headquarters at my 'convenience.' I was in the middle of building my house in Paradise and totally into it at the time."

"So, what did you do?"

"I went up there. The desk sheriff asked me a lot of questions. I said that I wanted Joe Kelly tried.

"Well, then they asked me what I would think if they promised that Joe Kelly would never be allowed to drive a car again if I dropped the charges. So, I thought, 'What the hell! That does it.' So I told them, OK."

"So, where's Kelly now?"

"I guess he's on a desk somewhere. People have told me that sometimes they call up and get him on the phone at the sheriff's office."

"Did they ever write down their promise?"

"No. But I sent a copy of all the stuff I mailed to the DA and head sheriff to Gary. So, I guess he's got it in his files."

THE county is getting restless over Paradise Valley. There is talk of abatement and various other legal measures because we have not applied for the proper permits: namely, building, health (water and sewage), zoning, subdivision, Coastal Commission, etc. It's about five hundred dollars' worth of permits.

We are working on a coherent list of our "violations" and proposed alternatives.

The big decision: will we apply for permits, be turned down, and work our way up the ladder of appeals or not? If not, the next step is the county counsel, the courts, more paper, and conceivably the bulldozers.

There seems to be a consensus that it would be pointless to apply for permits. Compost privies? Drinking from the creek? Houses without wires and pipes? No subdivision?

We'd just be turned down.

The decision to plunge on illegally is never quite specifically made our official policy either. There are disagreements. Some

feel we should draw up a plan, state our case and reasons, and then go ahead whether legally or not. Others adopt a "damn the county" attitude. They want to just keep going, wait for the sword-rattling from Big Pink, and then start fighting.

The matter is left unclear. But it doesn't look like anyone is going to stop working in the garden, on the houses, or with animals.

We have become the red flag waving in front of the bull-system. We hope that the system still has the flexibility to allow for the new, which in our case is mostly the old.

LEWIS, Peter, Burr, Judith, Rex, Bill, and I go up to Synanon (communal farm for ex-addicts) to see their package sewage-treatment plant. They have four small activated sludge plants and spray-irrigate their treated effluent onto nearby hillsides. But they still have not worked out any beneficial use for their treated sewage. Their plants are efficient and clean like American kitchens: use a lot of power, are immensely complicated, highly mechanical, subject to corrosion, equipment failure, and fatigue. They satisfy all the requirements. But they are ugly, hardly long-lasting, and expensive. Our sewer will be less dependent on technology and maintenance, and more reliant on natural processes.

Meanwhile, our sewer fights for its life in the state and federal bureaucracies. Each month the construction costs seem to rise. People are beginning to be worried about the monthly hookup cost which is certain to be $13 or more (not to mention the $.29 cent per $100 assessed tax hike). The question of cost makes it ever more difficult for people to fit the sewer into the larger picture of land use, beneficial side uses of treated effluent for agriculture, esthetics, and effect on the community. All such considerations seem to be easily submerged by practical, technical, and financial concerns. They all constrain against viewing the sewer as belonging to the whole pattern of life and town. The government grant requirements are like a howling gale blowing us back toward a mundane colossus with a chain link fence around it. Each requirement and agency gives permits and grants to solve one limited problem without anyone to oversee any interconnectedness. No money for anything but the grim minimum.

UP early.

Too early. Wait at the top of the hill and watch the reef until Bill swings by to pick me up. We drive out to the ranch for a meeting with Rolf about his partnership's development plans for their land.

He arrives with $6,000 worth of plans showing a lodge, 200 condominiums, tennis courts, an amphitheater, and a man-made lake. The whole development is all very tasteful in that genteel style of prize-winning architecture.

We all talk. Rolf is open, fair, sensitive. He is miffed about a town meeting to which he was lured while we were away where people came down pretty hard on him. Feels he got unfairly roasted in public and cast in the role of a crass rip-off developer, which he is not. But he *is* a developer. He still feels he has a right to develop these beautiful 210 acres of canyon and windswept pasture. Rolf is caught in a powerful contradiction. He is searching for some form of development which will turn a profit, which means something large which will cater to outside money.

"Well, I think if the town doesn't like what I'm doing," says Rolf, "you all ought to pass a bond and buy it."

But the resources of this town are small. It cannot buy all the land that needs protection.

We talk again about the possibility of Rolf subdividing the land into four sixty-acre farms with access and water. He seems curious.

"OK," he says. "If you can get me the first buyer, I'll. . . ." Then he closes up. I tell him I know they could be sold as multifamily farms. But he is apprehensive. The idea is untried. And what would his financial backers say?

ATE no breakfast today, save for the glue on seven hundred stamps. Several nights ago I decided to write a letter to the town. Things seemed to need a summing-up.

Today the letter goes out in the mail.

AN OPEN LETTER TO THE PEOPLE OF BRIONES

Dear Fellow Townspeople:

All summer long I have thought about writing a letter to everyone in town. With summer gone, it seemed like a good chance to clarify some of my thoughts about what is going on in Briones and share them with others. So, besides the presumptuousness of it all, I could see nothing to lose except some stamp money. I decided to give it a try and see how people reacted.

First, let me say that I do not come up for reelection at the PUD next month. In fact, I intend to resign from the board once we get the sewer squared away. So, in the narrow political sense, I am not campaigning for anything. But my mind has been spilling over with general thoughts.

Over the past two years I have often felt a wide gap between Board Directors and the people who elected us (you). It sometimes has seemed as though the elections or occasional crisis are our only point of contact. People find out what they can, vote, and then withdraw in relief leaving their new politicians to mind the store. There are exceptions, of course. But there is something dangerously amiss about a process which finds the majority of the people seldom participating. It breeds an unhealthy distinction between those who are politically involved and those who are not. The goals of the former become as unclear as the wishes of the latter.

Sometimes I think that I still feel the pulse of this town. At other times I have felt uncertain that I know what people want and care about. And, at times I have wondered if most people cared at all. Perhaps we as elected officials have been equally as enigmatic to you. Hopefully this letter will give you some sense of where at least one politically involved person's head is in this community.

The word "community" is a really powerful one for me. It is the reason why I think I am still living in Briones. It implies a group of people which is not so large that it is unable to share concerns. It implies the absence of anonymity or gaping spaces between people which make them feel afraid of each other, unfamiliar with each other, and uncertain about how to go about effecting changes around them. In a community, people are not strangers. The question of scale and size is crucial.

Some people still speak of Briones as a village; the county planners, for instance. But I think that we have already outgrown that appellation. Some refer to us as a town. That sounds more accurate. Others see us as kind of a weird bastard suburb combining our mud roads with commuters and dependency on the city. There is some truth here. But I don't think we have gone quite that far. The road over the mountain is still our guardian.

Whatever we are, we have been growing at an alarming rate, at least since I arrived here four years ago. I remember living on the mesa and feeling moments of real isolation; walking on dark winter nights and seeing virtually no lights or people. Many houses were empty. Many, including my own, were as yet unbuilt. A house could be rented for $125 a month. It was not uncommon to drive all the way downtown without running into another car (or having one run into you).

When many of us decided to leave the desolation of city life, we became refugees to other people's territory. We gave up the cities to look for a fresh start. But in doing so, I think we acted on an illusion which has a terminal disease. The illusion is that there will always be some new place ready to receive us to which we can "move on." But somewhere it must end. Our country and our world do not have an infinite capacity to absorb our mistakes, our negligence, our unwillingness to deal with problems, and our discarded beginnings. We will not be allowed forever to start over. We simply cannot continue to rely on this mutated pioneer ethic. We must get rid of this underground railroad in our minds which continually holds out the promise of unspoiled land ahead, from New York, to San Francisco, to Briones, to Oregon, with Canada as the final panacea in the background. Only the fast ones will make it. The rest of us will be left with the mess the others made while passing through.

But, worst of all, this faith in our ability to "move on" allows us to stand mutely by and watch as a seemingly inevitable process eats away at our present homes. Conservative or radical, we can all identify it. We all talk about it, and we all fear it. Even a child knows what is on the list: smog, asphalt, too many cars, crime, drugs, over-priced housing, high taxes, freak-outs, fear, depersonalization, and, above all, people losing touch with those other human beings who live around them.

Somehow this process has become so all-pervasive that we have

almost educated ourselves to accept it and give into it—and, then, hopefully to move on. We are in a constant retreat.

I find myself reluctant to grow attached to a place, to call someplace my home because of the knowledge that it is the rule rather than the exception that it will be destroyed. And I cannot help but think that if we decided we would not "move on," we might be able to stem the tide on this small peninsula, so that in ten, or even twenty years, living in Briones would still give us a good feeling and a good life.

The other grand flaw in the "moving on" syndrome is that everyone wants to go where it is still nice, and where they can enjoy themselves with a minimum of effort . . . a kind of parasite with no name. But things get crowded fast and stop being nice. Then what?

Briones is still an incredibly beautiful and satisfying place to live. But largeness is a threat, not just because of what large numbers of people do to the land and environment, but because of what they do to that fragile balance called community. In this sense, we are all part of the problem. But that does not mean that we should resign ourselves to it in guilty surrender. There have always been people moving from one place to another. But at some point the process becomes so accelerated that it becomes destructive. It is at this time that I think we have the right (obligation?) to get a grip on it even if some accuse us of elitist exclusion.

The concept of the small town is one of the most cherished in American history. Do we want to continue to live in such a town? Does it really matter if we can recognize most people on the roads, in the Store or in the Bar? Do we want to live in a place where you always have to lock the door? Do we care if Annie at the post office knows our name, or whether credit can be got in a pinch at the Store? Is there any benefit in being able to confront our adversaries for a welcome chat in the laundromat? Is it important that Joe, the fire chief, be personally known by most people? Should we actually try to develop a much stronger local economy so that more people do not have to make the grueling trip over-the-hill each day? Do we want to be a town of busboys, waitresses, gas monkeys, and motel clerks to serve strangers? Or would we rather be a town of farmers, carpenters, fishermen, ranchers, merchants, and craftsmen to serve ourselves?

It's our choice.

Does it make sense that each of us drive around in our own car when a simple inexpensive jitney service would provide a pleasant way to move for the old, the young, and everyone in between? Should we allow the beautiful pastureland which surrounds our town to be subdivided into second homes for the wealthy when it could be put back into agriculture and provide fresh vegetables, meat, and dairy products for the town? Should a town such as ours have three restaurants (and possibly a fourth), and several curio shops, but no dry goods store, no bakery, no feedstore, no brewery? Why should a town blessed with an ample supply of wind power send thousands of dollars a month over-the-hill each month to Pacific Gas and Electric when we could have windmill generators or solar collectors? Why should a town continue to allow itself to grow, necessitating expensive new roads, sewers, waterworks, school buildings, and police forces so that we become so overtaxed that none but the rich can afford to stay? Is beauty reserved for the rich in our system? Is it an inescapable law of nature that men must allow things they love to be despoiled?

The questions are indeed endless. Many may seem hopeless and insoluble because of the way that money and political power are organized. But we should not underestimate our own strength. Often I think that we do not even pose these questions to ourselves as much as we might because the answers might come back too clearly. And then what would we do about it?

Success will certainly not just happen or be delivered. First, we will have to be able to articulate what we want, and we will not always agree. Then we will have to ask, explain, struggle, and even take. A lot of people will have to do a lot of work. People will have to get together, and there are bound to be some dull meetings, but some good ones as well. And then, we'll have to work.

But, above all, people will have to decide that they have had it with "moving on," that they are sick of being like Indians moved from one reservation to another.

Even if we expend vast amounts of energy, nothing is guaranteed. There are too many examples of places which have not made it to allow for such confidence, and most of us have lived in such places. But somehow we must allow ourselves to dream what the future might look like for one small town. This may sound far-flung in this era of presidential criminality and political brutality. But regeneration will come from someplace. And I have a feeling it will come from the bottom; from some small place where people are still in touch, and cohesive enough to trust each other and act.

Perhaps we are such a place. What do you think?

Best wishes,
Orville

THE PUD election gathers momentum, but not much passion. Judith has organized a series of candidates' nights at various people's houses. Candidates as well as people seem to enjoy the chance to get together and talk.

The field of candidates seems to have broken down into two rough slates, with one or two others buzzing around the edges searching for issues.

The big issue dividing the three incumbent directors (two of whom were appointed to vacancies) from the other slate (composed of a city fireman, a high school follower of Maharishi Yoga, and a middle-aged woman who runs the Bar) is the question of whether or not the Utilities District Board should view itself broadly and serve as a kind of de facto town council. Since we are unincorporated and have no town council, there is a gap to be filled. The present directors (myself included) feel that the town desperately needs an official forum in which to consider community problems. We feel that the State Public Utilities Code gives the board such broad powers to deal with parks, roads, energy, and land use, as well as sewage and water. The other candidates are more "strict constructionists" and feel that the PUD should keep its nose out of wider issues.

Of course, behind the specific questions lie more important disagreements, such as the district's role in the question of growth and local self-sufficiency.

TONIGHT, the whole pack of aspiring PUD candidates troops down to the Community Center for what is billed as a "debate." About a hundred people are there. But it is creepy.

There is something listless about it. It is the same hall where the whole recall election was fired up two years ago. Now, the election pitches sound strange and scrambled as various people grope for issues to distinguish themselves from the incumbents. Everyone playing politics in this laughably narrow context.

Patrick, who is running, does an amazing flip from his days as coordinator for the Planning Group and comes out for motels, the flag, and know-nothing government.

Can people believe that red is green on alternate days?

THE Property Owners Association has risen again, and has sent out a mailer blasting the PUD for fiscal irresponsibility. They claim that our sewer is too expensive and that we are buying too much land for spray-irrigating the treated effluent. They are, needless to say, backing our opponents.

So, at last, the election campaign begins to heat up. The issues are becoming somewhat more clear. Judith and Paul are working on a mailer to all registered voters to answer the Property Owners' charges.

People around town are beginning to get more curious as their mailboxes are filling up with propaganda.

Susan has made several beautiful silk-screen posters telling people to support the sewer: "Keep the vision—Yes on H."

The candidates are getting scared and meeting more often. The three incumbents, Lewis, Bill, and Paul, are beginning to come out of their corners.

Five more days until the election.

This town will be a very different place if they lose.

THE mailer war is escalating. All candidates are deluging the voters with paper. Annie going crazy at the post office.

Paul and Lewis set up a card table down in front of the Store. Talk to people. Show them the sewer plans. See who they are, what they think about what is happening; confirm or deny myriad rumors. They enjoy the day and feel more optimistic about the election.

The Store is like the eye of the needle through which the town threads.

PRE-election jitters.

We are discovering more new people on the election rolls than we had anticipated. Summer houses are filling up with all-year-round residents. New people moving into converted garages and shacks.

Sometimes it feels as though this town may be perched on the edge, on that almost undefinable line where small becomes large and where town becomes just another place to live. It is not that the new people are bad people. By and large they are not. It is just that it takes time to assimilate, time for the new faces to be worked into the town's fabric.

And who is to say what the magic number is. Is it 1,500 people? 1,750 people? 2,000 people? When does anonymity begin to dominate familiarity? How many people?

We still survive as a community. Yet, it is still hard to know how thoroughly we have been able to touch people with the message: sewers, community, smallness, local control, self-sufficiency. In talking with the populace, we find that many share the vision but trust that it will materialize without, or in spite of, them.

We all feel so unfamiliar in our new role as the incumbent "establishment." We are in the unaccustomed position of asking people to vote for the continuation of something, not to help end some dramatic evil.

Perhaps, in the future, all big votes will be against, rather than for.

We are at a crucial point. Will we be able to finish what we started? *Can* we finish what we started? Can we and the people of this town stay with a project all the way from the early groping, to the plans, through the red tape and building? Can the ideas become incarnate? Can the gears be meshed?

TONIGHT is Halloween.

There is a party at the Community Center for kids. All the stores in town donate candy, prizes, and decorations. Susan makes a horror house featuring a hastily constructed dead man made out of bones and raw meat from the butcher. One small kid cries.

The party is followed by a dance. Every few weeks there is a rock dance in town, usually with a band somewhere from the county. People smoke a lot of dope and drink a lot of beer and wine. Things often get pretty rowdy.

Tonight a couple of local guys go berserk. They tear the sink out of the bathroom, rip a door off its hinges, destroy the refrigerator, break windows, and smash up the back door. Meanwhile, a bunch of younger kids are out in the street smashing bottles. Later in the evening, someone throws a firecracker into the Bar, which is packed.

Danny the piano player, who is the Community Center live-in janitor, writes a public letter:

Halloween, a grand bazaar night, was turned into a gross blizzard of blight, tricks with no treats. Our community center was ransacked. Names escape me, but pictures (mug shots) flash across my mind. These atrocities were witnessed and/or accomplished, but no one stopped the flood of destruction.

The aggressive negativity overwhelms me.

The heartbreak; again, the innocent shall pay for the works of the wicked.

HOWLING wind. Driving rain. Huge white breakers churning in over the gray ocean toward the reef. Sheets of rain chattering on the windows.

Phone chain going. Head over to Lewis' house in search of another voters' list.

He feels quite confident, and confidence has a way of spreading.

We drive downtown. Paul is standing out in front of the Store in a raincoat collaring people and talking to them. The card table is up and covered with soggy sewer plans and election propaganda.

People's reaction seems good. Some are just confused. Don't know that there is an election. Don't know if they are registered. Don't understand what the issues are. "What's Proposition H?" asks one. "For a sewer? Wow!"

No one hostile. Just a few who don't want anything to do with anything political.

"Voting sucks!" says one youth of this persuasion.

Go up to Paul's to get some crayons and pasteboard to make a few more signs. Head back down the hill.

Knock on a door to ask if I can hang a poster on a tree.

One guy with weird eyes which keep crossing is quite hostile. Two women are really curious. They say they feel "cut off." Agree that Briones is "far-out." Say they enjoyed the letter-to-the-town, but they are pissed about PUD directors taking salaries.

I offer some explanation. They seem relieved to know it was not all pure venality.

Drink a cup of coffee. Talk some more about town affairs. They thumb through all the mailers which they have stacked up on the table; many of these unopened.

Confusion.

It is obvious that we should be stopping at every house. But no time.

Put up the posters and head back downtown to the Store. Several groups of people are standing around the card table chatting and trying to stay under the overhang out of the rain.

Lewis buys a bottle of brandy to fight the chill. Various people have a nip as they go in and out of the Store. People clad in rubber boots, baggy coats, and odd hats. Scruffy dogs soaked to the skin patiently await their masters making the interminable journey into the Store, past the checkout counter, through several conversations, and then past the brandy bottle.

The election feels better. Contact is being made.

Kiss my first electoral baby.

IT'S the last day before the town goes to the polls.

Lewis, Bill, and I drive around the mesa in Bill's truck knocking on doors, talking, reminding people to go to vote. We are warmed by most people's friendliness and support.

Get into one long discussion with a quasi-absentee couple who have what they call a "country house" in Mendocino from which they have just returned. They work at a university and live here on weekends. They lead divided lives. They blame us for not keeping the community informed, although they basically agree with what we are doing and the direction the town is taking. They make the presumption that it is the job

of the politician to keep people informed. (Even if they do not pay attention?)

"You guys must be doing something wrong about keeping in touch because I do not know what is happening."

WE win . . . all three seats!

THE rain is still coming down.

Bill, head of the PUD maintenance crew, invites us out for a victory feed.

The wind is blowing the fog across the pastures around Bill and Sally's old ranch house. It is surrounded by an array of old barns, sheds, water towers, upturned Buicks, and rusted farm equipment. Wet cows, heads down into the wind, keep up their insatiable munching as we pass.

Inside, we eat roast beef, baked potatoes, peas, salad, home-made coffee cake, with cups of hot coffee. Bill is nodding off after spending the day at home with a broken rib and a case of beer.

We stuff ourselves on Sally's incredible feed. Talk about trucks. Drink a beer. Smoke a joint. And bid adieu to the hospitable head of PUD maintenance.

Stop off at the hardware store. Ambrose upset over the outcome of the election. He is past retirement. Runs a fine hardware store with his wife. Five days of work a week. Feels he is being forced out of town by high taxes and high water rates.

"And this damn building moratorium has driven the contractors out of town," he says with unaccustomed strain in his voice. "I'm sixty-seven years old. I sold everything to set up this hardware store. I mean, hell, in San Anselmo we didn't pay as much taxes as here and we had sidewalks, streets, lights, sewers, and curbs."

I try to listen patiently. Am not quite sure what I could say to make him feel better.

[134

BILL

REPLIES are coming back from the letter-to-the-town.

Do you think we can do it? I'm sure tired of being on the run.

T.H.

I am wishing to thank you for your letter where you spoke of Briones. You spoke of much as well of what I believe we as a living community can be.

[Unsigned]

We don't need this crap! PROMOTE AMERICANISM!
Fred

Dear Orville:

I would like to see the BCPUD changed into a town council and the town run with regular town meetings to pass on major decisions.

If Briones could set up a pilot program of some sort to make use of entire community resources—especially human ones—to achieve self-sufficiency as a community, it could be a prototype and attract the kind of attention and money that Briones needs.

In any event, people are not as apathetic as they sometimes seem, and your work is appreciated.

Marjorie

THE first clear day in a week and a half.

Lewis comes over with Ocean, his son. We make some coffee and talk about water.

Lewis figures that under no circumstances should the proposed new system supply more water than what is needed for the present town plus a 1 percent growth rate. Over twenty years that means approximately 120 new houses above the 650 existing ones. That's a lot.

"But you know, my feeling is that some growth is OK," says Lewis. "I mean there's growth and there's growth. We want to encourage agriculture and the kinds of growth that makes people self-sufficient, don't we?

"Like, the carpenters here do really fine work," he says. "It's good energy. And they're not out to rip anyone off. And I think that the town would be poorer, for sure, without them."

If every town and city implemented some sort of population or growth limit, soon people would have no place to live, right? Right!

Now most people are appalled at this idea, and think of it as a disaster. They picture thousands (nay, millions!) of people lined up refugee-style with cardboard suitcases, runny-nosed kids, and all their worldly possessions with "no place to go"!

But actually, maybe people would just stop peopling the globe with so many kids who could not be adequately provided for. It's like the energy crisis: unless there is not enough gas, people will not get out of their cars, travel less, or work out new and more efficient ways of traveling. Until there are NO VACANCY signs, people will multiply and fill areas beyond the natural carrying capacity. As long as there are more pipes being put into the ground, people will use them.

A recent US Geological survey reports that 900 million gallons of municipal and industrial waste are discharged into San Francisco Bay and tributaries *each* day. And, in spite of improvements in waste water treatment, the volume has increased.

The report projects that discharges will double if future population estimates are accurate. Bay waters will continue to deteriorate even with strict new federal controls because of the increasing volume, which has more than doubled since the early 1960s. During the same period, the toxicity of the waste water rose 16 percent. The report finds a direct equation among increased population, urbanization, and water pollution.

The main household polluters are garbage disposals that overload municipal treatment plants with organic solids and phosphate-bearing laundry detergents. The vast bulk of water pollution in the Bay comes from petrochemical plants, paper plants, food processing, and metal mills. Power plants are now the cause of the major thermal pollution problems in the area.

The report predicts a 120 percent increase in waste water discharge into the Bay over the next twenty years.

Altogether, two million acre-feet of waste water runs into the ocean from California cities each year. One acre-foot is one acre of water, one foot deep.

JUST as the county seems posed for the kill by issuing a "final warning" to Paradise Valley, some new wrinkles develop.

A big banner headline in the local county daily proclaims, CODES MAY RELAX ON FARM COMMUNE. PLANNING CHIEF PROPOSES WAIVING COUNTY RULES.

The article goes on to explain that the county planning director has proposed in an "unofficial position paper" that certain zoning and building regulations be waived in order to legalize the Paradise Valley experiment. He says, however, that there should be no softening of health and safety regulations.

"It seems probable that subjecting the experiment to all normal standards, procedures, and regulations could spell its early demise. . . . Ways should be found to adapt the county's regulations and procedures in order to allow such experiments a chance to survive."

Rumors have it that several planning commissioners unofficially agree. A major furor seems to be brewing within the county over whether to take a flexible or inflexible line.

The same newspaper (one of the most conservative in the Bay Area) surprisingly supports Paradise Valley by editorializing that the snarl is just another example of too much governmental interference in people's lives.

"If the ordinances and regulations are too complicated, and force too much expense, maybe they should be changed, but for all, not just a special few who are trying a "life style" that the County Planning Director wants to encourage."

Now you see it, now you don't!
Today the planning director denies that he proposed waiving county ordinances for Paradise.

Says, "Violations must be dealt with in accordance with existing codes."

He is obviously sympathetic, but cannot find a loophole through which to squirm without losing his job.

Once you get the county arguing with itself, there is hope.

RUMORS abound and spread fast in Briones.

The most recent is that there is a rapist in town. Then we hear that one woman, who lives on Grove Street, has been raped.

People are horrified, scared, and uneasy. No one quite knows what to do. There are no mechanisms besides the sheriffs to handle the problem. There is no local machinery for clarifying what has happened. There is no discernible way to prevent fear and give people a sense that everything isn't completely out of control.

Ilka is wary. She cannot quite believe that anything will happen to her, but she keeps talking about it. Today, as I frame the new back door, she inspects it carefully.

"Where's the lock?" she asks. Logical reaction.

There is some discussion that the women's group could do something. Put up signs? Send out the word that people are getting it together? Get together? Write a handbill for women which tells every lady in town how to handle or protect herself if she is attacked?

Someone needs to take charge.

ONE of the several women who have been raped calls a big women's meeting at her house tonight. About fifty women, all ages and all types, show up.

They talk.

Finally decide to call up Mike, a local sheriff who patrols the coastal beat.

He arrives and helps sort out fact from fiction.

The enemy is the lack of communication.

No one quite knows what the complete picture is. Some people think there are two rapists. One has been described as short and fat, wearing a mask and speaking with a phony German accent. Several people claim to know who he is.

Something is happening. The meeting helps. People seem a little less inclined to shrink back into their private fear and isolation.

IT is a raw, cold night. The weather hovers between frost and another storm. People file slowly into the Community Center out of the dark.

Someone has lit a fire. The lights are dim.

Sheriff Mike A. and Sheriff N., the local substation lieutenant, arrive and take seats up front.

Several hundred people fill the room. It is the largest town meeting anyone can remember.

The subject is rape.

GORDON (*chairman of the Community Center*): Because in a town the size of Briones rumors play such a large part, I think it might be helpful if the sheriffs told us what has actually happened, rather than just what we *think* has happened.

SHERIFF N.: OK. In detail, about the assaults around: There was a stabbing case which has already been disposed of. The suspect was arrested. He went through the jury process and was acquitted. The suspect in that case claimed self-defense.

The three rape cases which have so far been reported are under investigation and suffering from a terrible lack of accurate information. Our problem is to try to put all the material into a workable investigation so we can make an accurate arrest. To date we have talked to one individual who we feel is the primary suspect.

VOICE: Is this guy a local or a transient?

SHERIFF N.: The gentleman whom we have talked to is considered a transient, although he is now living within the confines of Briones.

VOICE: Are all the beats in the county manned by resident deputies?

SHERIFF N.: No, sir. The resident deputies were phased out two years ago. So, maybe you can see our problem. We are spread way out over four hundred square miles. We are spread thin and confined to our cars as our offices and communications centers. We are really dependent on the populace to help us by reporting crime and giving us information. The town of Briones has amazingly turned around in the year I have been here by starting to come forward and help. But in solving crime, we're like the doctor. A doctor receives patients after they are sick. Our preventative medicine is very, very minuscule. The chances of us preventing a crime in an area like this with normal patrol is little more than a dream. But when we have to do investigative work, this is where you, the citizen, everyone in this room, can help the police suppress crime.

You are the people affected by crime. You are the victims. We as the police try and bring justice to you by arresting the perpetrators of the crime.

BOBBY JEAN: Well, how can we help?

SHERIFF N.: Well, one of the big problems for us here in Briones is finding people. (*Loud and prolonged laughter from the audience*) For instance, with one of the rape calls, we could have been there twenty minutes earlier if we could have found the house. There are no house numbers in this area to speak of, and the roads are not marked. And speaking for a majority of the other officers, they are just *miserable* to drive on!

VOICE: Right! (*Loud laughter*)

VOICE: Do you really think that fear is the only way we can protect ourselves?

SHERIFF N.: No, ma'am, no, ma'am. I hope by the time I finish to be able to respond to more specific questions.

REX: You know, about two years ago the Planning Group had a questionnaire that got passed around. The gist of the replies suggested a strong sense of community here, and that people wanted to see a variety of life-styles. And it seems to me that this is a good chance for people to get together.

I look back on the oil spill as a really positive thing in many ways, because it showed people how to get together and make things happen. So, I think that we should look at this problem not so much as a police problem, even though they will help us, but as *our* problem and see what the community can do.

ELLEN: I know there are a lot of women in town who are alone with children. And I've heard a lot of rumors about guns and knives being used in the rapes and the lives of children being threatened.

I would like these rumors dispelled or confirmed. I want to know the facts. Is the guy breaking down the door? Is it at nighttime? Is the house locked? You know . . . how did it happen?

SHERIFF MIKE A. (*lives in town*): OK. First of all, we've actually had three reported rapes, two unreported rapes, and one sexual assault. We cannot classify it as attempted rape. It was a borderline.

On one of the occasions the victim was told that someone was holding a knife on her children. Now, whether or not that is true, I have my doubts.

We have three suspects. One we have talked to. One has split and is now over-the-hill. The other is bouncing back and forth between the beach and Briones. We have heard also that one of the guys is picking up hitchhikers, and we think that two others may be working together.

MARIA: How are these guys getting into people's houses?

SHERIFF MIKE A.: Well, what they're doin' . . . Well, one time, I believe, the suspect came to the residence, told the victim that he was running from the cops, and she let him in. (*Loud laughter*) She said that he could hide in her house and she got raped.

VOICE: Well, if there is something going on here, why can't we find out about it, and why aren't there more officers here?

SHERIFF MIKE A.: This town is getting a heck of a lot more attention than you would on average patrol. Right now, you're getting at least twice as much attention than your neighboring towns.

VOICE: How come none of the police know how to find the

streets? What are they doing? We all know them.

SHERIFF N.: We're bound as police officers by quite a few restrictions. Just because we suspect someone doesn't mean he's guilty. I mean, this is what we're talking about when we're talking about civil rights and justice. Someone we suspect is someone we're interested in talking to. We can't fall into the chasm of saying, "Well, he's a suspect, so he's gotta have done it."

Now, another thing. There's a lot of talk about vigilance committees in this town. Well, I want to warn you people. When you start taking the law in your own hands, you're going back a hundred years. And we're no better off than the lawless then. And if you think you're any better for hanging a man, hurting a man, or running him out of town because you suspect him of something, you're not. You're just as bad as he is. You're a criminal! (*Clapping*)

PETER: I'd like to say that it is obvious that Briones is fantastic for rumors and also for exaggerating them. But right now the town has no real filtering mechanism or screening-place for rumors. I have been talking to people at the Presbyterian Church to see if there might be a room available next to the clinic for a volunteer switchboard. It could field rumors and possible scares, and be a place where people could come or call if they had suspicions or fears. Perhaps we could check out and see how valid these rumors and fears are. I mean, we've even had some regrettable suicides and deaths. If people had a means to pass out and filter information, like tonight's meeting, it would be good. We could even use a social hangout like the old Future Studies. Maybe we could keep up with the emotional ups and downs of the town.

And finally, there are obviously women who do not want to officially report a rape. But they might report it to a group of community women with whom they feel an affinity.

So, anyone who is interested in this idea, sign this sheet that will be passing around.

ORVILLE: I think Peter's idea is really a good one. There has been a tremendous amount of fear around town over the rapes, and that more than almost anything else has been debilitating. I also sense that there has been a feeling around town which would make a burglar, a rapist, or any kind of criminal feel safe. If I were a rapist, I would be able to sense when people were isolated from each other. When there are no real overarching ways for people to get together, a criminal could just melt into our disorganization, be just another faceless person passing through.

If I were a criminal coming into town, and knew that people had it together behind a switchboard or something, I'd say, "Whoa! Wait a second! Maybe I'd better go someplace else!"

VOICE: One reason we women do not like to report rapes is that we don't want to go through the whole interrogation scene. It's heavy enough to get raped! Maybe it would be better if there were some women with some legal knowledge or something who could go over and advise a woman.

JUDITH: You know, we're always talking about a sense of community and "the vision" for our community. But even here tonight, I look around and see an amazing number of people that I do not know. And it kind of shakes me, because I thought I knew most people in town.

Maybe during the next couple of weeks, people could go around their block or area and introduce themselves to their neighbors and exchange phone numbers and say, "Feel free to call me if anything strange comes up." Maybe we would get a better sense of who we are, and be better able to take care of each other in the neighborhood.

The other thing is, why don't we have a few parties and invite . . . (drowned out by hollers of approval and clapping)

VOICE: My case is one of the ones which has been kicked around tonight. And I think the problem which we have is just what is going on around here tonight. And it shouldn't go on.

After I was raped, I spoke to the officer the next morning. And at least three pages were filled out about the case. It was in black and white that I did not open the door for this man. The door was open, and he just walked in.

And the feelings that I am having are ones of . . . ah . . . well, that the police think I let him in. And I just have a kind of feeling that they are being insensitive in talking about it.

It was heavy. It was heavy afterwards, too. And it's kind of the reason why people don't report it.

VOICE: One of the sheriffs on the scene sort of implied that she invited the guy in.

SHERIFF MIKE A.: This is what I was advised by the recording officer.

VOICE: But you heard her at the first women's rape meeting saying that she had *not* invited him in!

SHERIFF MIKE A.: Well, don't get the misunderstanding that I am laughing at all, because this is no laughing matter. And the way I explained it was the way I read it from the report. Now, I read the report at least three times.

LES (*the town doctor*): Do the authorities have a real sense of whether the difficulties are coming from people who are residents of the town, or from people who are coming from somewhere else to town to have a good time, get it on, and then split?

If we are getting the bad vibes and hassles just from residents, that's one thing. But if we have people coming from San Francisco to Smiley's, getting drunk, and ripping off a house before they go home, that's another problem entirely.

My reaction to the problem is that we have to create something besides Smiley's. Anyone who has come downtown at night knows that there is only one thing happening, and that is drunk people making noise in the street.

LANA: I mean, I work downtown here at Tarantino's every night, and I see what happens. Most people know who the troublemakers are. I think most people are just afraid to come out and say who's negative. I know! I live in the center of this town, and I know exactly what's happening.

But what can the police do? Just because someone is wandering around doing nothing with his life, you can't arrest him. And if they're into being negative, what can you do? That's what's driving this whole town crazy. And ya know . . .

well, ya can just take all that for what it's worth. But I really feel sorry for the cops. They can't do anything about it. The only people who can do anything about it is us. And we just have to put out the message to those particular individuals to get it together, or get out! *(Clapping)* And teach their children, too, all about this crap! *(Hoots of agreement)* And their dogs and their cats! Too many down here! *(Hysteria of whistling, clapping, rebel yells of agreement)*

SHERIFF MIKE A: Yeah. Well, a lot of people . . . well, maybe half, feel the way you do. And when they come up with some information about one of these pains-in-the-town's-back, they call the office. And when you get a certain amount of information against an individual, you can do something.

Meeting ends. Many people seemed relieved. They stand around in clumps talking while others fold up the chairs.

A large contingent drifts off down the street to the Bar.

BREAKFAST at Tony Tarantino's Seafood Grotto is an event. Tony has run his restaurant for thirty years. Crazy Tony. Seventy-six years old. Gray beard. Round potbelly that hangs out over his pants. Can often be seen on winter mornings in something that looks like an old nightcap and a sweat suit.

He talks fast. Moves slow. Talks endlessly on subjects which are not always clear. He can argue without another side.

Tony is selling his restaurant to the Tacherra boys, who own the ranch outside town. Tony doesn't really want to move, because he lives at the restaurant upstairs. The boys are running the whole show now except for breakfast. This is Tony's swan song. He ministers to the few red-eyed dispossessed who are up and hungry at 7:00 in the morning.

The restaurant itself is homemade. It is in the middle of town and covered with strange, out-of-place garish signs announcing such specialties as CLAMS in three-feet-high black letters. Another oversized sign announces Tarantino's fine HAMBURGER.

The interior of the restaurant is lit year round with oversized Christmas tree lights connected with a custom wiring job. There is an AstroTurf carpet inside the vestibule, the most recent area which Tony claimed from the sidewalk by quietly extending a few walls, securing them with a roof, and setting a door between two posts sunk in garbage cans of cement.

The inside is a maze of painted-over exterior shingled walls which used to be outside before they were superseded and consumed as interior walls. It is a building without a center. Growth through mitosis. What year did Tony first cross his property line as he expanded? Did anyone notice? Will Tony keep right on building until he reaches the broken yellow line running down the center of Wharf Road?

THE UBC (Uniform Building Code) is a fat, dull, 704-page book. All houses must be built to its specifications in order to pass building inspection.

The building code developed over the past century, and was originally designed to insure that houses were built safely, and that plumbing and electrical work was neither unsanitary nor hazardous. As tract houses swept the nation after the Second World War, the UBC also functioned as protection for those who might unknowingly buy a substandard house from an unscrupulous developer.

But there is another side to the building code. It is strongly supported by the building supply people because it requires that all building materials be "code," from stamped lumber and wiring and plumbing to heating, foundations, and fire-proofing. It stipulates minimum room and house square footage, ceiling height, number of doors, placement of certain windows, and such interesting fetishistic requirements as the distance or number of doors between the kitchen and the bathroom.

"We are worried about your safety," says Herb Winmer, head of building inspection at the County Department of Public Works. "And, the thing of it is," he goes on, "what if some guy just goes out and builds a house. And then he sells it. Now how is that buyer going to know if it is safe?"

But the UBC makes it more difficult for an owner to build his own house, particularly if he is constructing it out of scrounged materials, and wants to forgo some of the niceties of civilization.

Building a house to code is wasteful and expensive.

As an antidote, the building code of Hammurabi (2200 B.C.) is being circulated around town:

> If a builder builds a house and does not make its construction firm, and the house collapses and causes death of the owner of the house—the builder shall be put to death. If it causes the death of a son of the owner— they shall put to death the son of the builder. If it causes the death of a slave of the owner—he shall give to the owner a slave of equal value. If it destroys property—he shall restore whatever it destroyed and because he did not make the house firm, he shall rebuild the house which collapsed at his own expense. If a builder builds a house and does not make its construction meet requirements, and a wall falls in—that builder shall strengthen the wall at his own expense.

At home, I find a copy of a letter in our postbox from one of our distant neighbors to a supervisor who is not exactly disposed in our favor.

Sup. Peter Arrigoni
Board of Supervisors

Dear Peter,

When I endorsed your campaign for reelection, I did so in the hope that you would continue to support a sound policy of environmental custodianship. I am writing now to urge you to change your position regarding Paradise Valley Produce.

I have only heard your reactions to this matter as reported in the *Sun*, and it is to these that I must respond. Yes, codes have been violated. No, I do not believe that PVP represents a "wanton refusal to comply with health requirements," and no, PVP is not "a nuisance which should be abated."

The PVP families are attempting one of the most valid and significant experiments of our time. If, as an environmentalist, you share a genuine concern about suburban sprawl, the fouling of air and water, exorbitant consumption, and the insensitivities of industry, then you must also recognize the undeniable fact that these problems have a single root cause: the high standard of living which Americans have established, and the highly wasteful technologies which make this way of life possible. Production, with all of its attendant destruction of the land, is not possible without consumption, and we, not "they," are the consumers.

The environmental rhetoric is heard more loudly in this county than in most corners of the country. Yet, when the chips are down, how many people in our county would be willing to reach to the roots of the environmental problem? Concerning both income and life-style, we are one of the most extravagant counties in America. Our efforts to car pool and recycle are mere tokens in the face of the consumption we enjoy. They ease our conscience, but that is all.

The building codes, as presently structured, require a higher level of consumption and a more elaborate life-style than we may be able ecologically to afford. As long as health and safety standards are maintained, there is much room for the development of a new owner-built code which will allow PVP and others of like mind to pursue the simple life and test the ecologically sound technologies which someday we may all desperately need as replacements for the totally unproven experiment the rest of America is presently engaged in.

Mike Wornum's position is most sound. The codes are NOT sacred. They met our needs as we saw them when we thought that resources were unlimited. The codes must change to accommodate the clearer understanding we now have about the realities of the world in which we live.

As you know, I have been a teacher of young people in the county for a number of years. I have learned above all from my experience that the new generations coming along are not satisfied with the comfortable life and meaningless consumption per se. They are eager to learn new ways of living. Some of their experiments have failed, but you don't burn all books because a few of them are failures or offend established tastes. Life-style is the real testing ground of the environmental movement which is gripping this country. We are all going to have to face this issue in our own lives, and we desperately need all the visionary experiments possible in order to yield what we cannot have forever without undue hardship.

Our county is the perfect place for this test. We have a history here of visionary government, and you have played a significant role in this vision. I urge you to uphold appropriate community standards of health and safety, because that is your job. But I also urge you to work for a more sound, ecologically appropriate set of building codes, for protecting governmental flexibility is also your job. No issue facing this county, indeed this country, is more important.

Sincerely,
David Cavagnaro

THE Briones road signs are back up at the turnoff, companions of the energy crisis; sentinels for a dying age of transportation.

Will it in fact come to pass that Sunday driving will be outlawed because of the energy crisis? Will Briones become a quiet, self-contained town going about its own business on weekends? Will we learn to consolidate our lives and live more in one place?

Picked up a girl hitchhiking coming back from over-the-hill yesterday.

She said that Briones people were "weird." She told me that Briones was "an institution run by the inmates."

SOME days, the meetings, phone calls, letters, listening to gripes around town, the myriad problems that are generated by only six-hundred-some houses erode me to the raw nerve. My intuition tells me to flee for my life into some smaller, more manageable world. There does not seem to be enough time for myself as well as everything else outside. As a devotee of smallness, I sometimes find myself overwhelmed and confused by the obvious fact that people in politics easily get devoured regardless of the scale of their involvement. The only difference between here and Washington is that we ride bicycles and they ride jet planes.

WINTER

"I'm a person for change. I change things all the time.
One of the first things I'm going to change next week is
the front hall."   PAT NIXON

COOL, SUNNY, WINTER DAY. Trying to warm up, but can't. Misty dampness in the shade. Thousands of bright orange monarch butterflies have arrived on the yearly migration. They float lazily around town; bright orange wings against blue sky.

Get a ride back up from downtown with a guy I have never seen.

"Yeah. I just moved out from New York," he says, as only someone who has lived in New York can say (with eyeballs half rolled back into his forehead). "Fell in love with the place. Told CBS records I wasn't coming back."

"Where do you live?" I ask.

"Oh, um, up on Kale. I just bought a place," he replies.

"Really? Whereabouts on Kale?" I ask. "Which side?"

"Ummmm . . . Jeez, I can't even remember. I've been so busy installing a security system."

BUY a table saw from Mike to finish trimming out the back room. Some are addicted to a three-piece French Provincial bedroom set; for others it's a table saw.

We're all hooked.

For a town with a building moratorium, there are more carpenters per square inch here than almost any place I can think of. There is a fever for wood and a fever to build. It is a strange vestigial craving in a town so committed to re-examining the notion of growth.

SUNDAY morning. Greg drops by to see how we are. We get talking about putting out a Land Fund-Paradise Valley magazine issue on the whole question of land reform.

It is clear that we need some sort of vision for the land surrounding our town which transcends traditional planning goals and controlling land use through zoning. It is not enough simply to "allow" certain uses. Somehow a context must be established which actively encourages people toward the kinds of land uses which are productive and lead to greater self-sufficiency. Just as the present context encourages people to use property as a speculative investment, so a new context should encourage people to use property to provide the essentials of life.

Well-managed agriculture is one of the few ways by which men have learned to live on the land without creating the kind of irreparable damage brought about by residential, commercial, industrial, or recreational development. In farming, it is the land itself rather than the "improvement" which creates value. The land literally gives life. It gives food.

It is so obvious that the giant web of transport and communications in this country will eventually break down. There is lunacy in a refrigerator which contains mayonnaise from Chicago, beer from Los Angeles, bread from San Francisco, meat from Nebraska, fruit from Florida, and potatoes from Maine and Idaho. The system will (is) breaking down because it is both environmentally and economically too expensive. Eventually people will force it to break down when they finally realize that these transcontinental foods are not only tasteless and expensive but fortified with dangerous chemical conditioners and preservatives, artificial coloring, and hazardous wasteful packaging.

If our system of food production, distribution, and consumption is a dinosaur, then, it's no idle matter to wonder what will or can replace it.

I have seen no mention in the various governmental typhoons of words and hot air about any plans for the decentralization of agriculture and food production. Just how does Earl Butz think he's going to keep this mess running?

Does it ever occur to him that it might be on the verge of collapse?

How will people eat? How will they get from their suburban houses to the city to work? How will they get away to their summer houses?

THE family photo album shows an eight-year-old faded color snapshot of a young man who resembles Sal Mineo in his prime. Seated next to him is a beautiful dark woman with black hair.

Both are seated on a Castro Convertible in their 180th Street New York apartment. Richie wears a short-sleeved drip-dry shirt and has his hair neatly trimmed and parted.

Carmen wears a neat store-bought dress and has had her hair "done." A hi-fi console stands in the background.

The surrounding photos show pictures of Richie's Puerto Rican mother holding one or more of their five kids. They are pertly dressed in little socks, shoes, and ensembles.

As the pages of the album turn, the hair starts to get a little longer and a little more unruly. Richie starts a beard. Carmen's hair comes down. The children's clothes look somewhat rumpled.

It must be about 1967. Richie is in art school.

Richie appears with a huge bushy beard sitting naked in their New York City bathtub with four small children. All wear big grins.

In the background of many of the photos are amputated sections of Richie's dazzling paintings.

Carmen starts talking as the pages turn.

"Yeah. Well, here is where we split for the West Coast. No more photos with Richie's mother. We took this long Greyhound bus trip with the kids and the baby of a friend who was away for six months or so."

"What a trip!" says Richie. "When the bus would stop at one of those greasy spoons for a rest stop, I would run into town to a supermarket and buy fruit and bread. I mean, the food

RICHIE AND CARMEN'S
FAMILY WITH CHILDREN

was awful in those restaurants! We couldn't afford it, anyway. I don't know how many days we were on that bus. But we occupied a whole part of it."

Somehow they finally find their way to Briones. The next photo shows the whole family sitting downtown on Annie's steps. Seven of them. The day of the Rummage Sale. Hair tied back. All smiling. Kids in strange baggy Free Box clothes. No more little socks on the girls. Boys with full heads of hair.

More pictures: the kids climbing in cypress trees. Richie posing with a giant fifteen-pound cabbage in his garden. Little Greg holding a beet which is bigger than his head. Richie and Carmen on their porch with piles of potatoes, apples, and onions.

"Just takes a lot of chicken shit," says Richie.

Their house is a shed-like one-room box, transformed into an indescribably lovely place to live.

Rent is $150 a month.

There are a few fruit trees in the yard, and chickens in a coop out back with a big doe rabbit which they do not have the heart to kill. Their garden is mulched in straw waiting for the spring. Every inch of ground on the 100 x 100 foot lot is planted in something.

Two small connected sheds out back beneath a flowering plum house Carmen's pottery shop and Richie's painting studio. There is a feeling of great neatness and industry about these two work spaces. Good lighting. Well arranged. Crates of eye-popping Latin-colored canvases are stored in one room. In Carmen's studio, pots, plates, and planters are neatly stacked on shelves waiting to be fired in the kiln. Both parents are at last getting back to their craft, after years of children.

Inside the door of the house, five small lunchpails are lined up waiting for Monday when the kids will troop off to the mailboxes to wait for the school bus.

Jars of homemade applesauce and sauerkraut stand on shelves. Jars and cans of beans, rice, flour, granola, macaroni, and sugar line the wall.

A large wood stove with blue enamel panels stands in the center of the room. It cooks, heats, and adds life to the room. An old red, white, and blue freezer wheezes away beside a home-built kitchen counter.

Most things in the house are constructed from the residue of others. Tables, lamps, shelves are made from odd scraps of driftwood. An old basket chair which came with the house hangs by a rusty tire chain from a rafter.

Above the main room is a sleeping loft. Three small mattress-beds for the girls. A wall made of orange crates full of folded clothes. Then a double mattress for Richie and Carmen. The boys sleep downstairs.

The children sleep as we talk below. The house is one space, but there is a sense of privacy.

THE oil crisis has hit town. Gas prices are rising at Al's Mobil. People beginning to worry. The commuters are particularly upset. People are buying gas cans. The hoarding instinct is in evidence.

Today, the paper brings a report of yet another crisis causing panic buying: a toilet paper shortage.

How many people understand the difference between two-ply and one-ply toilet paper? Do they know that one-ply toilet paper is twice as cheap as two-ply because you get twice as much mileage (to borrow an oil crisis explanation) per roll?

Are people aware that they pay twice as much for "super-absorbent facial tissue," which is also twice as hard for your septic tank or sewage treatment plant to digest?

It's the small things in life.

"My grandmother used to cut up newspapers into neat little pads, punch holes in them, thread strings through, and hang them in the bathroom," says Ilka, recalling the paper shortage in Germany after the War. "And she taught us this special technique to ruffle the newsprint up on itself to make it less slippery and more absorbent."

The day will come when the entire city of New York will be wiping its ass on the *New York Times*.

FEROCIOUS storm last night. Heavy rain and wind made the house shudder and creak all night long.

Beautiful, blue, and clear this morning.

Stop by at Mike's house, which he built himself. Exquisite oiled eucalyptus banister. Fireplace made out of cast-iron buoy. Pegged floors. Handmade furniture. House all sided in secondhand wood.

Mike is working on a solar space heater which is made from hundreds of gallon jugs full of water behind an enclosure. The water in the jugs is heated by the sun. In the evening, air from the house is circulated by convection around the warm bottles and then back into the house.

We start talking about trying to get the town into some alternative energy project. We both get completely crazy behind the idea.

"What we really ought to do first," says Mike, who is a dropped-out engineer, "is do some sort of a study of energy consumption in town so we know how much people burn up."

We ramble on. Our enthusiasm carries us through windmills and solar collectors to methane and tidal generators. Think of trying to design some sort of alternative energy source into the new sewage treatment system.

We resolve to do something.

All the elements are present: water, wind, land, sun, and brains.

A headline in the San Francisco *Chronicle* announces, SKINNY DIPPER VICTORY. Paul wins on a technicality for the five arrested nude swimmers. It turns out that the beaches are actually private property to the high-tide line, and that the county does not have the constitutional right to "regulate nudity" unless it is on public lands.

Paul is delighted with his legal victory. He is quoted in the article as urging bathers "to do their skinny dipping someplace other than Briones," which he notes is still under quarantine for dumping raw sewage into the ocean.

Nonetheless, this victory is somewhat ominous.

Will we now be invaded by hundreds of be-shlonged young men from the city out to score some Brionesian coed?

The publicity will not help. Paul's aside about "raw sewage" may temper any such migration.

"Raw sewage": our teacher, our savior.

THROUGH our half-sleep, we hear a soft knocking on the door this morning.

Dan is on the front porch wearing a backpack full of funny little magazines which he has put out from the old library, a shop selling pottery, candles, jewelry, and other gifts. The magazine announces Dan's new stock.

He is trying to convert his store from a curio shop, aimed mainly at the tourists, to a dry goods store catering more to local needs. He's put in a potbellied stove and has started stocking clothes, boots, socks, raingear, etcetera.

He gives us a magazine, we exchange well-wishes, and he departs on the rest of his promotional tour.

"We've just realized that local trade is where our heart is," says the magazine. "Also, it's a way for us to best balance our year-round business. That's why all the changes in our merchandise. We're getting in what local folks tell us they want. A purchase from the Store literally helps support our trip. We'd deeply appreciate it if you would check with us before you buy out of town. Let us know what you want."

Just what we need. But most local stores have a difficult time making a go of it. Hard to compete with big chains over-the-hill. Hard to keep a large enough inventory.

The plight of the small shopkeeper is similar to that of the family farmer. The economics are all against them.

I drive up north today for groceries. There are deer all over the meadows alongside the road. Young fawns and does eat grass on the roadside in beautiful dark-buff-colored winter suits, the color of dead branches and chaparral. Supple nervous creatures with fluid bodies.

Round a curve. Cars parked in hasty disorder on the roadside. An old Plymouth with both doors flung open is angled half off the road. A fawn lies on the shoulder in a twisted posture making frantic sped-up motions that get it nowhere. It has been hit by a car.

Half a slender leg dangles on tendons like a child's mitten hanging from a fastening on the cuff. Dark red blood spurts out with each crazed heartbeat; a neat regular stream, like a syrup squirter at a soda fountain.

Crazy mad desperate eyes on this small delicate creature.

A girl is yelling. She is trying to hold the fawn. She tries to sweep her long hair out of her eyes. The fawn struggles in terror.

The girl is crying. Her whole arm is dripping with blood.

DAY before Christmas in California.

Some phantom has swept into town overnight and left fifty Christmas trees in the streets.

The kids have stood them up in a line right down the center of Brighton and Wharf Roads. There is a small forest in front of the Store and Scowley's.

Some people take them home to decorate them.

Young girls on horseback set up a slalom course on the street in front of the bookstore.

Everyone tries to explain this happy event. Some say it's the "good karma" in town. Others understand it as the cosmic banana peel: God delivering Christmas trees like loaves and fishes to the believing multitude.

The tree we take has a tag that says $16.95.

RIDE downtown to get the mail at the post office. David and Annie are listening to country-western music on the radio. A brightly painted yellow sports car pulls up. Two guys in their late thirties, clean mod clothes, expensive haircuts, get out and come into the post office. The soles of their well-shined laceless boots make a sound like high-heeled shoes on the linoleum floor. I watch as one picks up a fat eight-by-ten-inch envelope with an LA return address from David behind the counter.

There is an aura of money and credit cards about these two.

Richie and Carmen are outside in their Dodge Dart with the smashed-in rear end. He is worried. He says that he fears Briones could become a ghetto for rich young professionals, weekenders, and dope dealers in expensive cars who can afford $50,000 houses.

House prices have risen meteorically. Taxes are following. It becomes more and more difficult for people without money or steady, well-paying jobs to settle here. Retired people on fixed incomes will sell their houses. Perhaps these gentlemen from LA will remodel them.

THE state grants us a slightly tardy Christmas present. They inform us that our sewer has received "concept approval."

THE head of population studies in the US Department of Agriculture's Economic Research Division announces in Washington "the most dramatic demographic change" he's seen in this country except for the increase in birthrate in the fifties. People are moving back to small towns and small cities. In the 1960s the rate of growth for cities was 17 percent, while nonmetropolitan counties grew by an average of only 4.4 percent. During the past three years, cities grew by only 2.2 percent, while nonmetropolitan counties grew by 4.1 percent.

"What it means," reports another demographer, Conrad Treuber, "is that by the year 2000, we won't have the degree of congestion [in cities] that we would have had if we had continued with the growth rate of the '60s."

Both experts attribute the flow back into the rural areas to a growing disenchantment with cities and (strangely) an increasing availability of rural and small-city jobs.

COLD rain trying to turn to snow.

Rain, rain, rain.

Large rivers flowing down the hill past our house.

There are slides all around town. Earth turned to liquid, pulling away from hillsides by its own weight.

Piles of brown pudding slurp onto the roads like some giant tumor run amok.

Winter rain. The annual baptism of the mesa. Reincarnation as a rice paddy.

Everyone freezing and damp.

Wood wet. Hard to start a fire.

Black rubber boots with pink gum-colored soles are seen on all feet: winter plumage.

THERE is a big alternative energy confab at the PUD tonight. It is attended by an assortment of the two town electricians, an ex-engineer, several carpenters, two PUD directors, a handful of town agitators, and others.

Maybe we could convert some of that hot air into BTU's for space heating and just forget the sun?

The present state of alternative energy systems in this country is best described as "potential." Almost everyone has read an article or has a brother who has watched a friend build a solar heater or methane generator. But few people have actually experimented in any systematic way. We are no exception.

VOICE: Everybody is talking about windmills. I've seen drawings of the ones that NASA has developed. It's like a huge hoop that spins . . . with cups.

VOICE: You mean like an anemometer?

VOICE: Yeah. Too bad they aren't quaint-looking like Dutch windmills.

VOICE: No. These NASA ones look like huge roach clips. Ugly.

VOICE: Like everybody's TV antenna.

VOICE: It's very easy to figure out how many windmills you would need for a town this size just by eighth-grade arithmetic. You just figure out how many kilowatts this town uses in a day, and then calculate how much horsepower it would take to make that much power.

VOICE: I've never sat down and done that.

VOICE: Maybe it isn't even possible to have windmills. This town takes too much juice. Everyone's a juicer. Like, I haven't the faintest idea what the average monthly bill is. How many kilowatts do we use? How much money do we send over-the-hill each month to Pacific Gas and Electric?

VOICE: I'd say that the average bill is somewhat above twenty dollars a month per household.

VOICE: Well, just to give you an idea on what a hot-water heater is costing you, a fast-charge electrical unit uses about 4,500 kilowatt-hours a year. That's an average family. And you know, those heaters are on twenty-four hours a day. In Europe, they have ones which just go on when you use the water.

Anyway, here a kwh costs about three cents. So, your hot water is costing you about $135 a year. In New York, where one kwh costs nine cents, a year's worth of hot water costs about $405.

VOICE: If we generate power, then we have a storage problem.

VOICE: We could solve that by backfeeding into PG & E lines when we have a surplus.

VOICE: Yeah. But if you try to generate on their lines, you have a problem because you have to go along on 60-cycle. Electricity isn't just electricity. And the complications come when you have power outages. If you don't sync up, you fry all the wires.

VOICE: Whoa!

VOICE: There are ways to overcome this. But PG & E is just backward. They sit on power as their own resource. And that's not typical throughout the rest of the US. In lots of areas back east they have it worked out so that alternate power sources can be hooked onto the big commercial power grid.

VOICE: Is there anyone that anybody knows about who feeds into PG & E lines in California?

VOICE: No. Pacific Gas and Electric doesn't allow it. But it's very common for large users elsewhere with bills in the thousands of dollars. They have their own turbines and generators and feed into main lines when their loads are low. Consoli-

BOB AND HIS WINDMILL

dated Edison in New York does this a lot. Then the user can feed off Con Ed's lines when they are at peak load.

VOICE: You mean they just backfeed their meters with power that they generate themselves and run up a credit against what they use from the power companies at other times?

VOICE: Yeah. That's it.

VOICE: It strikes me that the answer to storage may be to *not* store, but simply admit that total self-sufficiency is unreal and hook some alternative system into Pacific Gas and Electric. You give when you got, and take when you ain't got. You might at least cut your bills in half.

VOICE: Yeah. But you got a situation where the generating equipment costs like hell.

VOICE: And also, we are just about wired into the typical voltage we use everyday because of appliances, power tools, etcetera. So there is not much sense in messing around with different voltages.

VOICE: Seems to me there are two things we gotta do. There's the big plan, and there's the little plan, which would get solar heaters, methane generators, and windmills to people's houses.

VOICE: Suppose the PUD got into the business of designing and installing solar heaters in people's houses?

VOICE: Or even providing tested plans?

VOICE: I did some calculations the other day based on a two- to three-thousand-dollar installation cost for a solar heating unit. That's high, and it could be used by any house in town not surrounded by trees. It would provide eighty to one hundred percent of your space-heating requirements.

If we assume that sixty percent of our energy use is consumed for space heating, we could cut the total community energy consumption in half by unplugging ourselves for space heating. And if you amortize the cost of that system over ten years, it would cost about a nickel a kilowatt. Over fifteen years it comes to about three cents a kilowatt, which is what we are paying for power right now.

So, over fifteen years, the cost of the new system would be the same as your heating bill. Then you would have your home virtually heated free. Once you're there, you're there. That's it!

VOICE: What kind of designs?

VOICE: Well, there are a lot. There's a roof pound system, hot water, hot rock storage systems, circulating water systems.

VOICE: What's the percentage of sunlight to clouds required?

VOICE: Well, it's hard to say. It depends for one thing on how many hours it's used and how well your house is insulated. That's the other important thing . . . insulation. If you did these individual systems, you would have to evaluate your house for sound insulation very carefully and calculate heat loss. I think that you could go around this town and insulate floors and ceilings, and save about thirty percent of energy consumption.

For instance, if you take a wood frame dwelling with no insulation and compare it with one totally insulated, there is about a fifty percent difference in energy you consume. It's an incredible difference. There is a considerable heat-loss factor in a hollow stud wall which is vastly improved by insulation.

VOICE: We'd have to get people to insulate existing houses.

VOICE: And you can do an existing house without tearing out any walls quite well. Just insulate floors and ceilings for between three and four hundred dollars.

VOICE: You can have rock wool blown into stud walls.

VOICE: There's a company in Santa Clara that makes a new insulation out of newspapers and wood fibers with some sort of fireproofing. I think it runs about twelve cents a square foot.

VOICE: I'm just worried that we don't have enough sunlight here.

VOICE: I figure we have twenty-six weeks of fog and rainfall here each year.

VOICE: Well, next time it's foggy, put a thermometer up on a black roof. The other day I put a thermometer in a plastic bag and put it in the window in the late afternoon. It got up to 110 degrees Fahrenheit.

VOICE: Listen, what this town needs is an official PUD energy commission. Get scrounging for grants, ideas, plans. But first

we better sit down again and figure out what we want to do.
VOICE: Yeah.

We agree to investigate grant possibilities. The meeting trails off. People sit for a while in groups talking and then slowly drift off into the darkness to their homes.

IN 1579, Sir Francis Drake sailed the good ship *Golden Hind* around the Horn to California. On his way up the coast of South America he plundered gold from several Spanish settlements. Once off California, he put into some harbor near San Francisco to repair and reprovision his ship. Where he landed is still unclear. The chaplain aboard his ship wrote in his diary of a protected harbor adjacent to steep white cliffs which reminded him of Dover. They called this unknown land Nova Albion, or New Britain. It was a land upon which white men had not previously set foot.

To date, people have assumed that Drake landed in Drake's Estero to the north of Briones. But today, several archeologists report that they may have found the remains of Drake's fort out in the back of Ben Meyer's trailer and horse pasture alongside the Briones Lagoon. The area and the harbor fit the descriptions left in the chaplain's log. In fact, there is a remarkable similarity between Drake's Estero and Briones Lagoon.

Our town may find itself the site of the oldest English structure on the North American continent. Drake arrived four hundred years ago, two hundred years before the Spanish settled California from Mexico.

The cosmic soothsayers in town are already saying, "For sure, man! I always knew this place was really heavy!"

A guard has been posted at the site, which was partially covered in the 1870s by some kind of fishponds. Samples of oak pitch found in the earthwork have been sent for analysis to ascertain whether it is from English trees. Curious people have already begun to show up. TV crews are coming out of the woodwork. On all the news shows there are big maps with stars denoting our small peninsula as though it were the center of the universe. The San Francisco *Chronicle* has banner headlines with quaint etchings of Drake being met by coastal Miwok Indians.

We become an historical epicenter. We, so much concerned with the present, suddenly spring roots which antedate anything that the white man has done on this continent.

"Oh, my god!" says one local commentator. "If they find Drake down there, are they going to turn us into a museum?"

IT is hard to know whether to laugh or cry.

Today a severed hand in a plastic Baggie was found on the beach where Canyon Creek flows out to the ocean. It was turned over to the police.

BILL is covered with hayseeds, as usual, from feeding his pigs, calves, horses, and goats.

He fries up a bunch of eggs and warms up some coffee. The kitchen is cold even though the wood stove is lit.

He makes some toast as we talk.

Conversation starts off on the usual: how to make some money. Our ideas always end up getting too visionary and costing us money.

Bill swallows the last few mouthfuls of egg, and then dives into the Yellow Pages. He starts calling insurance companies while I finish my toast.

We've decided Briones needs a service center with an insurance agent, a lawyer, an accountant, and a revolutionary realtor.

All the insurance for the town is now written over-the-hill.

The two local realtors take 7 to 10 percent of every land or house sale.

There is only one local lawyer, Paul.

No working accountant.

Why not have someone (maybe from the New Land Fund) match up good people and good land uses for a straight fee, just enough to keep an office open? Make real estate a service, not a business.

Bill calls up Mag, who just passed the bar, and is helping Renée build her house. She seems noncommittally enthusiastic. But Bill's all wired to go.

He calls a few more insurance companies. Starts shooting questions at guys at the other end of the phone. Seems like they have a hard time getting the picture. A small town? Where? What did you say you do? Pig farmer? Utilities District Director? One guy talks about taking a course. Another promises to call back. Several others are out to lunch.

It starts raining again.

THE Energy Commission has acquired de facto existence. Meetings, proposals, and conversations are its main ouput to date.

The problem is divided into two categories. Members agree to start looking into the various alternatives for community energy and household energy systems.

Community-Wide Categories:

1. Look into the natural gas potential out around Niman's which first surfaced when two different wells about a half-mile apart failed to hit water but hit gas.
2. Investigate various turbine generating equipment large enough to supply the town.
3. Compile a statistical survey of KW use in town and ways to cut down on high use of electricity.
4. Investigate the use of electrolysis (from wind-generated electricity) to isolate the hydrogen out of sea-water and store it as a fuel source. Apparently, internal combustion engines can be converted to burn hydrogen fairly simply . . . and they burn clean.
5. Investigate the possibility of separating the solids from our sewage before it goes into the primary treatment pond of the new sewer and feed it into a large methane digester.

Household Systems:

1. Household methane generators using human and animal excrement, plus household garbage.
2. Windmills for single houses or block systems.
3. Solar heaters for space heating and hot water.

4. Insulation (to cut down on fuel requirements regardless of source).
5. Making wood-burning fireplaces and stoves more efficient.

A US District Court judge rules against Petaluma's growth rate limitation of 500 subdivided units a year. He declares its ordinance unconstitutional.

"No city," he says, "may regulate its population growth numerically so as to preclude residents of any other area from traveling into the region and settling there. . . . The city of Petaluma is violating people's constitutional rights to travel and live wherever they wish."

The judge orders the city to evaluate all future building applications without regard to the growth-control ordinance.

The word around Petaluma's City Hall is that US District Court Judge Lloyd H. Burke has suddenly become the city's chief planner. The judge hands down a hard-line opinion: Any subdivision building permit which was refused to a developer in the past must now be granted. (The growth limit never covered single-family residences. Only developments.)

"We've got sixteen hundred applicants right now," groans Vice-Mayor Jack Cavanaugh, "and if we don't cooperate it looks like we will have to answer to the judge."

"Where do we go from here?" asks Mayor Helen Putnam.

Apparently, the government and people of Petaluma (who voted four to one for the growth-control law), are just supposed to stand obediently by while the developers wipe out the remains of what used to be a lovely small city. They are uncertain about whether or not they will appeal the decision.

Decisions like this have led to terrorism.

So much for planning and all the high and mighty rhetoric of "leaving planning to the planners." Without any way of controlling growth, they are like a bunch of eunuchs at an orgy.

Water and sewage are still the place to grab this growth dragon by the throat. Judges can't sue an entire voting public if they refuse to pass a bond for utilities expansion.

The FDA attempts to regulate known carcinogens by banning harmful substances from the market.

ARRIVE home to find a label from a soy sauce bottle tucked under the door. It has a message written along the edges.

For PUD Director
Ikon Chanel
$175 a month.
Wed. night, Jan 20, 1974
Hard-working. Visionary. Enthusiastic. Interested in building community. Willing to work long hours.

Ikon is reported as having been seen walking up from our house early this afternoon wearing a red football helmet with white faceguard.

THE rapes have ceased. People have turned their minds to other things. The rapist or rapists remain uncaught.

"I don't know about you guys, but I'm just tired of goin' to meetings," says Mike. "I'm just gonna go out and build me a solar hot-water heater."
Another verbose gathering of the energy commission.
Impatience leads everyone to agree that the first priority is action: to build a solar hot-water heater for the School artroom.
Mike suggests making it a science project with some of the kids. He's going to the dump tomorrow to get used hot-water heater tanks for a dollar for storage. Rex going over-the-hill to get some plastic pipe for the heating coil.
Walk back home with Mike.
It's cold and clear. We pass under some tall eucalyptus trees arching out over the road.
"Feel that?" he asks. "Even leaves make good insulation, since they retain a higher constant temperature than the air."
We walk back out under the stars. The temperature immediately drops ten degrees.

THE North Central Regional Coastal Conservation Commission meets in executive session and requests that the attorney general initiate legal proceedings against Paradise Valley for failure to comply with permit procedures.
The state commission's job is to protect the coast as mandated by voters. Paradise Valley is in the coastal permit zone, although it is neither on the coast nor even visible from a road.

MORE letters today from the County Counsel threatening hellfire, damnation, and legal ruination if Paradise Valley Produce does not stop building houses without permits.
Paradise Valley is on the supervisors' agenda as well as the Coastal Commission's agenda.
Double-header.
Both bureaucracies are rattling lawyers and legal warnings.
Valley people settling in for a long joust with Big Pink. People in town seem to be slowly warming to the furor created by the valley. Understand more. Know more. Have a better sense why people in the valley are breaking all these rules, codes, laws.
The valley needs the town. The town needs the valley.
We wait in the supervisors' chambers for three and a half hours before Paradise Valley Produce is discussed.
Finally, at 6:30, just as the hunger pangs refuse to be pacified with another cup of coffee, our number comes up.
The supervisors miraculously agree there has been a misunderstanding. They did not realize that we were applying for permits and appealing those sections where we disagreed.
We are told to finish our environmental impact report and figure out where we are at loggerheads with the building code, planning requirements, and health mythology.
"We have given up trying to slay the dragon," says Greg, "and are now trying to tame it."

TODAY Rex gets back from over-the-hill with several hundred feet of plastic pipe for the School solar hot-water heater. Mike and Minor lay it out on the top of Minor's black asphalt shingle roof. They fill it with water, and let it sit for a few hours.

The temperature reaches 140 degrees. Burns the skin right off you.

Why do we ignore the sun?

In the Southwest, the Taos Indians used to perform a daily ceremony to help the sun rise and set. It was their belief that the precious sun would fail in its path across the sky without their assistance.

They were not right. But they believed they were essential. And they derived tremendous satisfaction and strength from their sense of instrumentality.

Mental health may be little more than the belief that one is able.

WE often shop at the Dented Can Store in the city. They have incredible bargains on salvaged goods which they buy up from insurance companies who get stuck with them after a train wreck or fire.

Today, among other things, we get name-brand beer for eighty cents a six-pack. Each can bears a label: "The alcoholic beverage contained herein is distressed merchandise, salvaged from fire, flood, wreck, or similar catastrophe."

Pretty frightening. But the beer is good.

In the doorway, a small child with chocolate on his face waits for his mother to finish shopping. I watch him as he peels a wrapper off a Mister Crunch Bar and lets it fall to the floor.

An intelligent-looking woman who exudes liberal causes walks righteously up to him.

"Do you always throw stuff like that on the floor?" she asks him quite seriously.

He looks bewildered. Says nothing. Picks up the candy wrapper and, without moving, throws it out the door onto the sidewalk.

SPRING

In the 1960s there was a 4.8% annual decline in farm families. In 1973 it dropped to .8%, a forty-year low. But, still, each year 113,000 families give up farming.

US DEPARTMENT OF AGRICULTURE

The law locks up the man or woman
Who steals the goose from off the common,
But lets the greater villain loose
Who steals the common from the goose.

OLD ENGLISH PROVERB

THE TOWN SEEMS to have arrived at an unannounced milestone. Whereas, in the past, almost all our collective energy was directed *against* something, toward *stopping* some outrage or other, now finally it seems to be directed *toward* building.

Only one major effort *against* something comes immediately to mind. That is the fight against Rolf's lodge and condominiums. We have spent so many dreary days with the Planning Commission, the supervisors, state agencies, officials, and so on, wrangling endlessly. We have fought sewers, road widenings, oil spills, marinas, restaurants, subdivisions, building codes. Much of that frenzy seems to have ebbed. We have gotten stronger and wiser.

The tourist cars still arrive in ever-increasing numbers. We still go over-the-hill to work, escape, shop. Land prices and speculation continue to threaten. But the town is brimming with activity directed inward toward itself rather than outward against various out-of-town menaces.

The days of heroics, when it sufficed to give some over-the-hill officials a good roasting seem to have slipped past. We are turned back on ourselves to see what we will make of our situation.

Paradise Valley Produce is chugging along. Numerous other agricultural projects are being started. People seem to be enervated by the notion of greater self-sufficiency as well as frightened by the apparent vulnerability of the world outside. A new school, Full-Circle, for neurologically handicapped children, is being founded and built by a group of people from town in an old apple orchard along the highway. They are already stockpiling building materials, surplus goods, and salvaged lumber so they can begin construction as soon as the rain stops. The New Land Fund has received its state tax exemption and awaits word from the feds. This would allow us to accept contributions (money or land) and allow the donor to write it off his taxes as a charitable deduction. The Briones Tabernacle Choir is rehearsing for its spring concert with Maestro Young, a concert pianist. The poets are reading. The PUD sits on the future of the sewer like a brood hen on an egg. The Community Plan is in the final stages of labor. Ocean Parkway is falling off into the ocean. David, the new postmaster, has hung plants all over the PO, taken the bars off the window, and removed the picture of Richard Nixon. The women's group is grouping. The day-care center is alive and well. The highway sign is down.

Scheming and plotting go on at every level.

MICHAEL the Butcher hails from Earling, Shelby County, Iowa. Michael learned meat-cutting from his father, who is presently mayor of the town. One should not be deceived by the fact that Michael is a butcher. He also has a strong literary bent.

He is one of the surprisingly numerous people living here who have split up with their wives, with both surviving the painful aftermath and both staying in town. From his watchtower position behind the meat display case at the Store, he has come closer than anyone to knowing everybody who lives here.

Today, he is walking around town with a smirk on his face. It's his day off from the Store. He has a pad in one hand, and a pencil in the other. He walks into Scowley's, the Bar, the Store, around the street, past the bookstore, up to the post office.

"Hey," he says, cocking his elbows out and putting the pencil to the pad in mock cub-reporter anticipation of a scoop, "you got any news?"

Michael has decided to put out a triweekly town paper on the printing press which people in the town bought several

DAVID THE POSTMASTER

years ago through endless bake sales, benefit dances, concerts, and contributions.

No one quite believes that anyone could get anything out three times a week in Briones. But when you ask him, Michael just keeps smiling.

SEVERAL dozen poets live in town. A handful are "well published" and quite well known. A large number of others appear to be just short of the big time. They publish a lot in small poetry magazines and spend a good deal of time reading and writing for each other and for the town.

Poets from elsewhere often cruise through town (frequently from New York). They make guest appearances, and often bewilder everyone but those local people who are in the poet's fraternity. It is a tight fraternity.

By and large, people in town have trouble relating to poetry which is not about them. But they love Briones poems. Particularly if they are funny. It is this genre of comic self-reflection which gets the biggest hand at the readings.

These poets are like animals of a single species in the jungle. They call, hoot, laugh, jeer, and mumble during each other's readings; a private preserve of intraprofessional communication; a Shriner's secret handshake.

So many undiscovered poets all baring their souls to one degree or another. Edging up to that great and artful moment of self-confession.

Tonight, Joanne has organized a group of poets to give a benefit reading at the community center to help buy a plate camera for the town press. There is a fire in the brick fireplace. Ikon is passed out in the corner. People sit on rugs on the floor. Terry and Michael the Butcher sell paper cups of wine for twenty-five cents.

Joanne draws names out of a pot. And one after another the poets read:

"OUR TOWN"

Faded army blankets stretched over the tops of
some huge fallen eucalyptus trunks
might not sound like much of a house
unless you are from the outskirts of Rabat
but that's how some folks live in Briones.
What we call a condo's three or four wrecked Chevrolets
strung out along a dirt road.
We live in palaces constructed of mud
where it's so quiet you can hear the rats
piss on Kleenex.

LEWIS MACADAMS
TOM CLARK

WE are drowning in paper.

We are knee-deep in writing a county-required environmental impact report for Paradise Valley, a forty-page *summa theologica* on our plans and their effect on the natural condition of the valley.

Conundrum: At the same time the state and county are requiring that we write this statement on the local environment, we are being required to compromise that same

environment with power lines, flush toilets, wide-graded roads, subdivision, oversized code houses, and extravagantly wasteful water supply systems.

Internal contradictions in the heart of the dragon.

As laborious as it is to write them, environmental impact reports are good things to understand. Their advent has changed the whole relationship between development and conservation. And if you are into stopping destructive kinds of development, their EIR is usually the place to start.

Environmental impact reports are now required by state and federal law (via the California Environmental Quality Act and the National Environmental Protection Act) for all public and private projects that would "significantly" affect the environment. If a developer feels there would be no significant impact, he can file a "negative declaration," just as the state did when

MICHAEL THE BUTCHER

it wanted to widen the highway. But since all projects are bound to have some "significant" impact on the environment, it is not difficult to challenge either a "negative declaration" or a finished EIR and show why it is not a true reflection of the project's impact. If inadequacy is proved, the whole project will be held up while the report is redone. In most cases, such a delay is incredibly costly, if not fatal. At best, a development can be stopped. At worst, it can be slowed down.

Sometimes, slowing down a project is sufficient to stop it. When a large project starts going off schedule and losing momentum, it often is finished for good. The interested parties go on to something else, or just give up, when they see increased costs to consultants for more EIR's, legal costs, taxes, and rising materials costs which throw their whole financial projection out of whack.

If one is willing to fight, there is almost no project which cannot be stopped by grabbing onto its EIR: roads, housing developments, dams, shopping centers, irrigation projects, resorts . . . you name it.

We work all day at Steve's writing, researching, compiling, rewriting. Everything from wild flowers and soils to sewage and seismic conditions is included.

Everybody starting to get punchy.

Russ puts *Songs of the Humpback Whale* on the hi-fi. We turn off the lights and listen in the dark.

Strange, lonesome, high-pitched howls. Squeaking. Peeping. Guttural rumbles and roars. French-horn-like sounds.

Eyes closed. Thinking of these mighty creatures. Gentle creatures who have been hunted to the verge of extinction by some small, distant relation who stands upright on two hind legs, wears clothes, smokes cigarettes, and lives in square houses.

The sounds of these whales fill my heart with awe and sadness. Singing unknown harmonies beneath the sea. Answering each other in haunting patterns of whale-talk. Eerie electronic music with a soul.

Sometimes it sounds like an orchestra tuning up. Sometimes,

only two thin high voices speak to each other in almost inaudible tones.

Whales have blood. Whales are warm. Their blood vessels are so large that a trout could comfortably swim in some. They nurse their young calves. Bulls, cows, calves.

They say that if you ever look into the eye of a living whale, you never forget it.

THE road is slick with rain driving back from over-the-hill.

Hit the intersection at 9:30. It's dark.

Sheriff's car blocks the road. Blinking lights.

Joe gets out with a flashlight and walks over to the truck. Windshield wipers slapping time.

"Tree down up by the cemetery," he says, peering into the dark cab. "Road crew oughtta be here any moment. But you might just as well go into Jerry's Farmhouse for a cup of coffee."

"Oak tree?"

"No, bay."

"Yeah. Shallow roots."

"Yeah. Right across the road. Wires down, too."

"OK. Thanks for letting me know."

Rain pouring down through the beaming headlights.

Bob pulls up in his truck. We stand outside in the rain talking.

"Jesus, I gotta get home," he says. "All my goddamn worms are gonna get away!"

"Worms? You got a worm ranch?"

"Yeah. I got a couple thousand. Tryin' to get somethin' together I can do in town. Man! I'm really worried! Got about two thousand dollars in those worms," he says, looking blankly down the road.

"Do worms split in the rain?"

"Oh, for sure! It's not just the rain. Like if the barometer drops, they split too. Like, in forty-five minutes, they're all gone."

"Fast, huh?"

"Yeah. I keep 'em in these earth-filled deals. I got home late one night when it was raining, and jeez! There were worms all over the place . . . like, crawling up the walls."

"How do you stop them?"

"Well, like take last night, for instance. I was up all night after the power went out in that storm. Had to run my little gas generator. You gotta keep a light on 'em or they split. I don't know how come I woke up when the power went off. Just lucky, I guess. So I had to spend the whole night fillin' that one-quart gas tank on the generator. Then today they wouldn't fill up my jerry can at the gas station 'cause of the energy crisis."

"So, you think all the worms will be gone by the time you get home?"

"Hell! I hope not. And the wife just left an hour ago."

"Maybe you could call a neighbor?"

"Naw. The dog would probably kill 'em if they went over. I keep him so I won't get ripped off. And, aw hell, it's a trip turning on the lights. Nobody'd be able to figure it out."

"Sure is a lot of trouble in these worms."

"Yeah. But even if they split, I'll have the eggs left. They'll hatch out. Ya know, those worms are all muscle. They can just stretch out and get through any hole at all. No stoppin' 'em when it rains."

"Earthworms?"

"No. They're a special bait worm, red devils. I'm getting the contracts all around the Bay for bait. There's one guy I heard about who made eighty thousand dollars a year doing worms."

"Wow!"

"Yeah. I want to get into the mail order business. Like in *Field and Stream*. See, I'm real worried about this energy thing. I think we gotta all get some kind of employment we can do at home."

"Right."

"I wouldn't mind doing the landscaping or planting trees on the sewer land. We gotta keep as much of that work as possible for local people. We're all feeling the squeeze. Isn't that what Alioto is all about in San Francisco? This business about a local economy or some kind of agriculture has gotta get going."

Highway Department grader arrives.

Hauls away a huge tree.

The small collection of waiting cars head south.

Hit the turnoff. Another tree is down and has knocked out the town power.

Darkness everywhere. No streetlights by the School. Dim orange kerosene lamps in house windows. Flickering candles.

The absence of electricity and light creates a wonderful disorienting feeling. The darkness is punctuated only by occasional headlights.

The answer to the energy crisis: Turn off the juice.

VERNON's proposed new restaurant has just faded away.

Money tight. Costs of building materials going higher and higher. Fuel crisis makes tourist mobility more uncertain. Town opposition confronted him with the possibility of a long, costly fight.

The Community Center announces that it will hold a town meeting on the pressing problems of dogs (too many) and motorcycles (mufflerless, and driven up and down the dirt roads for kicks by kids).

Irwin proposes a solution to both problems: Rub raw dog meat on the motorcycles.

WE are going to have a baby.

It took about one week for the news to spread all over town.

We are already being buried in bales of secondhand baby clothes, childbirth books, hand-me-down cradles, and maternity clothes.

SUDDENLY, like a bolt of lightning, the Energy Commission gets a grant for almost $10,000 from a foundation to do alternative energy projects around town.

The grant was made directly to the people who will do the work.

A fairy godmother story.

A sewer project in our neighboring town, to which we were once joined via the old regional Kennedy Plan, has been defeated at the polls.

People feared it would have allowed for too much growth and destroyed the "village rural atmosphere."

At present there is a ban on new septic tanks because of dense clay and poor percolation. The ban is, in effect, a building moratorium.

The night of the election, a fight erupted at Elwood's Bar, normally a peaceful watering trough. As one witness described it, in the paper. "The sewer issue caused one man to be arrested for assault with a deadly weapon (an ax) and resisting arrest."

Pickets appeared at the crossroads the day before the election. Their signs read, THE SEWER PROPOSAL STINKS. ALL POWER TO THE SEPTIC TANKS!

THE town's first gasoline line forms today.

The cars stretch all the way from Al's Mobil to just short of the beach.

At first, people are pissed at being delayed. But slowly the line turns into a social event of major proportions.

The weather is reasonable. Everyone starts getting out of their cars and chatting. To save gas, some push their cars as the line moves up (extremists). Hundreds of vital messages are transmitted. Ikon is hired by someone to sit in his truck and wait in line. Some people do their laundry at the laundromat while their cars are parked out front. Others drop by the post office and get their mail.

People speak of the possibility of a budding street vendor industry to serve the daily line:

"Getch yur nice hot coffee, folks! Ice cream, candy, hot dogs, and painted turtles for the kids!"

"Shine! Getch yur shoes shined!"

THE first issue of the *Hearsay News* hits the stands, hot off the town's Mesa Press.

Written by Mike the Butcher. Printed by Mick the Printer.

Item: "Billy Spangler fell off a desk at school while watching a movie and broke his left arm. Lots of other people seem to have broken bones lately, too."

Item: "The PUD voted last night to halt the growing number of buses in town by charging higher rates for multiple hookups. They also voted to lower existing water rates."

During the last few years, the town has found itself playing host to a growing number of "hippie-type" vans, buses, and converted delivery trucks which park on vacant lots, by the side of the road, or on a friend's property.

They use water. Kids go to school. But they pay no taxes. Many of the older people do not like this "element." Even some of the younger people agree there is a certain injustice in the presence of these transient vehicles while other property holders are not allowed to build houses because of the water moratorium.

On the other hand, some folks like the vans and the van people. Vans provide low-cost housing. People don't use up much resources. Most hand-carry water, use kerosene lamps, and heat with small potbellied stoves.

"And if there's enough old abandoned cars and vans junked around," says one longtime funkologist, "the price of land and taxes will go down. Rich folks don't want to move in and have cocktail parties looking out at an overturned hydromatic Olds 88.

"I say, keep it junky. You get a better class of people: a lower class," he says with a devilish grin.

MEET Mike, Lloyd, and Mark bicycling up Shoefly Hill. They announce that they have just put the solar collector on the School art room roof. They plan to hook up the tank and finish the whole hot-water heater in a few days.

Various other energy projects around town moving in fits and starts. Bob is working on a windmill to pump irrigation water out of an old well on his land for a garden. Mike is working on a solar space heater. Mark is doing a solar space heater and water heater for Scowley's.

A judge over-the-hill rules that a huge water district in the eastern developed part of the county cannot reject further hookups because of a "threatened" water shortage. He orders that water be furnished to a new 292-house development as soon as the EIR is approved. Clearly directing his comments to the no-growth majority at the district, the judge says that the district is "obligated whether it [is] popular or not" to supply water to present *and* future users. He finds that the water district has "no jurisdiction or powers in the field of zoning, land use, density or population control."

What seemed to lose the case for the district was that it had only a "threatened shortage" rather than an existing one.

We have an existing shortage. Our moratorium seems safe.

Slowly the courts and the legislature will be forced to deal with people trying to slow things down through utilities, because they sure haven't been very successful with planning.

PARADISE Valley.

Kelly, age ten, gets lice.

Michael, age eight, proudly announces that he has not had a bath in a tub for three months since he visited his grandparents in Miami. (But, he swims in the creek.)

Nina douses Kelly's hair with kerosene.

The lice are purged.

The county replies to Paradise Valley on permits.

It insists both that permits be applied for and that approval will be impossible without electricity, flush toilets, running water at twenty pounds per square inch pressure . . . the whole nightmare.

The health robots lead the field in lobotomized responses.

Essential problem: THEY have figured out that the average Joe uses at least seventy-five gallons a day. So all their septic tank and waste water treatment requirements are sized to meet this projection.

If you take away the demon flush toilet (illegal), you reduce per-capita-daily-average-Joe-consumption to about forty-eight gallons. But you still have to have a large septic tank and dig eight hundred feet of leach field calculated to their seventy-five gallons a day. Means more tractor work, more plastic pipe, more gravel, more money. Waste.

They haven't got a box to check for any variation.

Circuits are blowing.

Someone wants to save water and doesn't want a flush toilet, and the whole pyramid topples in chaos.

Greg has not had a bath in a year and a half. He thinks soap and water kill the good bacteria on his skin and allow him to catch colds.

I don't know how his old lady feels, but I don't think he's had a cold in recent memory.

"I wanna tell ya, now. We had fifteen volunteer firemen on this job, and then there was another twenty guys, and all of 'em worked just like hell. And the thing of it is, this whole town could have gone up in smoke."

Joe has on his white fire chief's hat. Cigar in his mouth. Bloodshot eyes.

It's late morning downtown. The smell of water-soaked charcoal fills the whole Wharf Road area.

Bill, Jim, and Ernie Tacherra are throwing burned wood on a truck. Charcoal all over their faces. Dirty black boots and pants. Tired, shocked eyes.

Tarantino's restaurant is totally destroyed. Burned right to the ground. They took Tony T. to the hospital early this morning. Crazy, sad, confused. Rubbing his eyes and his temples with his seventy-six-year-old hands as his restaurant exploded into a boiling ball of flame. His restaurant and home are gone now, just weeks before its sale to the Tacherra's was to come out of escrow.

Fire trucks are everywhere. Hoses crisscross, in the street from hydrants. There are large puddles of ink-black water in the street.

"Jesus, I'm tellin ya," says Joe, "if the tide hadn't been up so we could pump outa the Lagoon, I don't know what we wudda done!"

The loveable but large ugly signs are burned in half, blackened and flapping in the wind. Everything is dripping. People stand around talking, not quite knowing what to do. Watching. Commiserating.

The sheriff arrives with a badge on a civilian suit. Waxed mustache. Friendly face.

He talks quietly to several of the residents of the upstairs apartments. He sits with Lana on the bookstore steps. She is exhausted and spaced-out, and puts her head on his shoulder for a moment. All her things are gone except her daughter, whom she managed to rescue.

"Yes. All right. Now tell me everything that you lost," says the sheriff, taking notes.

"You mean, even family photos and things like that?" she asks.

"Yes."

Someone drags a smoldering mattress out onto the sidewalk. Rips it open. Sprays it with a fire hose.

The insurance agent arrives. Already several rumors about the insurance situation are floating around town. People wondering about the future. Someone mentions McDonald's hamburgers. Someone else talks of a town park.

"And ya know, we just bought a thousand dollars' worth of wine and another thousand dollars' worth of abalone steaks," says Ernie, standing in the street looking blankly at the mess. "Last night we didn't take the checks and cash home." He looks at the charred cash register in the back of Joe's pickup. "All gone. Just all gone."

Clarence and Bea, who arrived in town in the 1940s, stand and watch, shaking their heads.

"Ya know what we oughtta do?" says Clarence. "We should get a volunteer group and clean up this mess so they can build over. That's the way it used to be. But I suppose they'll have a bulldozer in."

"Ole Tony hadda coupla grand stashed away in there somewhere," says a surfer. "Must have burned. Guess he was lucky to get out at all. One guy jumped out of the second floor in the back and cut his foot up real bad."

A pickle jar appears on the butcher counter at the Store with a sign, TO HELP REPLACE LOST ITEMS IN THE FIRE. There is about three dollars in change and a single dollar bill in it.

TONY has been arrested for burning down his own restaurant.

They say he poured out several cans of vegetable oil and lit it shortly before dawn.

The local paper reports that the "seventy-six-year-old Tarantino was despondent over the death of his wife in 1971, and the thought of losing his restaurant."

They give Tony a psychiatric exam and put him in jail.

What is he thinking tonight behind bars at the Civic Center?

FOUR men in plastic raincoats, holding clipboards, stand around scraping the mud off their rubbers on the grass as though it were dog shit.

Gray skin. Faint odor of skin bracer. Smooth-shaven.

The county and state health authorities arrive in Paradise Valley to check out plans for waste water disposal and sewage treatment.

"Well, at least ya know if you flush it, it's gone. Down under the ground," says one official. Someone from the valley mumbles something about high winter ground water and danger of contaminating the creek.

"Gee willikers," says the highest-up county man (to whom the two others defer), "I spent five years out in the San Joaquin Valley with those migrant labor camps. All had privies. Pit privies. Those Mexicans just crapped into the ground, and . . ."

"Were they legal?" asks a Paradise denizen rhetorically.

"Well, I don't know. It was different out there," says the official.

"Same state health code, isn't it?"

"Well, this is Marin County. And we're not letting anything but flush toilets go in in this county."

"I seen studies where they've even found cysts that hatch out of wind-rowed dried treated sewage sludge," says the state man.

Feel like we are making application to bury atomic waste with a half-life of thirty-three thousand years.

You'd think shit was the number one killer in America.

Tony T. bailed out of jail.

He immediately jumps bail after declaring that he burned down his restaurant because he was in league with the police and Foreign Legion against criminal elements.

A bench warrant is issued.

A crazy old man somewhere near the end of his life is on the loose alone.

As gasoline prices hit sixty cents at Al's Mobil, the energy crisis expires.

No more lines. No more panic. Plenty of good, expensive gasoline is available.

Cars have once again begun to fan out across the country-side like swarms of locusts.

The Golden Gate Bridge reports an increase in daily usage.

Commuter buses report a slackening patronage.

The creeping meatball triumphs as Mr. and Mrs. America slide back in behind the wheel.

The man on the TV news says, "And it's gonna be a great day for a drive!"

Once again, the Sunday orgy of automobiles spills out along the coast. Wharf Road again choked with traffic. Passive faces behind clean, rolled-up windows. New cars driving obliviously down a dead-end road.

Winnebagos and Aristocrat motor trailers and other RV's (recreational vehicles) crawl forth from the chrysalis of the gas shortage to make timid trips north. Like model airplanes circling on guide wires, they dare not lumber more than a half-a-tank radius away into the uncertainties of the gasless unknown.

We are back where we began. But a fix for our cars costs twice as much as before.

We celebrate April Fool's Day with a planning meeting.

Long, animated discussion on the final growth-rate figure for the Plan.

People confused between what they want and what they think the county will accept.

Someone suggests that we stop talking for five minutes, and all try and think what it is we really want.

Lights go out.

People sit quietly in the dark. Deep breathing. Wind in the trees outside.

Slowly, Rex begins to speak again. One by one we go around the room in the dark. Each person speaks briefly.

Gail says she is thinking of moving away from town because Briones is getting too impersonal and slick.

Bob thinks we do not have the moral right to keep people out.

Francis thinks we should try to stick with the proposed county growth rate of 1 or 2 percent.

Bill thinks we should just say, "No more!"

Rex feels that Briones has always been the cutting edge, and that we should try for a lower growth rate, even if it's unprecedented.

Ponderosa Pine says we are already overpopulated with homo sapiens, and that the balance between man and other creatures has already been lost.

Libby thinks we should just decide upon a reasonable growth-rate figure and get the Plan done.

Amy thinks we should protect our home as best we can by stopping where it seems to be fit.

Mike thinks that more growth will only lead to more crime and a lot of fast rich people.

Now, does Briones need a community bath?

We could have a large hot Japanese pool, or a Finnish sauna with an ocean-water plunge at the end. Or an Indian steamhouse. A medicine house is really good for colds, backaches, depression, tiredness, and it would give everyone a place to get naked together in winter.

You could emerge from the heat into the fog at dusk and glow.

Dr. Mike

A proposal for the site of Tarantino's charred remains.

Only one problem in the way: Dr. Mike doesn't own the land.

But since we're only dreaming, how about a zocalo?

The zocalo is the Mexican town square, a park with a band-stand in the middle. Benches around it under trees. No town or city is without one.

The zocalo is a meeting place, a place which gives people encouragement to do nothing but sit, talk, read, think, get together.

In the zocalo, there is always hope for the lonely, always that sense that something might happen which is so totally absent from the company of TV.

And something usually does happen if you spend enough time in the zocalo. It is like a large, free outdoor café. It is a place for others to go just to escape the four walls that surround them at home. A place to flee one's loved ones. A place to hear music on Saturday night. A place to catch up on the news and gossip around town. A place for lovers to sit.

Cold drinks, kids selling balloons, children playing, old men sitting, shoe-shine boys chattering and snapping their rags, people staring, snoozing, searching. That's the zocalo.

The old New England towns made a stab at it with their town squares and commons. They too seemed to be groping to give their communities a center. But it ended up being too chilly, too formal, just too close to those beautiful, cold white churches for anyone to feel really comfortable hanging out or relaxing.

Towns need centers. They need the gravity that surrounds a center and ties together all the outlying parts.

THE rain is gone now.

Sun, wind, blue sky.

Spring is unmistakably here. People out strolling. Working in their gardens turning up the sod. Fixing houses.

The whole town feels alive.

Whatever it is that makes Briones special is present in a large dose today. Everyone seems to feel it. It radiates.

A group of thirteen or fourteen toilet revolutionaries gather at the PUD this morning. They reluctantly come inside out of the fine weather.

Judy, Gary's supervisorial administrative assistant, arrives.

The subject: The county's refusal to grant permits for flushless composting privies or Clivus toilets (dry Swedish model).

Same old issues. Want to save water, save shit for fertilizer, save expense, and stop ground water contamination. Behind the toilet challenge is the whole issue of building codes designed for suburbia and then being forced on people who want to get back into small-scale multifamily agriculture.

"You know, sometime the supervisors as legislators are going to have to face the fact that their laws run right across the grain of most of their goals, like environmental protection, low-cost housing, the maintenance of agriculture," says Greg.

"I know," says Judy. "Gary and I went to a Chamber of Commerce meeting out here a little while ago, and a whole bunch of ranchers were there. And, you know, they are really on your side. One old guy got up and was all upset about the health and building codes. 'We came here fifty years ago,' he said. 'We had a few thousand dollars to start farming. Hell, if we came now, we wouldn't get nowhere!' "

The talk wanders off to the subject of secession. Everyone

talking with some displeasure about the county's role. Lots of joking and bravura.

"OK," says Judy, "if you want to change things, don't go to the supervisors with four inches of paper. They'll just be bored. And if you go in there and start talking about the Kaka Dragon, they won't listen.

"What you ought to do is get your facts and experts together, and then go in and try and connect up how your hassle fits in with the building codes and health. Then try to make the connection of how these things make it impossible to do what everyone wants to see done.

"You know, what is so unbelievable is that the county's own ordinance on individual waste treatment systems specifically gives the supervisors or inspectors latitude to approve any kind of system if it works," says Greg. "But they just act like they are bound hand and foot to accepted practices. They confuse their own prejudices for law."

Finally, the meeting ends. Everyone heads down to Scowley's for a cheeseburger.

Mark already has most of the solar heater up in the back. It consists of a huge ten-foot-high plywood panel holding hundreds of feet of black plastic pipe. Mark claims it will supply ten days of hot dishwater and heat without sun.

He turns on the faucet. The water coming out the other end is so hot it makes steam.

The energy is sure here today.

NEW mural on the bathroom wall at Scowley's.

Lovely deep colors on the faded wall.

A mandala of intertwining morning glory vines and blossoms. A hummingbird drinks nectar at the center.

Painted by Steve. Shy street person. Arrived several years ago and crashed in the loft at Future Studies office. Loves animals. Plays piano. Has just kind of been around all this time without going too far over the edge.

In minuscule, carefully drawn letters around the bottom of the mural is an inscription:

To the people of Briones. You have given me a shelter from a stormy world. I cannot find the words to express the full measure of my love for all of you. So, therefore, I dedicate in your name and give to you this painting with love.

Backyard Steve

WHARF Road is crowded with people milling around and following the boat on its cradle as it moves toward the water.

Today Ebba and Angela launch the boat on which they have worked for years. It is masterfully built, and has attracted a processional of helpers and of people enjoying the launching as a social event.

There is a tradition of boat-launching in town.

Lewis writes a poem, which he is fond of reading at poetry confabs as if it were a Nordic saga.

THE LAUNCHING OF THE *ANNIE*

I was still drunk and pink-eyed from the previous night's consciousness seizure (liquid ozone mixed with Prell and chased by fire), so that by the time we got halfway to Johnny's I had to let Phoebe carry the baby so I could bear down on just walking and carrying what was left of the Yellowstone Bourbon. We were late, as usual. People had been working since sun-up, and by the time we got there a big crew of humans already had the boat up on Johnny's trailer and were trying to hold it in place while Johnny and Danny and another guy named Michael-from-Canada hammered in blocks and bracings and tied the boat down for the trip downtown. I jumped in between Shao and another Mike. The fog rolled back and I could see the words BON VOYAGE ANNIE painted in big red capital letters on the roof of a new house going up a few blocks away. Johnny and Danny were yelling out orders and jumping around and setting things up and hammering. The boat felt so mammoth, we were all having to lean into it to keep it in place. The bow above our heads was

EBBA AND ANGELA LAUNCH THEIR BOAT

dark green, with yellow, yellow eyes that Philip Whalen had painted on sometime the day before. Everyone around the boat I talked to agreed that, yes, Philip knew right where to paint the eyes for the launching of the *Annie*; and today is launching day, so everybody's here to see what they can do. Me, I can hold up my section of the stern with Peter and Shao, and I can hand my bourbon around to warm up everybody's belly around the boat. But I save the very last sip for Johnny himself, because Johnny's the chief of this operation, which is to wheel this boat into town and launch it and sail it north with his family—to an island in the Georgia Straits, it turns out. And Danny's own beautiful dory *Eucalyptus*, and his and Richard's *White Boat* to come, that took our friends Danny and Bonnie south, will soon follow the *Annie* into the water.

Johnny built the trailer too. "Local materials," I can still hear him saying. And I know the trailer will do, because about a week ago six of us tore down an old house on Fern Road and hauled about ten thousand pounds of wooden cement molds back to Hal's lot on it. Then, while Lynne, his wife, took pictures, Johnny cut open a fifth of Cutty Sark, took a hit, and passed it around. He said, "We got a jeep here to pull this thing down to the beach if you wanna do it that way." But of course, uh-uh. Everybody finished off the fifth quick, and about twenty men and women set out to push the boat and trailer down the dirt road to the pavement and into town. When we got on the pavement, Danny climbed up on the trailer and garlanded the *Annie* with eucalyptus, and a few new gallon bottles of Gallo wine appeared. Cars were forced from the road by the parade, with Danny from the prow of the boat shouting out chants and sounds like "Ye-ah BOAT!" (Frankly, totally ripped.) I was sweating and high and slightly crying. People were out on their porches to see the launching.

When we got to the parking lot on the cliff where Ocean Parkway turns into Terrace Road we stopped, and there stood Piero's Circus in the form of a white dragon with ten legs and a face covered with burnished shells. In front of the dragon, people were blowing long copper horns, and the horns boomed away anything that could hold the boat back as we rolled it carefully down the hill. Cymbals clashed and we swayed. When we made the

turn and then the dip at the bottom of Terrace, Lynnie sighed and said, "From here on, it's easy."

Down Brighton to Wharf Road, down the Wharf Road ramp to the beach and into the mouth of the bay. Everybody in town joined the parade that day. The joints came flying. I was waist deep in water helping drag the *Annie*, guide the *Annie* into the tide. And I sang, "Bless this boat, and bless the builders, and bless the captain and bless the bearers, and bless the fishermen and bless the blessers, and bless the Ocean that sustains us all." All the braces tore away, and the boat splashed in, riding high in the water. Johnny climbed on and Lynnie handed Annie and Josh to him. Then he helped Lynnie aboard. Danny, Bonnie, and Steve climbed aboard, and they poled the boat back into the Lagoon to fit the sails on Kent Island. And we all climbed onto the bed of the trailer, and let the jeep haul us back up to Armstrong's for a gigantic celebratory chicken-and-wine high-noon luncheon.

LEWIS MACADAMS

Lewis Mumford strikes from the bowels of the Associated Press in our Sunday paper:

I think the Dark Ages are here, only we don't know it.

I think the small community is going to come back into its own. We know by plenty of evidence, which has piled up over a long period, that people enjoy living in small towns more than they enjoy living in big cities. . . . Until the beginning of this century, almost until 1940, four-fifths of the population of this world lived in villages and country towns on about the same level as the neolithic village. Now only 15 percent of the population is necessary to produce our entire agricultural output. We have industrial farming. Industrial farming will cease to operate as soon as it becomes unprofitable. What are we going to do when the cutback begins in agricultural consumption? It's already happening in every family. People cannot afford to buy the food that is being raised at the inflated prices being offered.

This is going to get worse, not better. It will get worse until we have more local food production. That brings me to the second solution. The first solution to the energy problem is to use solar energy. The second is to grow food wherever it's possible to grow food, not just where it's profitable. That brings us to my neighbor's lawn. In another five years, they'll have a big garden.

Now, then, there's the third answer, you see: manual work. Doing more of the work that is done by machine by human beings. This doesn't mean to say that we abandon machines. We abandon our dependence on machines.

Bill and Amy pour the slab for their pigsty today. The pregnant mother pig arrives tomorrow. She will farrow in a few months. Already Bill is talking about building a cold-storage locker where local people could hang and store slaughtered cattle.

"If a bunch of us went in on it, we could do it," he says, and then gives a special grin which I have learned to identify as coming after proposed schemes which cost a lot of money.

"There's no reason this town can't be self-sufficient on pork. And do I love pork!"

THERE are cushions and rugs on the floor of the Community Center. Candles in dishes flicker around the room and make accentuated shadows.

Several people are softly playing music on flutes and guitars in the corner.

Barbara sells tickets as people enter.

Mike the Butcher stands behind a table of gallon wine jugs like a pinboy at a bowling alley. He serves people wine in small yellow and blue Dixie Cups.

On the floor is a large scaly green papier-mâché dragon head. Its eyes sparkle. A large red felt tongue hangs limply out of its toothy mouth.

Tonight is Dragon Night.

What is Dragon Night?

No one really knows since it has never happened in town before. Even Piero and his troupe do not know. And Piero, the town's self-appointed jongleur and circus master, has organized it.

PERHAPS Dragon Night is just an excuse to get together and perform for one another. Everyone is invited. Several hundred are present.

The door to the kitchen opens, and bowls of salad and trays of eggplant parmegiana and garlic bread are carried out.

People sit on the floor, eat, talk, and laugh.

The acts come on. A bizzare rendition of Little Red Riding Hood. No words. Just dancers moving against a movie screen playing Piero's movies.

The old ripped curtain on the stage is suddenly pulled back, revealing David and his brass band playing oom-pah-pah music and mariachi serenades. People clap and cheer.

Bottles of champagne appear from nowhere, and are served in plastic champagne glasses with a comic aura of fallen majesty about them.

Bill's movies blink on. Sometimes the eye of genius is even present in a home movie.

Piero calls for performers from the floor.

Craig the Dancer rises. He teaches a dance class. His motto is: IT'S NOT THE MEAT, IT'S THE MOVEMENT.

He dances with Betty Buns, garbed in a kimono with chopsticks in her hair.

One after another, unsuspecting people are called forward. Shyness is overcome by wine.

The room is full of a deep fascination which only comes when it is one's friends who are the entertainers.

Songs, poems, speeches, dancing, buffoonery.

The dragon head is picked up and marched around the room. Adults and children follow, clapping in cadence. The brass band inadvertently leads the whole assemblage out the door.

"No! No! There is more!" says Piero in his heavy Italian accent. The band turns back. Three unlikely instrumentalists. Grinning David playing trombone. Blue knit hat, baggy pants. George on sax. Tom Chestnut on horn, breaking periodically into exquisite Wagnerian solos.

The room is full of people with a growing number of years

PIERO   [171]

shared between them. Marriages, affairs, children, political battles, houses, causes won and lost. It is a room of relationships so complicated and fragile that no one could ever precisely plot it on a graph.

There are secrets shared between two people. Secrets shared with the town. People dancing next to others to whom they used to be married; separate lives that somehow meet and touch again on nights like this.

When did Dragon Night begin? When does it end? It just trails off. The actors and the audience are one and the same.

Finally, Piero takes the dragon head out into the street and places it on the sidewalk outside the Bar.

Inside, people are drinking and dancing to the jukebox.

There is a gladness about. It is Piero's magic. Ringleader of the circus of ourselves.

MOST officials remain convinced that agriculture is dead as a way of life on this coast. They will admit that existing cattle and dairy ranches can be expected to limp along with tax breaks, loan assistance for feedlot pollution control (manure which washes into rivers and creeks), and other assorted assistance. But they almost haughtily reject the possibility that agriculture on any smaller scale is "viable."

What is viable?

Mike has bought a cow, a $450 Jersey 4-H'er which he has been keeping up at Bill's. He has been getting about three gallons of milk a day, and is selling what he cannot use.

Bill has slaughtered his pigs. We bought a half of one, which fills our freezer like a solid block. It is delicious, sweet meat, unlike any pork I have ever eaten. Tonight we had breakfast: Bill's sausage, eggs from Paradise, local apples for dessert.

Bob has pressed and pasteurized fifty gallons of apple cider in old gallon wine jugs. He is making his own beer and wine, which he bottles in recycled commercial quart beer and wine bottles.

A community vegetable garden has been organized on a piece of the sewer land. Meetings and parties have been held.

The jars for contributions in the liquor store and the Store are filled with change.

At the ranch, Bobby Hefflefinger has slaughtered some beef cattle and sold the meat to the Store. Scowley's advertises "Heffleburgers."

Slowly, the notion that one can raise much of what one eats is becoming more of a reality. It is not easy work. But the food tastes good, and it gives me immeasurable satisfaction to sit at the table, look down at my plate, and know where each thing came from.

THE *Hearsay News* has been coming out regularly three times a week and now has a separate editor for each day. It's effect has been profound. Suddenly the town has a brain, a central information center.

The paper includes everything and anything from hot news on the latest development in Rolf's proposed subdivision to PUD news, poems, jokes, drawings, articles in questionable taste, ads, sports, schedule of events, lonely hearts column, tide chart, classified ads (twenty-five cents each), and political punditry.

Item: "It can be assumed that Paradise Valley was inhabited by middle- and late-horizon Miwok Indians as early as 2500–1500 B.C. (or 1000 years before the overthrow of Ilium by the Greeks under Agamemnon) until the 1830s and '40s when the majority of the coastal Miwoks were decimated by measles and 'manifest destiny.'"   —From the Paradise Valley EIR

Item: "To brighten the ashen ruins of Tarantino's, Oceana will set up a colorful French Sidewalk Café this Saturday and Sunday. The setting will include an umbrella, cheerful tablecloths, fresh flowers, music, and, most important, Viennese coffee, the best of Briones' home-baked pastries, organic fruit salad, and other choice goodies.

"In the tradition of singing waiters(esses), all orders will be served in the best operatic style."

(Café later closed down by County Health.)

SUE AND BERNICE

THE first community-prepared land-use plan is before the board of supervisors. Ours will be the second.

For months, they have been delivering grand platitudes about the sanctity and urgency of the "planning process." They hate water and sewer building moratoriums. "Leave planning to the planners" is the familiar refrain.

And today, the colossal cave-in. All the hot air about preserving the environment, controlling growth and limiting populations distintegrates into a three-two vote against accepting this model plan which citizens and county planners have been working on for two years.

The first of the area detail plans, which would render the already passed general planning goals into reality, is sent back to the planning commission like a prisoner to Siberia, where it can wallow in more staff "input" and keep the company of hundreds of other meaningless reports and studies.

People groaning with disenchantment and discouragement as the supervisors bring "the people" to that moment when you can hear their faith in government snap.

A gray-haired man in a business suit with a cigar in his mouth uncontrollably yells up at the supervisors as the vote is counted, "Can't you do *anything*?"

"The cosmic wet noodle," says a young man in a beard and blue jean jacket as he heads for the door.

Michael and Gary, the two supervisors who supported and voted for the plan, look pale and drawn.

The Plan is subsequently passed with some changes.

PETER finishes his survey on rents and housing for the Plan, which forever seems to be in the process of "final completion."

Summary: The present renting system in Briones works against the ideals of a strong, self-sufficient community. *Ideally*, every citizen in Briones would be a landed citizen not subject to the capricious and inflationary rent market. Landed citizens are more secure about their source of shelter and are more likely to be concerned for the community's land and water and its social existence.

A permanent resident does not have to "waste" time looking for a new place to rent, and is more likely to understand the history and needs of Briones community life.

The present trends—higher and profit-oriented rents, multiple renting units, over-the-hill advertising for wealthy renters, no leases, and increased pressure to stop the conversion of trucks and buses into semipermanent homes—exacerbate the transient nature of the Briones population, the need to commute, and the elimination of low-income housing.

Renting Conditions. In general, renters in Briones live an incredibly insecure life. Typical stories of "caravanning" between three homes in six months abound. The instability arises from an absence of leases, a fast market of house sales (so that the renter must move when the house is sold), and special conditions attached as conditions of rental (such as vacating on weekends or during the summer months for occupancy by the landlord).

One result is the welcomed acceptance of sheds, house trailers, converted trucks, or studios which serve as bedrooms without bathroom or kitchen facilities.

Costs of Rent. With the increasing popularity of Briones as a place to live, landlords have had no problem finding tenants and raising their rents. The demand for a place to rent, inflation, and a new type of profit-oriented landlordism have produced skyrocketing rents and crowding of renters into single dwellings.

The rents studied cover the period of 1967–74, and a total of sixty-five houses and rooming situations. The rents are minimums and do not include utilities, since most landlords require tenants to pay for these over and above the rent. Further, some rents apply to only "rooms" with shared kitchen, living room, and bathroom, while others represent complete houses.

The percentage of rooms, partially communal households,

and single-family dwellings renting for $100 or below, has decreased steadily from 1970 to 1974. Only 7 percent of the surveyed rents are now $100 or less per month. The percentage of rents above $300 a month has increased from below 10 percent in 1971, to 33 percent in 1974. The rent per bedroom with access to bathroom and kitchen has tripled since 1967.

Many low-income families (earning below $3,000 per year per family) have been forced away from Briones. Many renters have been compelled to find less expensive outbuilding housing with facilities shared in a central house. Others have had to double up, sub-rent part of their dwellings, or go semi-communal in order to make ends meet.

Even such minimal housing as a school bus now rents for between $35 and $100 per month.

The survey reveals two types of landlord: The first hopes to cover house payments (and perhaps insurance and taxes) by renting. This type is more concerned about whom they rent to, and find acceptable only persons who are well-known and have been residents in Briones for at least a few years. These rents have remained stable, usually between $100 and $200 per month.

The second type of landlord is interested in making payments, taxes, and insurance, plus profit. These landlords are not as concerned with who rents, and tend to advertise in newspapers to pick up the wealthier over-the-hill trade, or people who usually commute and are unfamiliar with Briones community life. The rents start at $300 per month. These landlords tend to work against formation of a strong Briones community since they prefer to supply houses to high-priced out-of-towners rather than to already established locals in need of a place to live.

This second type of landlordism has become prevalent only in the last year (mid-1973–mid-1974).

Conclusion. The County-Wide Master Plan recognizes the increasing difficulty for low- and medium-income families and individuals in finding housing in Marin. The elderly and young families with restricted incomes are finding it less and less practicable to live here.

The County Planning Department has suggested that the county try to maintain the 1970 housing-rental mix. But the rise in high-cost rental units in Briones has already made this goal nearly impossible to achieve.

Outlaw buildings and shared households are rapidly becoming the only low-income housing option in Briones.

THE PUD parking lot is filled today with unfamiliar vehicles. Pickups, ranch wagons, a Cadillac, and a few other unidentified large cars.

The office inside is filled with contractors who have shown up for a pre-bid meeting on our sewer contract (including the laboratory, landscaping, pipe laying, fencing, pump stations, etc.). The cost will come close to a million and one-half dollars.

The contractors sit on folding chairs quietly waiting for someone to begin. They are mostly older men. A pot of coffee has been brewed. But the mood in the room is not that of the usual conviviality. Everyone sits in subdued expectation. Only a few local people, who hope to bid on the smaller jobs, step over all the legs and wind their way to the coffee pot, although, for the occasion, Robbie has put away the regular collection of seedy cups and brought out a plastic bag of Styrofoam hot-cups.

Betty Buns has baked a large tray of muffins which sit on a side table. Several local people wolf them down. One contractor, near enough so that acquiring a muffin causes no disturbance, hesitatingly takes one and eats it. The others watch, unsure about their relationship to the muffins, us, the contract, the town.

It is a roomful of strangers.

A black woman from EPA abruptly starts to speak. She intones on from a poop sheet about "equal opportunity." She tells the assemblage that, since federal money is being spent,

12 percent of the labor force must be "Negro, oriental, Indian, or people with a Latin surname."

The contractors look slightly bored and wary.

"OK. But as you know," says Bill, "we are pretty much a white community, and one of the lowest income communities in the county. We would hope that most of these jobs could go to local people rather than to minority people imported from over-the-hill."

The black woman's boss, a white man, takes over to answer the question like a skipper relieving an untutored passenger from the helm of a foundering ship.

He is small. Large Adam's apple. Pleasant. Brooklyn accent. He says that it is impossible, and commences to describe the forms and certificates that bidders must file to guarantee equal opportunity. He explains that any contractor who takes a job paying federal money is bound thereafter to hire 12 percent minority on every subsequent job whether private or government.

The contractors sit stiffly. One man with a Ronald Reagan Brylcreem hairstyle and a can-do look on his face smiles to his foreman and shakes his head.

Will the contractors hire local labor?

Confusion. Several contractors mumble about union labor and picket lines. One guy grins and says, "Sure. There are ways to do it."

Judith breaks her silence and asks, "Well, why couldn't we fill our minority quota with local women carpenters?"

The guy with the Brylcreemed hair does a Roadrunner double-take, and comes up grinning in disbelief.

"That's all we need," says a guy in a blue knit suit and a brush cut. You can hear him thinking. "What's next? Dope addicts and queers?"

Everyone in the room is beginning to wonder if anyone at all will make a bid.

I toy with the idea of getting up and passing the muffins. But something about the response to the women carpenters tells me to stay seated.

ALMOST each day brings reports of more thefts.
Nancy's VW is stolen.
Some roast beef is ripped off from the delicatessen.
Ikon's entire wardrobe is towed away in a van.
Liz returns from camping to find all her bicycles missing.
Crime.

Three or four years ago people seldom locked their doors. Thefts were relatively rare.

Since then, the town has almost doubled in population (although not in numbers of houses), as is shown by the number of registered voters.

January 1970	474
January 1971	565
January 1972	645
January 1973	801
April 1974	912

One draws one's own conclusions.

PARADISE Valley scores major victory!

Having appealed the issue to the most exalted appeals board, Paradise wins an exemption from mandatory hookups to Pacific Gas and Electric. Waivers are granted to that section of the building code which appears to require that all houses be wired to code (costing from $1,500 to $2,000) and hooked into a central power source.

The building appeals board is composed of contractors, plumbers, electricians, and air conditioning specialists. Sounds like a real bunch of baddies, right?

Wrong! They are the most reasonable, thoughtful, considerate "board" we have ever had the pleasure to discuss anything with. They listen, talk, question, learn about our situation.

"Well, it certainly seems right with this here energy shortage. As long as it isn't endangering anyone, I say, OK," says one contractor member.

I start hitching from the Civic Center back home. I get a ride from a big shopping center with a girl who teaches ecology at a local school. We stop at a snarled intersection for a light. Rows and rows of cars wait patiently with their engines idling. Drivers steal furtive looks at the occupants of the adjacent cars. They want to see who their neighbors are in this fleeting traffic jam. Women looking at men. Men looking at women. Kids just staring at whatever fascinates them. Old people staring blankly in front of them, lost in some thought.

Stuck. Everyone stuck, alone.

Get dropped by a blackberry patch beside the road where the berries are fat and sweet.

I stuff myself. Then stuff a bag.

Hands turn purple.

Start hitching again, thinking how I might someday try to explain to some commission about the importance of there being blackberry patches beside the road.

CHANNEL 4 (NBC) reporter and cameraman arrive at Paradise this morning to shoot a short documentary.

Pleasant but speedy reporter with broad colorful tie and jacket with pouch pockets. He loves the valley.

The cameraman is a gardening nut.

Both sympathetic. Spend half a day interviewing us.

The reporter flips out over Nina weeding the garden and carrying wheelbarrow loads of cow shit around.

"Whew! What a beautiful lady," he says.

Greg gives the old $14.95 rap on toilets and growth. Russ and Susan are reluctantly coaxed into posing outside their Army tent.

"Well, the way I figure it," says Russ, not sure whether he likes being on TV, "if it was good enough for me in Vietnam, it's good enough for me here."

"Well, I just think it's fantastic what they're doing," says Barbara on camera, her gray hair blowing in a gentle breeze. "If I was thirty years younger, I'd be here with them."

THE bids on the sewer come in, and they are double the engineer's estimates.

Prices going crazy. Shortages in everything.

"Everything is back-ordered," says one contractor. "Shortages. You can't get delivery on ductile steel pipe for eight months."

Opines old "Tex" Edwards at the PUD meeting, "Wahl, the thing of it is, yew cud have jes as eezy bought up each of 'em houses in yer downtown and tore 'em down, 'stead o' buildin' this here sewer, ya knowwat Ah mean?

"Jes buy 'em up and close 'em down, and yew wouldn't have hardly no need for this here sewer.

"An' it wudda cost yew 'bout the same, ya knowwat Ah mean?"

LOOKING down at the feet in the front row, one sees (1) a pair of Army boots, (2) a pair of black sneakers with long brown laces, (3) a pair of Dr. Oepker's imported orthopedic wooden sandals with red rubber footpads, (4) a pair of white sweat socks and leather sandals, (5) a pair of smart two-tone Gatsby-type brown and white shoes, (6) a pair of bare feet, (7) a pair of cowboy boots, (8) a pair of dark brown wing tips.

These are the feet of the tenor and bass sections of the Briones Tabernacle Choir as they sing their second concert of the Fauré *Requiem* and assorted madrigals in the Briones Community Center.

Landon conducts. Bill plays the piano accompaniment.

The choir is excellent.

The audience is large. People enjoy themselves immensely.

Wine costs twenty-five cents a glass. Various people have baked cakes and cookies to pay for the sheet music.

The concert ends with cheering, whistling, and rebel yells.

SUMMER

Private property is a creature of society, and is subject to
the calls of society, whenever its necessities shall require it.
BENJAMIN FRANKLIN

THE HOT, BRIGHT SUN has drawn the last green out of the hills. The grass is turning gold. The ground has long since become hard and dry.

All afternoon we work building a corral in Paradise Valley. String barbed wire from apple tree to apple tree. Build a gate.

Just as we finish, a blue truck with a horse trailer arrives at the main gate.

It's Bessie, the new valley milk cow.

We unload her and herd her into the corral to get used to her new home.

She is a lovely beige Guernsey with a full udder and long teats.

The dogs are nervous. Torn between chasing her and cowering.

The kids are excited.

"Is that our cow, Mommy?" asks Debby.

"Yup," says Nina.

"Really?" says Debby.

Two-year-old Riviere stands with a dirty face watching the new cow intently as she cases out the corral and then gives her first Paradise Valley mooooooooooooooo.

"And this cow is going to give us milk, butter, ice cream, and cheese," explains Susan. Riviere remains unmoved.

Harriet pays the girl who brought the cow in folding green. The girl looks at the $325 in semi-amazement.

"Our reserve cash fund," says Harriet with a grin.

"Jeez! I didn't think you were going to give me all this real money," says the girl.

It's four o'clock. Russ and Greg set up an old stanchion from a barn we wrecked. Time for milking.

Russ starts off. He sits on the small stool under the apple trees and starts squirting jets of white milk into the aluminum bucket as Bessie swings her tail in his face.

Slowly, everybody gets a try. Greg has trouble getting anything to come out.

"It's sure not like milking our goats," says Nina.

"Whew! Gets you right in the forearm!" says Russ.

Three to four gallons of milk a day. With milk at thirty cents a quart, that comes to $4.80 a day, $33.60 a week, $134.40 a month.

TODAY Ikon appears in town after a long unexplained absence. He is sweeping the wood boardwalk in front of the Store, garbed in a woman's white plastic raincoat covered with large black polka dots. On his head, he wears a hat fashioned out of what looks like an old pocketbook and the chrome rim from a Volkswagen headlight.

He smiles and bows as each person he knows passes by. He reports that he did some time in jail and then ended up in a mental hospital. Or perhaps the sequence was reversed. It is unclear.

"Finally, they just let me go," he says.

This afternoon, an ad appears in the classified section of the *Hearsay News*:

IKON NEEDS RESIDENCE: Will work for bucks, babysit, houseclean, caretake, or marry for home. Women with children only. I've been on the street too long. This is my song. I'm singing it to you.

Ikon

Harriet and Greg have bought some drop calves, young calves which have just been born. They live in Paradise Valley beside the garden. They are fed by bottle twice a day until they are old enough to eat solid food.

Greg figures that one grown calf will yield two sides of beef which will price out at about eighty-five cents a pound average for all cuts.

As I near the nursery on my bike, a Duster with racing stripes stops to a screeching halt. The driver waves me over.

"Hey, man," says a young man in medium-long hair and a Mark Spitz mustache, "can you turn us onto the nude beach?"

A new book on nude beaches in California has been published. Briones is listed as the northernmost recommendation.

There are rumors that *Penthouse* is planning to shoot a story on nude women at the beach.

THE day-care center is now firmly established at the PUD building. During the day the dark old Grand Ballroom is filled with children's toys, furniture, and junk. The coffee-colored particle board walls are festooned with bright pretty paintings done by the children. Fat ropes hang from the rafters for the children to climb on.

The room has been transformed.

Susan has been hired with county money to organize the programs and volunteers.

The day-care center keeps a log:

Monday
Native walk to Arroyo Hondo with 16 children. Examined banana slugs, ferns, erosion, town water supply and pipes, and many kinds of seeds fallen from the trees.

Tuesday
AM—Mellow, quiet.
PM—Short-staffed again. Understaffed and overworked! A COMPLETE WIPE-OUT!!!

Thursday
Oatmeal for morning snack. A big fire in fireplace. Stories, songs.

Friday
Took a tour of Briones mesa houses. Casually rode by,

and the children decided which houses to visit—mostly large ones with mysterious fences around them.

Took in ten houses, mostly exploring play yards. People taken by surprise, but were friendly since each visit was no longer than ten minutes.

In future, might give people notice as they might prepare snacks if they know you're coming.

An almost final draft of the Community Plan is finished. One hundred thirteen pages, excluding maps.

Judith gets fifty copies and circulates them around town for people to read before the town meeting and dessert feast Saturday night. Michael is printing highlights in the *Hearsay News.*

Most people feel good about the final plan. Many are amazed that it ever got finished after almost three years of work. We hope the message is buried deeply enough in the structure of the Plan that the county will have trouble nitpicking and emasculating it.

HIGHLIGHTS:

Plan Goals, Objectives and Recommendations:
A Summary

The goals of the Briones Community Plan are an expression of community consensus based on an extensive questionnaire.

COMMUNITY: The concept of community, including all living organisms and land forms, exists in rare form in Briones. The planning process shall attempt to understand, protect, and engender the elements of community as they apply to Briones.

GROWTH: A small annual growth rate shall be adopted and controlled by the community. Speculation on Briones land is not considered an essential element of this community, and, therefore, will not find encouragement in this plan.

TOURIST DESTINATION: While Briones will always have a flow of tourists, it shall not become a major tourist destination. Therefore, those elements of Briones which attract the tourist must be controlled to maintain a healthy balance between tourist and resident.

AGRICULTURE: Agriculture on this peninsula shall be encouraged as a source of food and income and as a way of life.

STACY'S BIRTHDAY

LIFE-STYLES: It is essential to this community that a wide range of life-styles be accepted and encouraged.

LOCAL JOBS: A Briones economy shall be fostered which increases the number and quality of local employment options.

CIRCULATION: The impact of the auto on the community shall be minimized. Other forms of circulation (pedestrian, bicycle, and equestrian) shall be encouraged, especially within the gridded Mesa (subdivision) and downtown.

WILDLIFE: The planning process shall recognize the various wildlife systems, including habitat, food source, nesting places, etc., and respond accordingly to achieve a healthy coexistence between man and nature.

LANDFORMS (OPEN SPACE, PARKS): Areas of geologic and hydraulic hazard shall be defined and exempted from development. The unique esthetic value of Briones landforms shall be preserved both spatially and visibly.

BRIONES LAGOON: The Briones community shall be responsive to all the elements of this extraordinary lagoon, including the effects of human activity on its watershed and on its shoreline.

The Plan calls for the formation of a local town planning board, mandated by the county supervisors and elected locally:

It is proposed that the composition of the Briones Planning Board be, insofar as possible, an expression by the community of its intentions, Therefore, the draft Plan proposes that a popular referendum be held in November to select a five-member council.

Any local resident over the age of eighteen, who is interested in the implementation of the Plan and the future of the community, would be eligible for a two-year term.

Implementation of the Plan would begin as soon as the council has been elected.

COMMUNITY INDEPENDENCE: In essence, the Briones Planning Group sees the job of successful planning as one which must be carried out on many fronts. This plan is not aimed simply at putting fewer houses in the right places. It is aimed at fostering a whole and healthy community which can provide its own necessities, protect itself from harmful outside intrusion, and work out a rate of growth and a kind of growth which are consonant with the long-term well-being of the inhabitants. For a community exists primarily for those who make it their home, not for transient spectators or absentee developers.

Finally, it should be clearly stated that the Briones Plan does not so much seek to stifle growth, as to direct it and suggest which kinds are constructive and which kinds are destructive.

Any means which are available must be pressed into service of this task. The above are only a few.

On the thorny question of tourism, the draft Plan proposes:

Eighty-six percent of the residents responding to the questionnaire agreed that Briones should not become a major tourist destination, and that elements which attract the tourist should be controlled. However, in any town, there is a need to provide overnight lodgings for friends and relatives, and for a limited number of people who wish overnight accommodations. We therefore propose that these visitors to Briones be put up at guest houses, much as one would find in small towns in Europe. The guest house proposal has gained favor in Briones for several reasons: First, it does not involve any new buildings; second, it channels money to many local individuals; third, it provides low-cost places to stay in that a range of prices could be assured. At a time when the average motel room costs just under twenty dollars per night, a room and breakfast in the five to fifteen dollar range would be refreshing and possible under this system.

People who wish to take in guests have been leaving their names at the bookstore, which refers visitors to them.

So far, the guest house idea has been a pleasure for all.

HERB Coon is not his real name.

He got the name Coon because he resembles a raccoon. Once he became Coon, people quickly changed it to Herb Coon, after the renowned San Francisco *Chronicle* columnist Herb Caen. Coon has also become the sports columnist for the *Hearsay News*.

Coon has been around town a long time. After his father died five years ago, Coon and his two brothers took over the family café, Scowley's. In the daytime, Coon and his brothers are hunched over the grill, turning out avocado and bean sprout sandwiches, cheeseburgers, and breakfasts for the hungry multitudes. They invariably have the local hip FM rock station on full-tilt boogie, regardless of whether someone has put money in the jukebox.

HERB COON AND GANDOFF

At night, Coon can usually be seen across the street sitting at the Bar drinking beers and shooting pool.

How he gets up every morning to cook is a mystery to many. One way or another, Scowley's usually opens.

Now, Coon's life has blossomed into the public arena as the writer of "Alternative Sports," a triweekly column. His handwritten commentary is the literary talk of the town.

A hot, sunny Saturday.

Ten or twenty people are doing a volunteer paint job on the Community Center and library. Free beer. No one working too hard, but the work gets done surprisingly quickly.

"Well, you know, I can remember giving this building its first coat of paint some forty years ago," says Hurford, one of the local realtors. He paints the cracks with Barbara doing the siding with a big brush. Hurford's gray hair makes a sharp contrast against the red paint.

"I always wanted to have a bank here in town. I even offered to build one. But my bank, Crocker Citizens, was just not interested," says Hurford, pondering one of his life's dreams which will now probably not come true.

Inside, Rex, Judith, and Ilka are setting up for the town meeting tonight on the Community Plan. Hanging zoning, wildlife, slope, habitat, land ownership pattern maps. Ilka puts up a display of town photos. Paradise Valley sets up an agricultural table. Cheese and pickles made by Susan. Renée's hand-dyed and spun wool. Butter that Luigi and Michael made by shaking some of Bessie's cream in a jar. Some of Dennis's potatoes, newly dug. Jam. A dozen eggs, containing some whoppers and a few tiny pullet eggs. Ten different kinds of herbs from the herb garden, and some free zucchini, parsley, and Swiss chard for the masses.

All afternoon long, people come and go. Look at the maps. Read the finished Plan, talk, and ask questions.

Evening.

The town meeting begins. The room is mobbed. People stand around drinking coffee and eating desserts that various individuals have baked. Finally, Rex coaxes people to sit down and be quiet.

Different people rise and explain the diverse parts of the Plan as the audience listens, tries to understand, gazes at the many pretty-colored maps hanging on the wall behind.

Presentation goes slow. Growth, housing, zoning, agriculture, animals, utilities, downtown, roads, the School.

Two weekenders leap up before the floor is thrown open to questions.

"I want to say that I am sick and tired of paying more taxes for every damn crazy scheme," says one particularly venomous man in brick-red pants and hair so well groomed that it looks like he is trying to force it back into his head!

"I got nothing against socialism or even communism. But that is what this plan is calling for," says a balding man with a thin pale mustache who owns a house but does not live here.

"Well, I just want to say that I live here, pay a lot of taxes, and am pleased to pay some more to bring about what this plan calls for," says another younger speaker who has a small farm.

"For thirty-five years I've been coming here," says an older man with a British accent. "And there used to be coveys of quail all over the mesa. Now, they're mostly gone. I think that anything this plan can do to give the wildlife a break is completely justified."

"Well, I'm sick and tired of paying more taxes! What rights do property owners have any more? You can't build a house, so you can't live here, so you can't vote," says the balding man. "I don't think you residents should be telling us what to do!"

"I just wanted to say," says Peter, "that my guru is Thomas Jefferson. And, you know, back in 1776 the Founding Fathers were going to put down 'life, liberty, and the pursuit of property.' And then Jefferson, Franklin, and a bunch of others got together and decided they'd better change it to, 'life, liberty, and the pursuit of happiness.' 'Happiness'! Not 'property'! And they had a reason! And that's just the way it's been ever since.

And if you think otherwise, you'll probably end up in the Supreme Court. In fact, I think the Briones Plan will end up in the Supreme Court." (Laughter)

"Everybody's so freaked-out about the taxes we pay the county. Yeah. It's a bummer," says Conrad. "Well, let's incorporate. Everybody sell their houses and land to the town. No taxes that way. Then we all lease them back at a dollar a year and get out from under the whole mess. And this isn't just another crazy Conrad idea!" he adds hastily.

The Plan moves on toward hearings at the county where parts of it will doubtless be scrapped. A small but well-spoken group has organized around the Property Owners Association in opposition to the Plan. They feel that planning is the prerogative of landowners only.

GREG starts a pigpen in the valley.

Two more calves arrive.

Thousands of board-feet of lumber from a wrecked warehouse in the city wait beside the half-finished barn.

Renée's house is the only one finished.

Most of the men in Paradise Valley have jobs during the day. The task of building a farm goes slowly. Money, time, energy. All resources in finite supply.

A colossal yellow bulldozer is parked right in the middle of Hurford's cow pasture.

Our sewer has begun.

It's the first time in a long while that my heart has felt gladness at the sight of a bulldozer.

JUSTICE William O. Douglas grants Petaluma a stay in its growth limitation case. He stays the decision of the lower federal court against the city's planning department, which would have required Petaluma to grant building permits to as many subdivisions as applied. Justice Douglas' intervention will allow the city to continue with its growth controls until the case is heard on appeal.

"This is going to be a landmark case," said Petaluma city planner Frank Gray last year. "It'll probably end up in the Supreme Court and will decide if cities can control their own growth."

It's on its way.

How does Mayor Helen Putnam feel about Douglas' decision?

"I feel very good about it," she says.

A year later, the US Court of Appeals for the 9th Circuit reversed the lower court decision. The Court of Appeals found that the City's housing plan was "not arbitrary or unreasonable." It said: "The local regulation [of 500 houses per year, exclusive of single-family dwellings] is rationally related to the social and environmental welfare of the community, and does not discriminate against interstate commerce."

In so ruling, the court cited previous Supreme Court rulings that upheld the right of communities to restrict land use, saying that they had "ample . . . power to lay out zones where values and the blessings of quiet and seclusion and clean air make a sanctuary for people," and that the growth-control ordinance was "a reasonable exercise of the city's police powers."

Subsequently, on appeal, the Supreme Court refuses to review the 9th Circuit Court's decision . . . a victory for growth control.

FALL

The question is, how to look at waste; from which point of view and with what attitude. From the metaphysical point of view, waste cannot be used and should be gotten rid of. On the contrary, the materialist dialectical point of view holds that what is waste and what is not waste are relative terms. There is nothing in the world which is absolute waste. Waste under one condition may be valuable under another. Waste materials left from one product can become good materials for another product.

THE WRITING GROUP OF THE
TIENTSIN MUNICIPAL
REVOLUTIONARY COMMITTEE,
PEOPLE'S REPUBLIC OF CHINA

DARKNESS IS JUST FALLING. As we head downtown, we meet Mike the Butcher hitching. He gets in the back of the truck.

Downtown, the orange school bus is parked outside Hurford's real estate office. Jay, who drives the bus each day for the kids, is standing out front talking with a gathering group of people. Richie sits in the front seat wearing a huge floppy chintz Easter bonnet-like hat on his head. He and Ebo are collecting money; a dollar from each person.

Bernie, the school principal, didn't want to lend the bus for non-school activities. He said he was afraid the state would cut off some school bus maintenance fund. Bernie is not accustomed to being illegal.

Somehow the bus was procured for the occasion. There is a hearing in San Francisco tonight with the Transit Authority and National Park. They want to run more buses each weekend from the city to Briones. People in town are wary. Don't like the idea of being an official tourist destination at the end of a weekend bus line.

All week long, Paul has run notices in the *Hearsay News* advertising the trip: WE NEED ELOQUENT VOICES AND BODIES. BUS LEAVES COMMUNITY CENTER AT 6:00 PM. BRING INSTRUMENTS AND MUNCHIES.

It's dark before the bus fills up. George has his flute and kazoo. Yvette has a guitar. Piero has his Super 8 movie camera. (He has an idea of making monthly 8mm newsreels of the town's activities.)

Just before the bus leaves, Susie runs over to the liquor store for a gallon of wine. Inside the bus, bags of oranges, brownies, cheese, sandwiches start appearing. Bottles of wine and beer circulate down the aisle. Finally, Jay sweeps his long hair over his shoulder, and swings into the driver's seat.

"OK," he says, laughing, as we pull out onto the road. "If we get stopped, I'm just going to say that I was forced to drive." He is answered with a thunderous ovation.

We head out of town.

"Hey, Jay!" someone yells from the back. "Better turn off the inside lights so no one can see what's going on in here."

"Well, at least if we get arrested we'll have a good time together in jail," yells someone else as we head down the hill past Ben's barn.

Everyone is heavy into eating and drinking when we hit the highway. The atmosphere is one of children at a Saturday matinée. People are shouting comments above the sound of the engine as inspiration strikes.

"Hey! Does this tour include the free rhumba party?"

"Just call us the Briones boosters!"

"Hey! I got it! Let's paint this bus psychedelic and go to Albuquerque!"

Greg has a six-pack. Harriet passes some salted peanuts across the aisle. A number of joints are circulating up and down the bus.

"Hey! What meeting didja say we were going to?" asks a voice from the back.

"It doesn't matter," yells a replier. "They're all the same anyway."

Someone yodels.

We wind down the hills. Suddenly there are bright lights everywhere as we approach the freeway.

"Hey! We gotta stop at the Arab garage. Gretchen's gotta pee!" yells Peter.

Jay pulls off on the shoulder in front of the Arco station. Three or four ladies get off to a big hand.

We hit the tollbooth at the bridge. Jay, who is staying straight, pays. The toll collector looks in the windows of the school bus as we glide through. He sees many grinning faces. We leave him scratching his head and wondering what school kids have come to.

The hearing is in a church. We file off the bus into an almost elegant ecclesiastical meeting room. There are about fifty of us. We outnumber the other people in the room two to one. They stare and smile.

Our group is quiet, considering our trip in. We take seats, mostly on the floor. There are transit route maps taped to the wall over the fireplace next to an imitation Renaissance oil painting of the Virgin Mary, Jesus, and several other religious groupies.

"Well, I guess we can get going. I see we have the Briones syndrome here tonight," says the vice-chairman with a mixture of boredom and distaste. He continues on to briefly extol "citizen participation" while gazing out over the heads of the people from Briones as though we did not come under such a rubric.

Two different men are called on to discuss the proposed new bus routes. They address themselves to the problem of better connecting up the city with the National Park.

When they conclude, the vice-chairman says, "I'd like to say a few words here if I may."

There is one black man in the room. He has his hand up. The vice-chairman sees him and suggests that "we hold the questions for now." The black man tries to ask his question anyway. The vice-chairman cuts him off almost without noticing that he is doing so. The black man gets up and leaves.

The hearing continues.

The Transit Authority now provides four buses a day on weekends to our town. On weekdays they provide two. They now propose to increase the weekend service to nine by adding five buses to the highway turnoff. They will not increase the weekday service.

"OK. Why not increase the weekday service instead of the weekend service?" asks someone. "Is this bus line designed just for tourists?"

"Listen," says Peter. "The real question is how to get people out of cars. The buses just bring more people, and the others still come in their cars. People may come once on the bus, and then come again with their family in their car. The average family just isn't ready to take a bus. And if you just keep on flooding our town, eventually we'll end up with parking meters and tollbooths just like Carmel."

"You guys are supposed to be getting people to the parks, not our town," says someone else. "We're not a recreation area or a park. Briones is our home. I mean, if you're going to run buses, run them to the park that the people paid for, not into us."

"Well, if you're going to be running all these buses into someone's town, just for starters you might try to provide some places for them to throw their garbage . . . and maybe some rest rooms," says Michael the Butcher.

"Have you ever seen what a bus looks like in our town?" interrupts Desloge.

"OK! That's enough!" says the vice-chairman.

"It's huge!" says Desloge, ignoring him.

"OK. OK. I think we have an idea of what you people in Briones think! And we've got a long agenda . . .."

There is still a forest of hands in the air. People start protesting. But the vice-chairman is insistent.

"Oh, for god's sake! We come all the way over-the-hill and listen to a lot of crap about citizen participation, and then you want to shut everybody up," yells an angry voice.

"Hey! How did *you* get here? We came in a bus," says Greg, provoking some sniggering and cheers.

"I came in a car because there was no bus," says the vice-chairman. He's getting pissed. But he grudgingly allows the discussion to continue.

"We're only presenting a proposal," says a Transit Authority man. "And of course, what you all are saying will help us determine the final decision. We really thank you for taking the time to come."

"I'm just here to listen to people like you," says the National Park director, an intense, youngish man in shined black shoes and a suit. His political acuity has taught him to take large crowds seriously. He is an attentive man.

The meeting moves on to discuss transportation demonstration programs. People have already started drifting out onto the sidewalk.

Jay brings the bus around, and everybody piles into it. A debate arises about whether to stop for ice cream or eats on the way home. The ice cream lobby wins, and Jay swings the bus around to a Baskin-Robbins.

The whole bus empties. But the store has just closed. Several women stand outside the plate glass window imploring two pimply young attendants who are mopping the floor to open up.

VISITING TOURISTS

The women are like frantic deaf-mutes standing outside the window using sign language. The attendants stare transfixed at the growing assemblage outside.

"Jeez. I hope there's not going to be an ice cream riot," says Piero, laughing, as the crowd surges off down the block. Someone has discovered an open liquor store. The two men behind the counter look a trifle edgy as the place fills up; fifty people from Briones loose in a liquor store like monkeys in a peanut factory.

"Where did you say you were from?" asks one man behind the counter. "Brolognas?"

People are grabbing bottles of wine, fruit juice, quarts of beer, potato chips, canned mixed cocktails, and Fritos. Customers who have found the drink of their choice line up in quasi-obedient fashion in front of the cash register. Michael asks for some extra paper bags to clean up all our bottles, cans, and trash from the bus. The liquor store man offers to sell some. Michael pays.

Ikon appears. He finishes off someone's bottle of burgundy.

"Supper," he says. "Oh, yeah. I was in Sausalito and came over special for this gig." He is wearing a promotional button given away by the Transit Authority.

Gradually, the liquor store empties. The bus fills up and quiets down.

We drive back over the mountain to the sound of popping beer cans.

RANNEY must be about forty-five. Tall. Very quiet. Handsome.

He began showing up at PUD and planning meetings (any meetings) about two years ago. Almost never fails.

He rarely speaks. He usually just sits quietly in the back row and listens. People say he is an "anarchist," although he sure doesn't look like one. Finds a strange fascination in watching the goings-on of the town in which he lives, although he is not moved to act similarly. He believes that acting to achieve some vision or socio-political goal is futile, or perhaps even compounds the original problem.

Ranney reads the Plan, and writes a public letter to the *Hearsay News*:

Please remove my name as a representative of the Briones Planning Group and as an implied supporter of the Plan. However delightful the Plan alleges life would be in a back-to-the-turn-of-the-century (and therefore bogus) Briones, I am not interested in endorsing these unrealistic elements of the Plan:

1. Population control measures, whether or not selective and discriminatory, will probably be viewed in 2024 with the same regret we now feel as we study the Oriental Exclusion Act of 1882, and the immigration laws of 1921 and 1924.

2. "Self-sufficiency." The disadvantages of a Fortress Briones policy will continue to accelerate as the world sees the value of independence, specialization, and cooperating on a wide geographic basis. Presumably, most people see the value of not trying to provide from within Briones coffee, books, bananas, foreign and domestic travel, tea, wine, salt, washing machines, automobiles, oranges, pumps, beer, timber, pepper, knives, wire, paper, glass, copper, iron, and 95 percent of the ideas we have. Nationalism writ small is not a very inspiring concept.

3. Agrarian romanticism. The peasants of the world reject it, and are fleeing from the land as fast as they are allowed to by their rulers and by mechanization of agriculture, heavy application of chemical fertilizer, use of insecticides, and improved transportation. It is not just a coincidence that China is now dependent on Japanese nitrate fertilizer, and that the Chinese government has recently signed a contract with M. W. Kellog to build eight large chemical fertilizer factories. Even now, 80 percent of the people are still scratching away in the fields, unable to feed 100 percent of the people without reliance on imports. Fortunately, 100 million tons of grain from the US will be available for export again this year to many countries which are still saddled with obsolete agricultural systems.

4. Populist rhetoric against profit-taking, speculation, absentee developers, and landlordism. Perhaps the final version of the Plan can add to this rogues' gallery a sprinkling of fascist capitalists, moneylenders, and other enemies of the people.

5. One more level of local government ("Power to the people in power"). I have yet to meet anyone in Briones who wants to be

governed *more*. Most people want *less* of it. The nostalgia fad may be amusing, but let's not congeal it into law.

To paraphrase a Chinese proverb, "A great plan is a public calamity."

Ranney J.

P.S. I'll keep coming to planning meetings as an observer, as a self-appointed watchdog.

PAT'S old father, George, is dead. He was seventy-one years old.

They buried him in the cemetery by the Catholic Church, not far from Pablo Briones.

"We planted a redwood tree on his grave," said Pat. "It was a beautiful ceremony."

One of his poems was read before they pushed the earth back over his coffin.

AGE

I have no time to think of age
symbols crash
        and visioned youth
fill my eyes.
Gray hairs in morning sun
           turn brown
Wrinkled shadows show in gold
Who and why should one grow old?
I have no time to waste in fear
        of death
strange specters haunt the land
for those who dread the cold
        of passing
I have no time to think of age
In living youth I look
blue skies beckon
        I heed the wonder
of a turned land, a browed hill
        quest and live.
In the time of my living, past vistas
open wide the gates of life
        and like a croupier
I rake my gains, and live.

GEORGE M. HAINES

Downtown, I meet Tom, a retired minister who is now coordinator of the Craftsmen's Guild. Although no longer officially a clergyman, he performs occasional marriages and funeral ceremonies.

We talk about how remote death seems from our town. We try to count the recent deaths. We can only recall three or four.

"It's true," says Tom, starting the engine of his truck. "This is a town of youth."

LONG, long, long meeting.

PUD finally bites the bullet. Decides to put the water moratorium on the ballot this November to see where folks' heads are.

If they vote against expanding the water system and refuse to approve funds, what can a court do?

Postscript: In the election the town votes overwhelmingly against passing a bond for a new reservoir or pipe system which would lift the water hookup moratorium.

SOMEONE has hung a sign painted crudely on a piece of pegboard out by the Christian Science Church:

QUIET!

Approaching Sensitive Community!

The annual Briones Rummage Sale opens, proceeds going to the Community Center and local churches.

Mountains of junk.

People line up eagerly before the doors are opened hoping to get first crack at the jewels.

The fire whistle blows. People stampede in past the boxes of zucchini, fruit, cookies, and cake to the real stuff.

Clothes, toasters, lamps, hats, books, whiskey bottles shaped like plantation slaves, hats, kitchenware, crafts, shoes, old mattresses, baby carriages, evening gowns.

I score a large jar full of toothpicks for two cents.

Lunch is served "by the ladies."

STEVE C. comes out from the County Planning Department to help with the final revisions on the Community Plan.

We are sitting and talking.

We see flashing red lights out in the parking lot. Look out the window. An ambulance turns around and speeds back down the road.

Richie and Carmen's small daughter, Jenine, has been hit by a truck while riding her scooter near her house.

She is taken to the intensive care unit of the county hospital over-the-hill.

She has a badly broken pelvis and various cuts and bruises. The doctors want to operate. Richie and Carmen sign the papers for the surgery.

It's happened.

"HORSES are as much at home as cars on Wharf Road in Briones, the peaceful seaside community that beckons to refugees from Marin's urbanized eastern corridor. Though little more than a half-hour away from the farthest places in the county, a Saturday or a Sunday spent there can seem a trip well back into time."

This caption appears underneath a photo showing a horse walking down the road in front of the Bar. The headline below says in large black letters: BRIONES, AN IDEAL ONE-DAY TRIP.

The article goes on to describe Briones as a "charming spot," and describes how to get here, where to park, where to eat, where to buy, and recreate.

All this appears in the weekend edition of the largest county daily paper.

On our way home, we notice that the sign has again disappeared, leaving two sawed-off stumps sticking up out of the grass on the roadside.

Near town, a bobcat lopes across the road and disappears into the brush just as our headlights round a bend.

JENINE is still in the hospital.

Various people around town have been helping Richie and

Carmen take care of their other four children while they are over-the-hill at the hospital each day.

Mike writes a letter, printed in longhand in the *Hearsay News*:

Last week somebody suggested the need for traffic control bumps.

Someone even offered to form a committee to get the county to install bumps!

Forget it!

The county doesn't use bumps, and can't install them . . . something about not wanting to deal with lawsuits from owners of vehicles damaged by the bumps.

However, if you want bumps on your block, don't form a committee, form a work party.

Here's how to make bumps: Take a pick and dig a series of holes across the street—holes about the size of one's head—and place stones in the holes leaving about a four-inch projection above the pavement level.

Then, pack a stiff mix of concrete around the stones. Do one side of the road at a time, leaving room for cars to pass.

Barricade the lane until the concrete sets up. Some friendly signs ½ block either side of the bumps should finish the job nicely.

THE Property Owners Association has sent around an "information sheet" on the Community Plan (they oppose it), and on Rolf's subdivision or lodge north of town (they support it). Their information was appropriately polemical.

The town is in an uproar. Once again, everyone is talking about "Rolf's development." On Monday, the California North Central Coastal Commission is coming to town to have hearings on the new coastal conservation plan. There are rumors that they support Rolf's development and his claim that it will help provide access for people to the coast.

Some people are worried by the thought of such a development. Others are positively invigorated by the idea of fighting it. They see it as another Kennedy Sewer issue around which the town would congeal.

"It's not going to get through," says John. "If it did, it would definitely be time to move."

FINISHING THE SEWER

"I could see a motel," says Nancy. "But a hundred fifty units multiplied by two people equals three hundred people! What's the population of Briones? [About seventeen hundred.] What kind of an increase is that? What about limited growth?"

The *Hearsay News* is full of information and predictions of apocalypse. Everyone is being urged to attend the big hearing on Monday.

Rolf and his partners do not live here. But everyone is talking about them.

THERE is a banner stretched between two telephone poles as you come into town. It says WOMEN CELEBRATE WOMEN, PUD, 8:00 P.M. POTLUCK.

Tonight, 150 women from town each cooked a dish and then went off to the PUD Grand Ballroom (which had been rented) to the dinner and festival.

"The food was incredible," reports Ilka. "We all sat around small tables with flowers and candles and ate."

Reports filtering back into the outside world tell of fondue, caviar, spring rolls, brandied fruit, homemade bread, and twenty gallons of wine.

"Almost everyone I knew was there," says Ilka, my particular informant. "It was a really high time."

Sandra, who is a daytime bartender at the Bar, was the Ms. of Ceremonies for the four hours of entertainment that followed. Judy played a piano solo. Carmen and Ellen did some folksongs. Judith brought the house down with a song by Oceana called "He's a Wolf."

"I don't know," says Ilka, laughing. "It was something about Little Red Riding Hood getting warned by her grandmother about what big teeth and paws this wolf has. It had everyone rolling in the aisles."

Dottie and Sarah read poetry. A different Sandra than the Ms. of Ceremonies performed a mad scene from *Medea*.

"We were all stunned by it," says Ilka. "There was something about how she got into it which made it awesome."

O'Brien sang an aria from *Die Fledermaus*. And then the belly dancers came out.

"It was Susan from the Store and Elaine. They got up there with tambourines and started dancing, shaking their breasts and bellies and really going at it. Pretty soon people from the audience started getting up and moving into the semicircle to dance. It was wonderful. Everyone just let go. There were a couple of guys outside watching the whole thing, looking in through the windows. But nobody seemed to care."

Kathy writes in the *Hearsay News*: "I'm glad to hear that the profits accrued from the evening (75 cents) will go to buying Sandra a drink at the Bar, if 75 cents still buys a drink. Thanks, Sandra, and everyone else, for one of the nicest evenings I've spent in Briones."

Of course, I was not at the evening, being a man. Ilka says this description leaves no doubt about that.

DR. Mike writes in the *Hearsay News* today: "Have you seen the other side of where we live? Is Rolf the devil? Our shadow? Winter death or summer life? In any case, whenever I read of Rolf in the *Hearsay News*, I momentarily feel poorly. Things around me look dark. I think of moving, get images of a completely changed village. But then I see the sun and the Lagoon, and come back to my senses. So, Rolf is necessary to provide the jolt that holds it together . . . to make me think about it all."

How will it end?

No one is sure.

Again, I talk to Rolf about subdividing into family farms with water supply, access, maybe houses and barns. Says he will talk to his architect.

Is he desperate enough yet? Will his investors laugh him out of the room? It's hard being a developer.

But I feel that the conspiracy of tight money, good town energy, and Rolf's reasonableness may make this development end up with a new and hopeful twist.

MOST of the cats and other heavy equipment have left now. The earthen berms of the sewer ponds slope in rolling lines up from Hurford's old cow pasture. The land now belongs to the town. Almost one hundred acres. All around the ten or so acres of ponds, the land has been slightly dished out to catch and retain all winter rainwater.

"Wait until you see it in the spring," says Peter. "It's going to be covered with migratory ducks, waterfowl, and wild flowers."

The pile driver is still slamming away downtown and blowing out everyone's eardrums as the pump station is being dug.

The laboratory and the apartment for the maintenance man, which Don designed, are finished.

The sewer is almost completed. Driving past it today coming home, I felt glad, and older.

Four years of many people's lives for a sewer.

A new art gallery downtown opens with a show of Briones artists.

The Briones theater group presents a play.

A new self-defense class is forming.

A monster dance is held at the PUD with notable rock musician Mark Beno et al. playing.

Alexandra's new book about macramé, embroidered hip clothes, crocheted maps, and various and sundry other avant-garde fashions—is out.

The town is bubbling with energy. Brimming over with activity. Articles about it keep appearing. Mention of it pops up in columns, in conversation, in books, on the radio, on TV.

The crews are out there digging up what they hope will be the remains of Sir Francis Drake in front of the School.

"God! Remember three years ago? Nothing ever happened. Now there are several things every night," says Ilka. "You couldn't go to a fifth of them even if you wanted to."

Like everything, this "growth" of energy and activity is a double-edged sword. With it comes a kind of notoriety which forever erases the possibility of the town being something for itself.

We may expire, victims of our own genius and creativity which act as a magnet to the outside.

People come for inspiration, for hope, for relief.

Our successes may be our undoing in a way as yet unfathomed by us. The signs marking the way may be down, but people find this town. Our ability to absorb the consequences of our own actions may well be insufficient. Success and hope are commodities to be devoured with a vengeance. Our town is filled with doubt, but also with hope.

Will all our efforts to preserve and fashion a community make us so interesting that we will be buried in attention?

The line of cars coming into town today, a beautiful Sunday, was almost unbroken.

I'M just back from the job, after spending all day nailing down roof decking. Wash the stale coffee out of my thermos.

Ilka comes in the door. Just hitched back from the doctor's office thirteen miles away.

"They said the baby could come any time now," she says. "But I've had pains on my way home."

"Maybe it's false labor," I reply, feeling that I am in uncharted waters. My first reaction is that it must be false labor, since I cannot yet fully realize myself as a father and Ilka giving birth to our child.

She sits down on the couch. We look through some childbirth books for some hint as to what is happening.

The fog is rolling in now across the point in great gray moving snowdrifts. The sun is still orange on the mountain across the Bay.

The pains are coming more frequently. We call Jane.

"What does false labor feel like?" Ilka asks. "Could it be so regular?" She doubles up under a sudden surge of pain. She gives up trying to talk through it.

Ilka does not want to call the doctor yet. Feels embarrassed.

She has heard too many stories of hysterical mothers calling the doctor several times before real labor has begun.

Jane says to call Aggie, the midwife.

The contractions are obvious, now. Only several minutes apart. Dusk is settling. The dogs are outside on the porch waiting to be fed, oblivious to what is happening inside.

We call Aggie.

"Well, Ilka, what I suggest you do is to come over here and let me check you. I would come up to your place, but I am all alone, and just can't leave my children." Aggie is one of several midwives who work with the local doctors.

I eat a fast dinner. Pack some sandwiches and fill a thermos with orange juice.

We walk up to the truck with a bag full of baby clothes and a few things for labor which Ilka has packed weeks ago.

Bea, our neighbor, comes out on the porch. She has had four children of her own. She immediately knows.

"Good luck," she says. "Don't worry about the dogs. I bought some dogfood for them. Make sure you call me when it's born. It doesn't matter what time." She waves as we drive up the hill.

Ilka sits on a pillow. I try to massage her back as the contractions come.

We drive down to Aggie's. She lives in an old white farmhouse near the Christian Science Church. She is canning pears from her trees when we arrive.

Tall. Hair tied back. She is wearing blue jeans. Very open face.

"Why don't you go right into the living room, Ilka, and lie on the couch while I fix a cup of tea."

Aggie is English.

A wood stove is burning in the living room; an old cast-iron parlor stove with chrome trim and something which looks like a bowling trophy on the top.

The pain is inescapable, now. Ilka gets down on the rug on all fours each time a contraction hits. I massage her back. Hold her. She is beginning to retreat into the process of birth. Few words. Gripped by inner concentration.

Aggie comes in with the tea and a black doctor's bag. The top opens like a fish's mouth. She puts on a pair of membrane-thin rubber surgical gloves.

"All right, now. Lie back, please, Ilka. This may hurt just a little." She sits sideways on the couch, reaches her hand in between Ilka's legs, deep into the birth canal. Ilka freezes in pain. I start to do deep breathing exercises with her. Her body relaxes.

"Well, Ilka," says Aggie. "Everything's just fine. Perfectly normal. You're already dilated about three centimeters. And you're welcome to have your baby here in our house, if you like. We have a guest room." Aggie pauses. Purses her lips together. Waits through the next contraction.

"Are you sure you don't mind?" asks Ilka. Both of us feel warm and secure here with Aggie. The idea of having our baby in Briones feels right. Neither of us wants to drive over-the-hill to the hospital in the fog in our small truck.

"Do you have anything here in case the pain gets too much?" asks Ilka.

"No, we don't," says Aggie. "Only in the hospital. Why don't you think about it?"

We talk. The decision is hard. The contractions come, sweeping her away into her own world. Suddenly Ilka becomes nauseous. She throws up. The thought of moving seems unthinkable. We decide to stay.

Aggie leads us up the stairs, past the freshly painted white doors of her sleeping children to the guest room. Double bed, clean white ceiling. Fresh new wallpaper. Windows which look out to the Lagoon and the daffodil field.

Aggie puts down a rubber sheet. Gets some pillows. She checks Ilka again. She has dilated six centimeters. The head of the child is forcing its way through the cervix. Aggie massages Ilka's back. I hold her head and shoulders and breathe deeply in her ear. Try to get her into the rhythm of abdominal breathing, and above the grip of the pain, as we were taught in our natural childbirth class.

"Follow me now," I say. "Open your eyes. Watch me. Breathe

like you're trying to make yourself yawn. Try to breathe the pain out of your body."

She follows.

"Don't go away," she says. "Stay here."

Short, simple statements. "Push, Aggie! Oh, Aggie, push! higher! Please, more!"

The contractions get harder, but there is more time in between.

The phone rings. Dr. Whitt wants to know how it's coming. Aggie gives a report.

"Easy. Relax as each breath goes out. Try to get out of your skin into mine. Relax. Breathe deeply. Keep the rhythm." She watches me intently with a look almost of pleading. I am her only frame of reference outside the pain.

We're four hours into labor. She sleeps now between contractions. Aggie and I talk softly.

The phone rings. It's Liz at the women's meeting. Jane has let the grapevine know that Ilka is in labor.

We tell Ilka she called. She smiles faintly.

She sucks on a wet washcloth before each pain. I cool her forehead with a wet towel. She is completely preoccupied now.

Aggie checks her again. The cervix is dilated seven centimeters. She reaches in with a sterile hook and breaks the water bag.

The doctor calls again. Aggie says it is time for him to come.

Suddenly, Ilka sits up with her eyes bulging and the veins swelling on her temples. "I'm pushing! I'm pushing! Is it OK, Aggie? I can't help it!"

She is in her final labor. There is blood and mucus on the pads beneath her. All her clothes are off now. She is hot and working hard. She squats on the bed. We hold her arms.

"Push through the pain, Ilka!" says Aggie, sitting on the bedside. "If it feels good, push! Push your baby out! It will soon be here!"

Ilka is grunting, gasping deep breaths, eyes wide open now. She pulls her thighs back to her breasts as she again lies on her back and pushes with all her might.

Headlights turn into the driveway. Feet sound on the stairway. Dr. Whitt comes in the door. Looks tousled and tired.

He puts a large brown doctor's satchel on the floor. Sits on the bed and watches. His sudden presence is both reassuring and unsettling.

A new face has entered our intense group, and there is no time for introductions.

He watches. Sits somewhat aloof. Seems slightly bored.

"Push! Push! Why don't you push?" he almost barks.

Ilka pushes while emitting a deep, throaty, involuntary growl.

"Push it out! Push as though you were emptying your bowels," he says, sitting, watching, hands clasped.

Ilka's breathing becomes chaotic. I try to get her to pant through a few contractions for rest. She worries that she is not performing properly.

Dr. Whitt feels her bladder through her abdomen. It is full. We go to the toilet. She sits through ten contractions in the darkness. I hold her on the toilet and massage her back. But nothing comes. The baby's head is blocking the escape of the urine. We walk slowly back to bed. Whitt and Aggie try to catheterize her. I hold the flashlight. They can't get it in. Everything is too swollen from the contractions and the force of the baby's head inside, pushing outward.

The contractions keep coming. They wrack Ilka's body. She puts every muscle into pushing.

"I think we're getting an involuntary reaction against the full bladder," says Dr. Whitt. "It's just hard to push against a full bladder. I think we ought to head over-the-hill to the hospital where we can get you into some stirrups and catheterize you. Don't worry. Your baby is going to be fine."

The bed is covered with surgical gloves, gauze, bloody pads. It's 3:30. Dark. Foggy. Ilka is scared.

"You better take my station wagon," says Aggie. "Ilka can ride in back."

"I'll follow up behind you," says Whitt.

We swing out on the road. The fog is so thick it is hard to

see two dotted lines ahead in the center of the road.

Curves. Endless curves. Past ranches, the lake, the turnoff, the cheese factory, more ranches. Through the dark and fog. Ilka softly moaning in the back with each contraction.

"How far? When will we be there?" she keeps asking like a small child on a long trip.

Finally, we come down a hill, and the lights of Petaluma are below us in the fog. We drive up to the emergency entrance. We ring. A nurse comes with a wheelchair. Whitt is right behind us.

"That was some fog," he says.

They put Ilka on the table. Whitt scrubs up. We all put on green surgical gowns, caps, shoe covers, and masks.

Ilka is in great pain. She keeps saying she will never have another baby. I give her a cold wet cloth to suck on.

"Take it easy," says the nurse. "Soon your baby will be out."

Whitt comes in. Shining lights. Sparkling silver surgical instruments. The delivery room.

"OK, now let's push!" he orders from his position between her legs.

The pushing begins anew. Ilka is coiled like a spring trying to release itself. The tendons in her neck are taut as piano wires. She strains against the grips on the delivery table.

Whitt gives her a local anesthetic before he slips a pair of low forceps in around the baby's head to ease it out. They look like some grotesque implement for serving salad. Ilka is in intense pain from back labor, a kind of pain which was always gently skirted in our natural childbirth class. But she is completely into it now. Getting the baby born is the only way out of the pain.

There is a kind of slithering pop, like a greased champagne cork coming out. The baby is there. Miraculous. Blue. Crying. Covered with blood and bits of flesh. Still connected like some bizarre telephone component by a purple cord which disappears inside Ilka.

The pain has ceased, like a storm which is suddenly becalmed. Whitt starts to hand the baby to Ilka, but the cord is too short.

"I'll just cut it," he says. There is the sound of shears cutting flesh. He ties it off. Puts the baby on Ilka's breast.

It is a boy. Small fingernails, penis, ears, weirdly shaped long head. Ilka counts its fingers. Wants to make sure.

We watch this small, writhing, magical creature that is ours.

Whitt works quietly away on Ilka at the foot of the table like a shoemaker at his bench. He is washing and rearranging the ragged, bloody hole from which the baby has emerged. His green gown is covered with blood and shreds of tissue from Ilka's insides.

"OK. Now, let's just push one more time and get the placenta out," he says.

Ilka pushes. Whitt pulls gently on the umbilical cord.

"Here it is," he says, holding up the afterbirth like a large piece of liver. The purple cord droops down. This bloody Portuguese man-of-war sits in the box with part of itself hanging over the side. I watch it, and think about planting a fruit tree on it.

The door has been open to the delivery room the whole time. Nurses have been coming in and out. One brings in a wheelchair. We put Ilka in it. She sits there with our baby on her breast chatting and smiling.

I leave her in the hospital and head back home.

The word is already out. I stop at the job to tell them the news. Ron gives me a big hug. John looks down from a rafter he is setting and says, "Well, congratulations."

I stop at the post office. Everyone is glad. Lots of hugs, congratulations. Liz and Nina want to go up to the hospital in the afternoon and take Ilka some goat's milk from Paradise Valley.

At home are a stack of baby clothes and a freshly baked loaf of bread on the porch from Mary. Just as I get in the shower, Harriet comes bounding in with a big hug.

ILKA comes home from the hospital today. We put our

still unnamed son in Susan's old cradle. I take the day off from work.

Burr comes over with a bottle of champagne and a beautiful belt handwoven by Sarah. He offers to cook dinner.

EACH day, new people come to visit. They all bring presents or some food.

"Happy times," says Val, the contractor on our job.

Gail brings a chicken.

Liz brings two stuffed squashes.

Tissa comes to cook while I'm at work.

Everyone brings some new tip, advice, or suggestion from their own experience of having children.

Strangely, almost no men come to visit in the first days. Only women.

But I have a good feeling in me these days, and I know this is the place where I want to raise our child.

ABOUT THE AUTHORS

ORVILLE SCHELL is a writer who lives in northern California. He is co-author of several books on China and has written numerous magazine articles on contemporary social and political issues. He was born in New York in 1940.

ILKA HARTMANN, a photographer, also lives in northern California. Her work has been exhibited in museums and published in numerous books and magazines in the United States and in Europe. She was born in Hamburg, Germany, in 1942.